INFORMING DIGITAL FUTURES

Computer Supported Cooperative Work

Volume 37

Informing Digital Futures

Strategies for Citizen Engagement

by

Leela Damodaran
Loughborough University, U.K.

and

Wendy Olphert
Loughborough University, U.K.

 Springer

A C.I.P. Catalogue record for this book is available from the Library of Congress.

ISBN-13 978-90-481-7161-3
ISBN-10 1-4020-4784-3 (e-book)
ISBN-13 978-1-4020-4784-8 (e-book)

Published by Springer,
P.O. Box 17, 3300 AA Dordrecht, The Netherlands.

www.springer.com

Printed on acid-free paper

"...the future, unlike the past is always newborn. To involve all living persons in constructing the future is to release and facilitate growth and change all round..."

Margaret Mead

Contents

Preface

Several decades of involvement in a myriad of projects, programmes and initiatives concerned with designing for people, have revealed to us and to many others a pattern in which successive waves of new technologies each raise hopes and expectations. Too often we are then disappointed with their shortfall in delivery. Of course many of the systems, products and services many of us take for granted in our lives have brought innumerable benefits, and we sometimes pause to wonder how we ever managed without the capability to use, for example, email, internet banking or mobile phones. But such capabilities are not yet enjoyed universally, and often come with unanticipated, sometimes negative, consequences. The benefits have by-passed many people in our society and are out of reach of many others on economic, physical, educational, social and other grounds. Our explorations of cases where the use of technology to enhance human capabilities and quality of life has succeeded have convinced us that it is only with 'people-power' that the awesome capabilities of information and communications technologies (ICTs) can be shaped to meet the needs and aspirations of citizens.

The design of complex, multifunctional, ICT-enabled environments, products and services typically involves many role holders with responsibility for different aspects of design and decision-making. We hope the contents of the book will be of interest to all those stakeholders in the Information Society who are involved in the many roles associated with planning, design, implementation, delivery and support of digital technologies for use by citizens. This growing cohort of people, in many different roles and with a variety of objectives, is working to achieve the participation and active engagement of members of the public in matters relating to technologies – especially the digital technologies – which permeate the Information Society. The intended audience for this text is commensurately diverse. It includes the research community attempting to understand the engagement process and to develop theoretical models of engagement; practitioners in domains such as local government, healthcare, community housing and education who face the challenge of engaging apparently uninterested, even apathetic, citizens in local matters of consequence for the community; and policy makers and strategists in central government and international agencies.

In particular we hope that those of you who have not sought to involve citizens in designing technologies will see what you have been missing and be inspired to make up for lost time. For those who have attempted to engage citizens in design efforts of one form or another but have been disappointed with the result, we offer a framework and strategic approach. We also describe tools and techniques to facilitate the process of engaging with citizens and gaining the rewards that have perhaps eluded you before.

One aspiration for this book is that it will enable people working in this diversity of contexts to share perspectives, experiences and emerging best practice of citizen engagement processes. Practitioners have perhaps the hardest task in setting up processes for engaging citizens in shaping technological futures in which they will be stakeholders. It is for them that this book includes material on the available 'know-how' for achieving effective engagement of citizens. To ground the substance of the book, examples of good practice in citizen participation and engagement are drawn from projects and programmes around the world. A wide range of the processes, mechanisms and media used, as well as a considerable array of tools and techniques, are identified and discussed.

Acknowledgements

On the journey to this book there have been numerous influences and many contributions. To acknowledge them all adequately would take a full chapter. Some contributors have been so significant for us, however, that it would be remiss of us not to thank them individually.

Among the key people for Leela to thank is a most important benefactor, Laurie Thomas, for his mysterious power of inculcating self belief in his students and for the inspiration of his rich creativity.

We both thank Lisl Klein, not only for the many insights she shared with us in working together and in her books, but also for providing an inspirational role model to all social scientists through her intellectual rigour and uncompromising commitment to the integrity of the research and consulting process. We are also both grateful to Brian Shackel and Ken Eason for the unsurpassed learning opportunities provided in the HUSAT Research Institute, and to John Spackman, for his vision in creating groundbreaking opportunities to develop and apply social science concepts and principles to the design of large-scale complex ICT systems. Enid Mumford must be mentioned for her pioneering work in raising awareness of the human aspects of computer systems and the importance of involving users in design, as well as for her warm personal endorsement of our professional endeavours.

In the production of this book, we are indebted to a number of our colleagues for their professional inputs, enthusiasm, and commitment. These include Sue Hutton, Joan Stenson, Rachel Hardy, Steve Phipps, Beverley Kent, Lynda Webb, Kayla Tomlinson, and particularly Mark Shelbourn who deserves an additional special mention for staying the course, for his good humoured support and for his inspirational talent with production of the diagrams. We have also enjoyed brainstorming ideas, and the laughter and friendship of our colleagues in the Research School of Informatics through difficult times.

Finally, our families, especially Mitty, Gerry, David, Wray, James, Joel and Glyn, and supporters, Margaret Fox, Linda Grimbley and Sandra Clifford all deserve mention for their encouragement and support over the months of writing this book.

1 Introduction

We have written this book to begin to fill a significant gap we perceive to exist between the rhetoric of inclusive, user-centred design of information and communications technologies (ICTs) on the one hand, and the ideology of participation and engagement in civil society on the other. The former has developed from a recognition that effective ICT-based systems, services and products result from a central focus upon the characteristics and needs of their intended users. The latter promotes consultation and debate with the public in order to achieve consensus on future plans and desirable outcomes in relation to a wide range of planning and policy issues. In the UK for example, citizens are familiar with this type of public consultation on issues such as the location of shopping malls, new housing developments and road bypass schemes. The early 21st century is characterized by the increasing pervasiveness of ICT into all aspects of our lives. Some individual ICT development projects have adopted a participative approach and sought to include end users in the design process. What are conspicuous by their absence are public consultations and discussions in relation to the scope, shape and implications of new technologies which will nevertheless impact on our lives. We, as individual citizens, do not have the opportunity to learn about and discuss emerging technologies, to discover what is becoming possible in our increasingly 'connected' world, or to consider the implications and explore what might or might not be desirable – in other words, to inform and influence our digital futures. Many putative developments occur in the research labs of the manufacturers and software providers, shrouded in secrecy to preserve competitive advantage until the 'chosen design outcomes' are launched upon the public.

In both civil society and in the design of ICT systems and services, there is a growing body of experience and knowledge about what does and does not work in terms of engaging people in decision-making. Unfortunately, both practitioners and researchers in these two separate domains operate largely without reference to each other. The apparently impermeable boundary between these two communities seems extraordinary when both so intimately and profoundly affect the lives of citizens across the globe. This is especially true when one (the use of digital technologies) is increasingly being seen as a means of achieving the other (enhanced social inclusion and citizen engagement in civil society). Both communities face resource-intensive challenges to successfully address key issues. For instance, identifying which groups of citizens are at risk of exclusion in a particular design context, and engaging 'hard to reach' stakeholders in the community will be critical common objectives. Any sharing of knowledge and good practice could ease the burden for both 'sides'. At present, there is no forum for capturing and sharing the rich knowledge and experiences of participation across the different design domains. Thus, a primary aim of this book is to draw together emerging principles and practices of citizen engagement from across domains, disciplines and territories in a new unifying and integrated framework.

1.1 Scene Setting

The theme of the book has its roots in the studies and ideas of sociotechnical change pioneered by the Tavistock Institute in the 1940s and of planned change published by the Harvard academics, Bennis, Benne and Chin in the 1960s (Bennis et al. 1969). The key contribution of sociotechnical theory is that by focusing on the interdependencies between human (social and organisational) and technical systems, it overcomes the traditional 'splitting' of these two activities such that technical design is performed by technologists and the social and organisational aspects are dealt with subsequently (Klein and Eason 1991). The application of change management principles and best practice in winning over all stakeholders (in government, in business and in the community) will be key to achieving a shift towards sociotechnical design.

The use of terms in this book has posed some problems. Whilst terms such as design, designers, users, stakeholders, citizens and technology, participation and engagement are in frequent use, it is surprisingly difficult to arrive at coherent definitions which are not to a particular context. We have tried to adopt the broad definitions which we present below, but our preference for using these is sometimes at odds with the need to be context specific. We hope we have achieved a workable compromise such that readers can be clear about the meaning of our material in each context.

Throughout the text we use the term design in its widest sense, to mean the process of making decisions about the function and form of an object or system. However, there are many different areas of design, and each profession tends to use the word design as though it applies primarily or exclusively to their field of expertise. So, for example, industrial designers will tend to use the word design to mean the process of combining stylish appeal of the appearance and form of products with their necessary function. Mechanical, electronic and software engineers on the other hand tend to be focused primarily on the often very complex and detailed design of the functionality of products or systems, and that is what they mean by design. We also share the perspective of Iversen and Baur (2002) that *"design is a social activity that takes place among people that negotiate. The design process is an ecology of participation, communicating both internally and with the rest of the world, depending upon the socially constructed values participants assign each other."* We realize that there are some situations, e.g. technical design, where this definition does not fit and will certainly not resonate with the individuals involved. For instance, many engineers and programmers frequently work in comparative isolation in research and development laboratories. The context of design activity is therefore, clearly crucial. Design with a particular focus or goal which relates to people, can be defined more specifically. Thus, inclusive design means designing products which as many people as possible can use (Disability Rights Commission 2001).

Defining designers proved particularly tricky. We generally refer to designers as those who have some professional training or skill in design. But, as Norman (2000) points out, most of those who have a hand in design are not professional designers – they are engineers, programmers or managers. Furthermore, as Seely Brown and Duguid (2002) note, *"in the digital world many of the distinctions between designers and users are becoming blurred. We are all, to some extent, designers now"*. This diversity among designers creates its own issues: *"designers are not users, users are not designers, and designers come from many different backgrounds, the inevitable result of the equation is that communication problems start to arise"* (Media Lab 2004). For the purposes of this book, however, the aim is that its contents have relevance to designers in all these contexts where the design outcome is intended for use by the public.

In the past, the all-important users of digital technologies were relatively easy to define as a group. As computers proliferated in the workplace, it was still relatively simple to distinguish users as those who operated them directly. But in the 21st century, as digital technologies become more and more pervasive, the user is of course, now potentially anybody and everybody – and herein lies one of the most significant challenges for the design of digital technologies. Each and every one of us is an individual, with our own different characteristics, skills and aspirations, and at different times and in different contexts, we may have different relationships to technology. All of these differences mean we have varied and changing needs and requirements of technology. The challenge for the design of truly effective technologies is to ensure that these differences are identified and their implications for design are explored. Therefore, unless we are referring to people who are actual, current users of technologies, we have tended to use the terms stakeholders and citizens to denote potential users.

The ubiquitous term stakeholders merits some attention as we use it quite often. The stakeholder concept emerged in the 1960s among academics at the Stanford Research Institute. They proposed that, instead of focusing exclusively on shareholders, a firm also should be responsible to a variety of stakeholders without whose support the organisation would collapse. The term was made known and expanded by Freeman (1984). He included in the stakeholder definition *"any group or individual who can affect or is affected by the achievement of the organisation's objectives"*. This expansion of the original concept resulted in widening the view of the firm from a strictly economic perspective to a political one (Correia 2005). In the context of ICTs, stakeholders are defined as *"individuals or organisations who stand to gain or lose from the success or failure of a system"* (Nuseibeh and Easterbrook 2000). In the past, it was a useful way of distinguishing between users (who operated computers) and those who were in some other way impacted by them. The list below (Hackos and Redish 1998) gives an indication of the range of people who might fall into this category:

- individuals who buy software and use it without assistance or interaction with others, either at home or in the workplace;
- individuals who use the interface and information as part of the work they do, even though someone else purchases the product;
- groups of people who use software and information as part of a larger business process;
- those who administer the software so that others may use it successfully and who are, themselves, users of the administration interface;
- individuals who repair products that are broken or who troubleshoot systems and processes that fail to work as intended and who are, themselves, users of maintenance interfaces and information;
- those who install products for themselves and others and are, themselves, users of installation software and information;
- customers of the users and others who are affected by users working with the interface and information.

Our perspective is that all citizens are stakeholders in the Information Society by virtue of the all-pervasive nature of ICTs. The sometimes unseen presence and influence of digital technologies on every aspect of our lives suggests that, in a democracy, citizens have every reason and right to be active participants in shaping them. The International Agricultural Centre (IAC) explains that *"without the understanding, commitment and support of different stakeholder groups, experts and governments often find themselves powerless to act. Further, the knowledge and experience of different groups must often be utilised to make good decisions and arrive at workable strategies for change"* (International Agricultural Centre 2004).

Citizens are a central focus in this book. Only by being well-informed and engaged in civil society is it possible for them to exercise their rights, fulfil their responsibilities, play their full role in the democratic process (Steele 1998) – and influence the nature of the society in which they live. In ancient Greece, citizenship was the privileged status of the ruling class in the city-state, while in the modern democratic nation-state, citizenship has been based primarily on the capacity to participate in the exercise of political power through elections.

The defining characteristics of citizen engagement are conveyed well by the following quote: *"…there are many ways in which people participate in civic, community and political life and, by doing so, express their engaged citizenship. From volunteering to voting, from community organizing to political advocacy, the defining characteristic of active civic engagement is the commitment to participate and contribute to the improvement of one's community, neighbourhood and nation"* (Philanthropy for Active Civic Engagement n.d.). On this basis, the concept of citizenship can therefore be described simply as participation in a community. We have chosen to use the term citizen in this broad and inclusive sense. This reflects our view that, regardless of whether they are formally recognized as citizens or have the right to vote, people who are impacted by technology should have the right to participate in shaping those technologies. In the 21st century the capacity and opportunity to participate in the design of our digital futures may become just as important as access to the ballot box.

Although the terms participation and engagement are sometimes used interchangeably, there are real differences in some situations. In their usage there appears to be a common understanding that engagement is a form of active participation. The Organisation for Economic Co-operation and Development (OECD 2001) has published a three stage model of public engagement:

1. information: a one-way relation in which government produces and delivers information for use by citizens;
2. consultation: a two-way relation in which citizens provide feedback to government;

3. active participation: a relation based on partnership with government, in which citizens actively engage in the decision and policy-making process (OECD 2001).

As Hashagan (2002) points out, engagement *"suggests that there is a 'governance' system and a 'community' system. To build the collaborative relationships on which a complex activity such as community planning would depend, it is necessary for the governance system to fully understand the dynamics of the communities with which it seeks to work, and to be prepared to adapt and develop structures and processes to make them accessible and relevant to those communities. In this way, the term 'engagement' warns us against making assumptions about communities: it asks for dialogue. It also implies that the development of the relationship itself will need to be a focus for attention: 'government' will need to engage with communities as well as asking communities to engage with it"*.

Our understanding of the term technology has changed over the centuries. Winner (1977) notes that the term was used in the 18th and 19th centuries to refer to machines, tools, factories, industry, craft and engineering. Today the term is used to refer to a much wider collection of phenomena *"tools, instruments, machines, organizations, methods, techniques, systems and the totality of all these things in our experience"* (Winner 1977). He further notes that so broad an interpretation risks becoming meaningless. Berniker (1983) states that technology can be understood as a *"body of knowledge about the cause and effect relations of our actions and of the machines and processes we build"*, and proposes that technical systems are artefacts, *"sets of tools (equipment, facilities, and computers) as well as methods (procedures, programmes, and software) all designed as a system to accomplish that transformation required by an organization"*. This is the way in which we use the term technology, although significantly for our purposes, we must emphasize that the transformations involved could be required not only by organisations, but by individual citizens, communities and civic society as a whole. As Castells (1996) says, *"technology (or the lack of it) embodies the capacity of societies to transform themselves, as well as the uses to which societies, always in a conflictive process, decide to put their technological potential"*.

Specifically, we refer throughout the text to ICT, meaning the building blocks of the networked world. ICTs include telecommunications technologies, such as telephony, cable, satellite and radio, as well as digital technologies such as computers, information networks and software.

1.2 A Desirable Digital Future?

In this book, we refer frequently to creating 'desirable digital futures', so it is important to define what we mean by this. What are the ends which people might want technologies to serve – what might a desirable digital future contain? It will undoubtedly have different characteristics for different people at different times. But in general terms, we would all benefit from technologies which are affordable, inclusive, easy to use, and promote sustainable use of the earth's resources (including human efforts and support). Equally, we would all benefit from technologies which fit in with our social systems, cultures and values, which have built up over generations.

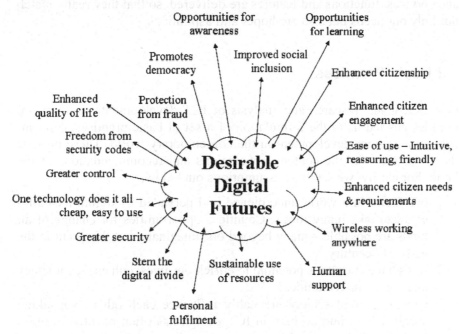

Fig. 1.1. Key Attributes of a 'Desirable Digital Future'.

We would also like communication which is always available to us, like the power of speech, and which we use when we choose. What we do not want is to be bombarded with unwanted communications from people we do not know, with unsolicited or offensive material, or demands that we engage in communication when it is not convenient or appropriate. We would welcome being able to undertake financial transactions which are as simple and secure as handing over cash to the seller. What we do not want are complex security procedures which, if we muddle them up or forget critical items, put us at risk of not being able to access our own money, or being electronically 'mugged'. We want privacy, safety and security for ourselves – and we would prefer to be in control of what we reveal about ourselves, to whom, and when. We would like government and local agencies to be democratic, open, transparent and accountable; we would like our companies and corporations to be efficient, productive, value-adding, ecological and ethical – and we would like the technologies which they offer for our use to behave in the same way. In other words, we want to be able to exploit what digital technologies have to offer – the vast resources of information, the speed and low cost of communication, the power to control aspects of our environment, to enhance our lives and the lives of others. But we also want to shape and influence the way in which systems and services, functions and features are delivered, so that they really match not only our needs but also our hopes and aspirations.

1.3 Basic Premises

Our experience, research and analysis of ICT developments over several decades has led us to the formulation of a set of basic premises about information system development in the contemporary world. These provide the foundation for the content, conclusions and recommendations in the book. For clarity, we set these assumptions out below.

1. our future in a world underpinned and pervaded by digital technologies can take many forms. Countless opportunities for change of all kinds are possible – many beyond our imagination at this point in the early 21st century;
2. ICTs have enormous potential to enrich our lives, enhance democracy and boost our economies;
3. technology and society inevitably influence each other. Not taking social factors into account in ICT design has often resulted in unintended and unexpected consequences following the introduction of new digital technologies;
4. while many of us enjoy extensive benefits from using ICTs, they have often fallen short of their expected promise;
5. one well-established reason for this has been that ICT design and development have tended to focus on the technical attributes of the ICT system and not on designing sociotechnical systems;
6. a further reason is that user/citizen participation has not been an integral part of ICT design culture. This deprives the design process of the benefits of citizens' knowledge and experience;

7. for technology to be developed in such a way as to benefit society demands shared understanding of what might constitute benefit in the eyes of the majority of people. This knowledge of what is important to people can only come from citizens themselves;

8. the potential of ICT is more likely to be effectively fulfilled if citizens develop and contribute their capabilities to inform and shape digital technologies;

9. desirable digital futures will not come about by chance. Extensive consultation and strategic planning in communities will be essential to achieving consensus on priorities through the participation and engagement of citizens;

10. engaging people successfully in ICT design processes throughout our societies will require energetic and imaginative exploitation of a vast pool of knowledge and expertise drawn both from academic theories and from extensive practice.

In this book we offer a rich understanding of citizen engagement processes and outline a blueprint for achieving a major shift in ICT design practice to incorporate citizen participation and engagement and from this deliver sociotechnical, rather than technical systems.

We examine common practice in ICT design and development, highlighting the paucity of involvement of users/citizens in the process. We then contrast this with examples of more extensive engagement and participation of citizens in planning and policy-making in civic society around the world.

From a theoretical perspective we identify five approaches that together offer a powerful multi-faceted theoretical framework to underpin design of digital futures informed and shaped by citizens. The intended outcomes are digital futures which are experienced as desirable and positive environments in which people can thrive and prosper.

The theory and practice are used to frame guidance on how to implement methods to successfully achieve such desirable digital futures. The final three chapters of the book guide the application of the state of the art knowledge presented in earlier chapters.

1.4 Structure and Content of this Book

In the next chapter we discuss some of the benefits and disadvantages of digital technologies for citizens, and examine different approaches to ICT design which have influenced the current situation. In Chapter 3, we seek to articulate the case for citizen engagement in planning, policy-making, and design of our vastly complex 'Information Society' which is under-pinned by an immense network of ever-evolving digital technologies. Chapters 4 and 5 examine current practice in citizen engagement – often enabled by ICT – through 20 case studies in 10 different countries. Chapter 5 focuses specifically on the widely-held aspirations for ICT to promote social inclusion. Case study material relating to some highly diverse and often marginalized groups reveals complex social needs and some innovative ways of meeting them. Chapter 6 provides an analysis of citizen engagement in the different case studies, and models the processes and outcomes. Chapter 7 explores barriers and facilitators to citizen engagement and pro-poses an integrated approach which draws upon related theoretical frame-works and approaches. The last three chapters are a suite of component strategies for achieving a shift in focus of ICT design. Chapter 8 draws to-gether the lessons learned and the best practices in citizen engagement to inform strategies for engaging citizens in defining and designing desirable digital futures. Chapter 9 describes some of the tools and techniques which are available to support citizen engagement. Finally, Chapter 10 addresses the challenge of making citizen engagement a mainstream activity i.e. the process of citizen engagement in design and development of ICTs for use by the public.

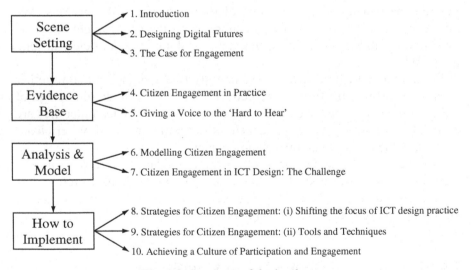

Fig. 1.2. Structure of the book.

References

Bennis WG, Benne KD, Chin R (1969) The planning of change. Holt Rinehart and Winston Inc., USA.

Berniker E (1983) Sociotechnical systems design: A glossary of terms. Productivity Brief 25. Houston, TX: American Productivity Center.

Castells M (1996) The rise of the Network Society: Information Age 1. Blackwell Press, USA.

Correia ZP (2005) Towards a stakeholder model for the co-production of the public-sector information system. Information Research, 10(3) paper 228, pp 1-32.

Disability Rights Commission (2001) Disability rights Commission presents: A guide to inclusive design. Disability Rights Commission, London.

Freeman E (1984) Strategic management: a stakeholder approach. Pitman, London.

Hashagan S (2002) Models of community engagement. www.scdc.org.uk/resources_reports/models%20of%20engagement%20web%20version.doc

Hackos JT, Redish JC (1998) User and Task Analysis for interface Design. John Wiley and Sons, New York.

International Agricultural Centre (2004) Appreciative Participatory Planning and Action (definition of) Technology of Participation. http://www.iac.wur.nl/iac/themes/msp_theme.htm

Iversen OS, Baur J (2002) Design is a Game: Developing Design Competence in a Game Setting. CPSR (Computer Professionals for Social Responsibility), Palo Alto pp 22-28.

Klein L, Eason KD (1991) Putting social Science to Work. Cambridge University Press.

Media Lab (2004) (MDR) Participatory Design 14/07/2005. www.mlab.uian.fi/participatory

Norman DA (2000) The Design of Everyday Things. MIT Press, London/New York.

Nuseibeh BA, Easterbrook SM (2000) Requirements Engineering: A Roadmap.

OECD (2001) Citizens as Partners: Information, Consultation and Public Participation in Policy-Making. PUMA, OECD.

Philanthropy for Active Civic Engagement (n.d.) Welcome to PACE. www.pacefunders.org

Seely Brown J, Duguid P (2002) The Social Life of Information. Harvard Business School Press, Harvard.

Steele J (1998) Information and Citizenship in Europe. Routledge, London.

Winner L (1977) Autonomous Technology: Technics out-of-Control as a Theme in Political Thought. MIT Press, Cambridge, MA.

2 Designing Digital Futures

For decades, new technology has offered tantalizing potential for tremendous benefits to people and society. Harold Sackman, in his influential book published in 1967, discussed ideas for augmentation of human capability through the concept of 'human-computer symbiosis'. He anticipated a world in which people would be freed from the drudgery of routine tasks and empowered by computer technology to expand their horizons and creativity (Sackman 1967). But, as computer technology proliferates and becomes ever more sophisticated, how close are we to realising this inspiring vision? This chapter outlines some of the benefits and costs of new digital technologies, and explores the way in which approaches to the design of ICT systems have developed.

2.1 Living in a Digital World

Certain technological achievements have far exceeded the predictions made in the early days of computerisation. The wonders of the Internet, the boundless capabilities offered by rich connectivity of both wired and wireless technologies, are a tribute to human creativity, innovation and ingenuity in science and in technological development. Immense technological challenges have been overcome successfully to enable some of us – a privileged minority worldwide – to enjoy a multitude of facilities undreamed of by most.

The pace of development is breathtaking. It has been said that human achievement is no longer limited by technological capabilities, but only by our capacity to imagine what technology can do for us.

These achievements have delivered an astonishing array of capabilities and devices that, together, offer significant advantages for professional activity, learning, leisure, entertainment, travel, health and every other aspect of human life to those citizens who are privileged to be able to access and use them. The Internet for example delivers the possibility of instant access to more information than we can imagine – and growing by the hour (estimates vary, but the rate is astonishing: millions of new web pages are added each day); the ability to communicate with one individual or with many, for whatever purposes we choose; to send and receive not only text, but pictures, movies and sounds; the ability to browse, order and buy a vast range of goods and services. Whether at an individual level, within organisations, or between communities and nations, the Internet is changing lives in innumerable ways.

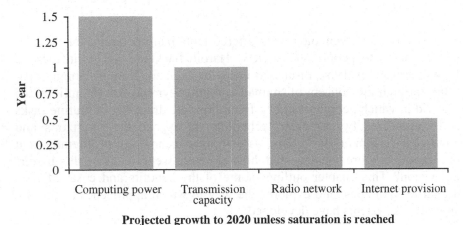

Projected growth to 2020 unless saturation is reached

Fig. 2.1. Growth rates for web-related technologies (European Commission 2000).

Devices such as personal computers, laptops and personal digital assistants (PDAs) mean that all this information and communication power can (theoretically at least) be accessed by individual citizens. High speed digital telecommunications deliver the services of the Internet; mobile phones allow us to communicate almost anywhere, accessing both voice and a wide range of other data. Broadband services carry data more quickly and at greater volumes. Wireless telecommunications mean that we can access these resources without the need for physical connections. Geographical Information Systems (GIS) enable us to gather, transform, manipulate and analyze information related to the surface of the earth, in a variety of formats. They are used by citizens as well as by agencies for navigating in vehicles, and also for locating and tracking. Virtual reality – advanced 3-D graphics and immersive facilities enable us to create and explore simulations for a multitude of purposes, including gaming. Digital media (e.g. CDs, DVDs, MP3 players) allow us to store, manipulate and retrieve digital information for a wide range of uses including entertainment and education. These capabilities are being exploited not just to provide new functions and features for individuals to use, but to deliver a vast range of services such as e-learning, e-banking, e-commerce, e-science, e-medicine, e-government – e-etcetera! As well as providing sophisticated new services, they provide new ways of accessing traditional services.

2.2 Fulfilling the Promise?

With all these miraculous functions and capabilities, it seems, to paraphrase Nardi and O'Day (1999), churlish to criticise. Yet, on the one hand, there are still billions of people across the globe who do not have access to the potential benefits of the digital world. On the other hand, for those of us who do, enjoyment and recognition of the achievements is often overshadowed by the shortcomings of the products, systems and services and the ramifications for society more broadly. Some examples of the limitations of services aimed at the general public are discussed below.

2.2.1 Government Services

In the UK a new computer system was implemented in 2003 to manage tax credits for families with lower earnings, an initiative aimed at alleviating poverty. However the computer system has been blamed for the fact that many who were eligible for tax credits either received underpayments or overpayments. Neither of these situations is satisfactory for people on low incomes – particularly since the agency involved (the Inland Revenue) has requested immediate repayment of amounts overpaid, totaling thousands of pounds in some cases. Unfortunately the recipients of overpayments were often unaware that they were receiving more than their entitlement and had thus assumed the money was theirs to spend. As a consequence when the Inland Revenue made demands for repayment, they had no funds available to do so. Some turned to loans at high rates of interest in order to make the repayments. Thus a system which was designed to help families on a low income has resulted in some situations where people now have less money to spend rather than more (BBC Radio 4 2005).

2.2.2 Digital Television

In the UK, the Government has embarked upon a process of switching over from analog to digital broadcasting, with plans to switch off analog broadcasting completely by 2012. Digital television offers a high quality signal and an enhanced range of programmes. It also offers the potential to access the Internet and its corresponding benefits from home without the need for a personal computer, by using interactive services. While there are numerous potential advantages, there are also some challenges. Although more than half the population has already switched over voluntarily (OFCOM 2005) a significant proportion of the population has not, and many cannot see why they should – they are not interested in the additional content and facilities that it would deliver. The new services require new equipment both to receive the broadcast signal and to access the new functions and features (precisely what depends on what you already have). The hardware involved is far more complicated to operate.

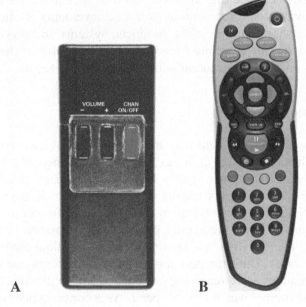

Fig. 2.2. A and B The difference in complexity of TV remote controls.

Figure 2.2A and 2.2B illustrate one of the consequences that the explosive growth in functionality and choice of features has for the user. Fig. 2.2A is an early remote control (circa 1980) for an analogue television set. This remote control enabled the TV viewer to remotely change the major parameters of their TV viewing with just three buttons. A simple toggle switch allowed the viewer to move between the four terrestrial TV channels that were available at that time or switch the TV off, and two buttons controlled the sound volume – one to increase it and the other to decrease it.

In sharp contrast, Fig. 2.2B shows the remote control for interactive digital television received via satellite. This has more than 40 buttons which greatly increases the complexity of the task facing the user to change channels and volume. In addition the user can also control and programme a range of other features. Because of the vast number of channels available, the user is given a variety of means of changing channels. For example, one button gives access to a seven day electronic programme guide, then there are buttons to navigate up, down, backwards and forwards through this, and another button to select the desired option. Alternatively, numbered buttons allow the user to enter the channel number directly, or (when watching a particular channel) the user can use the navigation buttons to move backwards and forwards through the channels in numeric order. There are other buttons which enable the user to move through the electronic programme guide day by day. Yet more buttons give access to menus of user services, interactive services, teletext, programme synopsis information, etc. The whole control process thus relies on the user having a mental model of the concept of multi-layer functionality and the capacity to memorize the procedure for navigating through these layers.

The remote control in Fig. 2.2A was an additional optional control device; the television could still be operated by buttons on its panel. However, with new devices (Fig. 2.2B) the only way in which specific features can be setup and changed is using the remote control, with the user no longer having the option of using the television set itself.

Studies have shown (e.g. Carmichael 2001) that these more complex controls present particular difficulties for the older citizen and those with certain disabilities – many of whom are perfectly able to operate their existing analog equipment. Citizens who face these difficulties may not only face the threat of losing access to a familiar and highly valued service, but also a sense of loss of control and a sense of powerlessness over their lives.

2.2.3 Local e-Government

Government in the UK had the aim of making all its services available online by the end of 2005. As a part of this process, all local authorities now have a website. A number of these are well designed and offer a range of useful services to citizens including the ability to pay bills electronically. However annual surveys of local authority websites carried out by Socitm (e.g. Socitm 2005) show that many of the websites at this point simply provide citizens with an alternative format for accessing information about their local authority and services. Other studies (e.g. Olphert and Damodaran 2004) have suggested that even so, local authority websites may not be fully meeting citizens' information needs. In a small pilot study, searches were performed on a sample of 20 local authority websites on queries of interest to citizens (such as the availability of local play facilities, or disabled access to local attractions). While the searches returned 'hits' in about 50% of the sampled sites, often the information that was found was not relevant or sufficient to answer the query. For example, in many cases the search brought up internal council documents (e.g. minutes of meetings) where reference might be made to the council's expenditure on play facilities, rather than describing the facilities themselves or their locations. Furthermore, the annual Socitm surveys reveal that a significant proportion of local authority websites are not easy to use or fully accessible to citizens.

2.2.4 Mobile Phones

Mobile phone companies have invested billions of pounds in developing new 3G services which allow customers to access the Internet and all its benefits from their mobile phones. So far, however, the general public have not rushed to adopt this new technology. Sales have been disappointing, and indeed there is evidence of a degree of 'backlash' in the market against the complex range of features which many mobile phones now offer. Some companies have recognized that some customers at least want a phone which is very easy to use simply as a phone, rather than as a camera, games console, music player etc. They have also recognized the difficulties that some users (in particular older people, who are under-represented in the mobile phone market) experience with small buttons and small screens. Consequently some companies are now making a virtue of producing simple, easy to use phones with fewer functions, large buttons and large screens.

2.3 Vision versus Reality

Four decades on from Sackman's predictions (1967), where is the freedom and fulfillment we were promised in place of human drudgery? Instead of freedom from drudgery, new forms of techno-drudgery have evolved. Thus, for example, a simple visit to the bank to raise a query has been replaced by the mind-numbing tedium and error-prone frustration of telephone banking: entering passwords, remembering how to negotiate security checks, and entering 16 digit account numbers. If you succeed in avoiding all the built-in traps in this process then you may have the privilege of speaking to a human being. Your communication problems may not end here however. The capabilities of modern technology may mean that the person you are speaking to is in a call centre on the other side of the world. They may be unfamiliar with your accent, your locality, your culture or even the country where you are domiciled and you may have trouble understanding each other.

Let us review Sackman's predictions (1967). One was that computers would free us from drudgery. And indeed there are now many digital tools available to relieve us of tedious chores in the workplace and in the home. The awesome 'number crunching' power of computers has freed us from the chores of mathematical calculation; word processing programmes and electronic publishing facilities make producing and manipulating text based documents a relatively simple task, compared to preparing them in the traditional way. Spell checking, formatting and reformatting, grammar checking, changing one word for another – all can be done with a few key presses. Optical character recognition can even remove the need to type a document.

Table 2.1. Sackman's vision and the reality of digital developments

Vision	Reality	
	Benefits include:	Drawbacks include:
Freedom from drudgery	data processing	neo-Taylorism
	'instant' printing and	loss of control
	publishing	tedious security proce-
	background processing	dures
Enhanced creativity and	tools for creativity	not everyone wants the
greater leisure time	office and factory automation	extra work
	mobile working	job losses
		work-life boundaries
		blurred
Augmented human	microtechnology	concerns about
capabilities, 'human -	immersive environments	security and privacy
computer symbiosis	pervasive computing	authority
		control

We no longer have to develop photographs using wet chemicals – we can simply slot the memory card from our digital cameras into the computer and print them at home. We can have computer programmes running in the background, with no need for supervision – to perform tasks like searching for signals from radio telescopes for signs of extra terrestrial intelligence, or (more mundanely) to print out a document, while we get on with more important or interesting things. But this same technology has also enabled the creation of call centers, which are growing all around the world and which are employing increasing numbers of people. Here often the jobs of workers are highly routinized with little or no scope for variation, imagination or learning, counter to well-researched principles of good job design (e.g. Davis and Taylor 1972). Work is paced by the computer and performance is closely monitored – an unwelcome return to the principles of Scientific Management developed by FW Taylor at the beginning of the 20th century (Taylor 1911). The need for security and protection of our personal information and systems brings other kinds of drudgery – such as the need to enter (and remember) numerous passwords and logins and registrations and PINs whenever we interact with a system; or the need to make backups and store copies of our digital data, in case of system failure; and the need to contact helpdesks when we find it has all gone wrong. We may find we cannot retrieve money or information from our own bank accounts because we have entered the wrong sequence of numbers, or we can't access all the work we did yesterday because the system has locked up. Computers have also given us 'information overload' – wading through 'spam' emails, throwing out junk mail, trying to find the right document in vast databases or even in the mountains of paper which we have too easily printed out – these are all chores that we can do without and which impact on our quality of life.

Sackman (1967) also envisaged a future where we would expand our creativity. Certainly digital technologies can offer us this. Not only can we store and access vast quantities of music, games, TV programmes, films and radio, but we can create and manipulate them too; we can make our own recordings, produce our own films, create our own radio shows, make our own digital artworks, build our own websites and write our own blogs – and make them available to a potential worldwide audience through the Internet. He also envisaged a world where we would have more leisure time (possibly even excessive leisure time) as computers took over aspects of 'work'. Indeed, we have automated vast swathes of traditional activities, with computer controlled production, office automation, etc. This has of course led to excessive "*spare*" time for some – i.e. those who have lost their jobs as a result of automation – but it has changed the nature of work. Service industries have grown, and in the information age, knowledge work and computer support have become important. The demand for these skills never stops – and thanks to computers and telecommunications, workers can be reached at any time or any place. For many people in employment, the work/life boundary has become blurred and the idea of excessive leisure time is pure fantasy.

Finally, Sackman (1967) envisaged a world of human-computer symbiosis. And yes, we have this too. Microtechnologies, embedded technologies, immersive environments – the future promises even more pervasive technology. Current research and development is making it possible to embed intelligence in our surroundings and in the objects or artefacts that surround us, which has led to the term "*smartifacts*" being coined to describe items that have embedded intelligence and sensors enabling them to detect changes in their environment. Computing, communication and intelligent user-friendly interfaces are converging to create the *"ambient intelligent landscape"* where intelligence will be embedded in our phones, in our clothes, in our household appliances, and even in our pets. But such developments raise significant questions about control, authority, security and privacy – who is in control of these technologies that we cannot see, are not aware of? How do we know what they are doing, what data they are collecting about us, how it will be used?

While new technologies have undoubtedly delivered many exciting and rewarding opportunities, it is clear that they have not come without a cost. The vision of fulfillment and opportunities to enjoy human-computer symbiosis can seem a long way off. Although there are undoubtedly many benefits from the advent of new technology, it could also be argued that, in many cases, the technology has simply brought new kinds of drudgery and different kinds of routine tasks. Since such systems now underpin every aspect of our lives in the Information Society their impact is considerable. In the sections below we consider some of the factors which might have led to this situation, and examine possibilities for influencing ICT design in order to deliver more desirable digital futures.

2.4 How Did We Get Here?

There has for centuries been a strong body of opinion that technology is deterministic, that is to say, that the developments themselves are inexorable, and that despite the benefits, negative impacts are inevitable and unavoidable. Negroponte (1995) for example asserts that being digital is inevitable, *"like a force of nature"*. It is suggested that both the speed and the scale of technological change that we face in the modern world contribute to this sense of inevitability; Toffler (1980) calls this 'future shock'. Nardi and O'Day (1999) make the point that the speed of communication in the modern world has had the effect of accelerating the speed of change in every aspect of life, and note the erosion of tradition and identity entailed by the constant necessity of moving on to the next tool, the next technology, the next fundamentally different way of doing things. *"We are adapting to technology rather than controlling its fruitful and pleasurable use."* They add that nothing about tool use is fundamentally new to us as a species, but that our ability to absorb new tools – and the different ways of *"doing"* and *"being"* that emerge with technological change, are challenged by the avalanche of innovation we are experiencing. The suggestion embedded in their observations is that it is our sense of powerlessness in the face of such diffusion and complexity that makes us believe that technological advancement is inevitable and inexorable.

In contrast to the deterministic view of technology is the belief that technologies are shaped by multiple factors in its social and political context. Williams and Edge (1996) assert that there are choices (though not necessarily conscious choices) inherent in both the design of individual artefacts and systems, and in the direction or trajectory of innovation programmes, and that these choices may have differing implications for society and for particular social groups. If this is the case, then technology can be seen as negotiable, with scope for particular groups and forces to shape technologies to their ends, and the possibility of different kinds of technological and social outcome. Although the form and direction of future technologies may be negotiable, there are many reasons why we may not exercise real freedom of choice. New technologies tend to develop cumulatively, erected upon the knowledge base and social and technical infrastructure of existing technologies, and where increasing returns are sought for investment, this can result in 'lock-in' to established solutions (Williams and Edge 1996). The way in which ICT design is approached also exerts a powerful influence on the possible outcomes.

2.5 The Influence of Design Methods for ICT

From the earliest experimental days up until the early 1970s, the use of computers was confined to specialist research laboratories, and computing operations were primarily carried out by centralized, mainframe computers. Since they were both designed by, and used by, programmers and engineers, there was no need to involve anyone else in the process.

During the 1970s, however, developments in electronics – in particular the very large-scale integrated circuits and silicon chips – made possible the microprocessor and visual display units with integrated keyboard and screen. This led to the advent of the personal computer, which in turn enabled the migration of computers out of specialized laboratories and onto the desktop. When their potential for promoting efficiency and reducing costs became evident to leading business institutions, large-scale IT system development projects began to proliferate both in commercial organisations and in the public sector. At that time, appropriate off-the-shelf software was not available and organisations wanting to take advantage of the benefits of computerization had to finance and develop their own 'bespoke' applications. This was a costly exercise, undertaken only by the largest and most well-resourced corporations. To achieve a return on such major investments needed large-scale implementations aimed at achieving significant cost savings and efficiencies. Computer system design of this nature was complex, hugely demanding of time and resources and embryonic expertise in IT development.

Consequently during the 1970s and 1980s, a number of methodologies evolved to support the development of large-scale, bespoke computer systems. Many of these were developed by systems analysts, such as DeMarco (1978), Gane and Sarson (1979), and Jackson (1983). Systems analysts tended to be drawn from the ranks of the computing profession, starting off as programmers, with formal training in mathematics, and then moving into analysis work. Such approaches to design tend to reflect this. They embody a technocentric focus, in which design is seen as the specification of a technical system, and where human activities are largely either automated or ignored. The focus of analysis is on the flows of information through a given environment and the different entities that make up that environment.

But although relatively influential, methods like these unfortunately did not solve all the problems associated with designing effective computer systems. Examples of truly successful computerization projects were few and far between and there were many examples of partial successes and even catastrophic failures (e.g. Mowshowitz 1986). The scene was set for what became an all-too-familiar pattern in large-scale IT systems developments. Typically the sequence begins with the statement of ambitious objectives, projections of significant improvements in productivity, forecasts of significant cost savings, and expectations of increased competitive advantage and improvements in service to customers. In reality the outcomes were (and, unfortunately, still are) often late delivery, escalating costs, a shortfall in performance and productivity, and user disillusion. Contemporaneous studies of the reasons for the lack of success of many high profile IT projects conducted in the 1980s (e.g. Kearney 1984) consistently highlighted the key areas of weakness as poor project management, inadequate definition of user requirements, and a failure to involve users adequately.

The realization that many design problems can be attributed to other than purely technical issues led to the development of new specification techniques and methodologies to assist in the design activity. Several were influenced by the concepts of systems thinking (e.g. Checkland's Soft Systems Methodology 1981) and sociotechnical systems theory (see Chapter 7 for more details). While these developed from a diverse philosophical and experiential base, they shared the recognition that the specification of requirements for information technology systems was the most difficult part of the design process, and that achieving a sound understanding of users' needs in turn required some interaction with users. It was also recognized (sometimes explicitly, sometimes as a by-product) that interaction with users helped to create user 'buy-in' which was an important element in successful systems implementations. But such engagement was typically confined to a small sample of users, who were relatively easy to identify because much of the systems development activity was targeted at 'bespoke' systems built for specific applications within individual organisations. User involvement was also typically confined to specific points in the design process, e.g. as part of the requirements definition process once the initial computer system had been scoped, and then again in user testing of prototype and final versions of the developed system. Users therefore had little opportunity to influence the scoping, planning and overall shaping of the systems, or to explore alternative options and their consequences. Yet at the level of the individual user, their experience of existing technologies and products will influence and constrain their expectations about the "*shape*" of future technologies and products.

An exception to this 'ping pong' approach to user involvement occurs in participative ICT design approaches, which have been adopted by a relatively small number of ICT design projects. Mumford, a pioneering advocate of participative design, who developed a method called ETHICS (1983) in response to the limitations of existing approaches summarizes her perceptions thus: "*my interest in changing system design practice was stimulated by observing the bad human effects of many early computer systems. Work was frequently routinized and controls tightened as a result of the new technology. Systems analysts, as designers were called then, appeared to have little understanding of the human consequences of their work. The difficulties of technical design appeared to displace any concern for human feelings....When computers first appeared in the offices in the late 1950s and 60s, their costs and limitations meant that they were often introduced in an authoritarian manner. 'This is what we can provide and you must have it' was a common technical attitude. Then as user resistance was encountered, strategies changed to a soft sell approach: 'This is what we can offer and it is just what you want.' Overselling of poor systems led to user scepticism and gradually analysts began to realise that they need to talk to users before producing a product: 'We think we know what you want but we'd like to discuss this with you'. This led to the practice of interviews with single users*" (in Schuler 1993).

The need for designing systems around the needs of users (human-centered design) is now well accepted by the design community (and indeed is embodied in standards such as ISO 13407 Human Centred Design Processes for Interactive Systems 1999). But, as Clement and Van den

Besselaar (1993) note, *"while modern methods for information systems development generally accept that users should be involved in some way, the form of the involvement differs considerably. Mostly, users are viewed as relatively passive sources of information, and the involvement is regarded as "functional", in the sense that it should yield better system requirements and increased acceptance by users."*

Designing technologies for use by a wide variety of citizens is currently one of the biggest challenges facing those involved in the design, development and delivery of ICT based products and systems (e.g. Shneiderman 2000). In addition to the well established procedures for human-centred design there is now a bewildering array of information, guidance, tools and techniques available to designers for inclusive design (known in the US and Japan as 'universal design' or by the goal of 'universal usability'; sometimes referred to as 'Design for All'). These provide, for example, information to designers about the physical parameters of specific groups within the population such as older people and disabled people – 'extraordinary users' (Newell and Gregor 2000) – who may have special needs compared to the 'ordinary' population.

Despite the growing recognition of the need for the involvement and engagement of users in the ICT design process, however, surveys of design practice suggest that in many situations designers still do not seek information directly from the end users they are designing for. Rather they rely on personal experience and imagination to define their needs and characteristics (e.g. Hasdogan 1996).

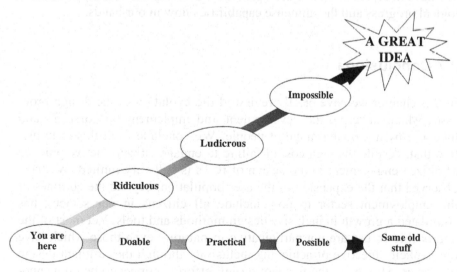

Fig. 2.3. Different approaches to design (Cooper 1999).

Another serious limitation of design methods is that they limit the scope for imagination and creativity. Cooper (1999) observes that *"when engineers invent, they arrive at their solution through a succession of practical, possible steps."* Because of this, their solution will always be a derivative of the old, beginning solution. What happens through successive iterations of prototyping and evaluation is that, while unsatisfactory qualities and features may be eliminated, it is harder to ensure that novel and desirable qualities and features are 'designed in'. To do this requires a different strategy from the conventional systems analysis approach – one which begins not with analysis but with imagination, and which encourages the widest exploration of opportunities and possibilities before commitment.

2.6 Did Anybody Ever Ask Us?

Our disappointment and frustration with the shortcomings of ICT are perhaps exacerbated by the underlying sense that we can't remember anyone ever asking us if we really wanted all these amazing widgets – nor were we told of the price we would have to pay in frustration, lost time, and loss of control over aspects of our own lives. We were never consulted about the desirability, the dangers, the consequences, what we might have been able to have instead, how we might want to interface with the technology, what we would like it to do most, and how much we wanted to pay for it. We have accepted what has been provided, awed by the wonder of technological progress and the immense capabilities now in our hands.

2.7 Conclusions

In this chapter we have briefly reviewed the evolution of the design processes which underpin the development and implementation of ICTs and their use by a growing range of people. We conclude from this examination that, despite the high cost of failing to engage citizens, active practice of citizen engagement in the design of ICTs is still very limited. We have observed that the expansion of the user population, beyond the confines of the employment sector to now include all citizens in our society, has stimulated a growth in inclusive design methods and tools. Yet most of the approaches in use are not participative in nature – even those which have the explicit objective of achieving inclusivity through the resultant design outcomes. Moreover, the focus of design effort continues to be on technological systems, rather than sociotechnical systems. For our nascent Information Society, this means that the design of the digital technologies fails to benefit from the immense pool of creative talent, wide and varied knowledge and expertise of many stakeholders in our society – its citizens.

References

BBC Radio 4 (2005) 'Inside Money' – Taking the credit – Broadcast on 13/08/2005 – 12.04 BST. More information at: http://news.bbc.co.uk/1/hi/programmes/inside_money/4740091.stm

Carmichael A (2001) Elderly Users of Interactive Television: Challenges and Opportunities. Presentation to ITC 'Easy TV' Seminar.

Checkland P (1981) Systems Thinking, Systems Practice, Wiley, Chichester.

Clement A, Van den Besselaar P (1993) Participative design projects, a retrospective view. Communications of the ACM 36(6), pp 29-37.

Cooper A (1999) The Inmates are Running the Asylum. SAMS Publishing, Indianapolis, Indiana.

Davis LE, Taylor JC (1972) (eds) The 'Design of Jobs', Penguin, London.

DeMarco T (1978) Structured analysis and system specification. Englewood Cliffs, NJ: Prentice Hall.

European Commission (2000) Information Society and Technologies Advisory Group Report 2000.

Gane CP, Sarson T (1979) Structured System Analysis: Tools and Techniques. Prentice Hall, Englewood Cliffs, NJ, 1979.

Hasdogan G (1996) The Role of User Models in Product Design for Assessment of User Needs, Design Studies, 17(1) pp 1-33.

Jackson MA (1983) System Development, Prentice Hall, Englewood Cliffs, New Jersey.

Kearney AT (1984) The Barriers to Information Technology – A Management Perspective. Orpington: Institute of Administrative Management.

Mowshowitz A (1986) Social Dimensions of Office Automation. Advances in Computers. 25, pp 335-404.

Mumford E (1983) Designing human systems. Manchester Business School Publications, Manchester.

Nardi BA, O'Day VL (1999) Information Ecologies: Using Technology with Heart, Massachusetts. MIT Press.

Negroponte N (1995) Being Digital. New York, Knopf.

Newell AF, Gregor P (2000) Designing for Extra-ordinary People and Situations CSERIAC Gateway (Crew System Ergonomics Information Analysis Center), XI, 1, 12-13.

OFCOM (Office of Communications) (2005) Digital television UK household penetration reaches just under 60%. http://www.ofcom.org.uk/media/news/2005/03/nr_20050330

Olphert CW, Damodaran L (2004) Dialogue with Citizens – the missing link in delivering e-government? In: Proceedings of the International Conference on Politics and Information Systems: Technologies and Applications, Orlando, Florida, 21-25 July 2004. International Institute of Informatics and Systemics, pp 95-99. ISBN 980-6560-21-3.

Sackman H (1967) Computers, System Science and Evolving Society. New York, Wiley.

Schuler D (1993) (Ed) Participatory Design: Principles and Practices. Lawrence Erlbaum Associates.

Shneiderman B (2000) Universal Usability. Communications of the ACM 43(5) May 2000.

Socitm (Society of Information Technology Management) (2005) Better Connected. SOCITM, London.

Taylor FW (1911) The Principles of Scientific Management. Harper, New York.

Toffler A (1980) The Third Wave. Bantam Books, New York.

Williams R, Edge D (1996) The Social Shaping of Technology, Research Policy, 25, pp 856-899.

3 The Case for Engagement

Citizens across the globe are facing an unprecedented rate of technological and social change. An unceasing flow of new products, systems, services and environments places demands on individuals to change their behaviours, attitudes and values. Collectively, the emerging developments offer the tantalizing promise of enhancements to our lives. The emerging technologies are transforming business, communication and lifestyle; they have the potential to enrich human life in innumerable ways, many of which we cannot yet imagine. They can simplify the mechanics of daily life, prolong independent living with smart homes and with 'obedient' domestic appliances, assist our learning, extend our skills and capabilities and enhance our leisure. For the transformational potential of these benefits to be realised in society, new systems and services will need to be accessible to all and taken up by the majority. Achieving positive digital futures, which deliver genuine improvements in quality of life, requires the active engagement of citizens in their planning, design and implementation. This chapter sets out the imperatives for citizen engagement, and identifies the benefits that it can bring.

3.1 Drivers for Engagement

Citizen engagement is not a new concept, and indeed there are many areas in which some form of engagement is already an established process. Public consultations are a regular feature in certain domains of public policy and civic planning; for example in 2004 the UK Labour Party launched its *"Big Conversation"* initiative, which was described as the biggest consultation exercise ever undertaken with voters, as a way of gaining public input into future policy making. The Scandinavian countries have led the way in developing participative approaches to the design of technology (e.g. Ehn and Kyng 1994), and there is growing recognition in the product and industrial design sectors of the need for some form of user involvement in defining requirements and evaluating prototypes. However, the pace and nature of social and technical change is now such that there appears to be a good case for these activities to become an integral part of all ICT developments.

There are a number of drivers for greater participation and engagement and four of the most significant are presented below. The first of these relates to developments in technology: nowadays it seems citizens are being offered *"e-everything"* with the proliferation of electronic services delivered by commerce and by government. The second relates to the consequences of the pace of technological change and the dangers of *"digital divides"* emerging in society between those who have access to the benefits of the new technologies and those who do not. The third relates to the goal of increased social inclusion, i.e. the process of reducing social exclusion by enhancing opportunities and equality to enable as many of the population as possible to participate as fully as they would wish in society. Finally, the fourth relates to the aspiration of many governments to capitalise on the potential for new technologies to enhance the democratic process.

3.1.1 "e-everything"

The changing nature of technology is now delivering *"e-everything"* to a vast and heterogeneous user population – the general public. Barely half a century ago, computers filled entire rooms, were serviced by armies of technical staff and were used by highly skilled experts engaged in 'big science'. Programmes took hours, if not days, to run. Today, more processing power than in those huge machines can be found in the average domestic washing machine, and millions of people carry devices in their pockets (PDAs, 3G mobile phones) which give them instant access to gigabytes of computer capacity. Carrying a terabyte of memory in your pocket is expected to become a reality within the foreseeable future. Analysis by the Institute for the Future shows the major shift which has already taken place since 1980 regarding the availability and usage of ICT and presents the projections for the future (see Fig. 3.1).

As a result of these developments, digital technologies have spread out from the science lab and the workplace to have a role in every aspect of citizens lives: schools and universities, hospitals and doctors' surgeries, shopping and service provision, transport and travel, entertainment and leisure, politics and government. The deep penetration of digital technologies into all aspects of our lives means that we often have little choice about whether or not to engage with new technologies: whether we realise it or not, we are all ICT users in some way or another.

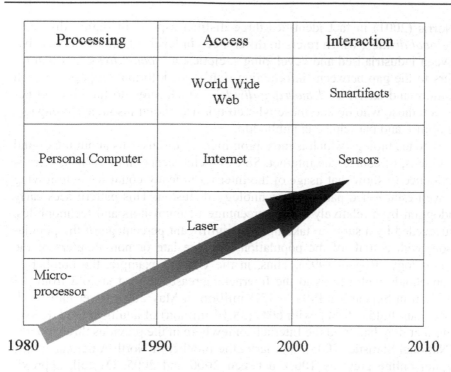

Processing	Access	Interaction
	World Wide Web	Smartifacts
Personal Computer	Internet	Sensors
	Laser	
Micro-processor		

1980   1990   2000   2010

Fig. 3.1. The shift from processing and access to interaction (Institute for the Future 1997).

Those involved in the design and development of new technologies have come to realise over recent decades the benefits of engaging directly with users, to define their characteristics and needs and to develop solutions which serve their requirements and aspirations. With a vast array of new and emerging technologies, and even more vast numbers of potential users, this is no simple task, but the active participation of citizens in the process becomes even more critical.

3.1.2 Stemming the Digital Divide

Another major driver for citizen engagement is the need to stem the digital divide. The term 'digital divide', popularised by the US National Tele-communications and Information Administration under President Clinton, is commonly used to describe the gap between those individuals and groups who have access to digital technologies and those who do not. While there is much debate about this term and its implications (e.g. Kling 1999, Warschauer 2003), there is no doubt that disparities exist. Pippa

Norris (2001) in fact identifies three distinct aspects of digital divide: a *"global divide"*, which refers to differences in levels of Internet access between industrialised and developing societies; a *"social divide"*, which refers to the gap between 'information rich' and 'information poor' in each nation; and lastly, a *"democratic divide"*, which refers to the division between those who do and those who do not use digital resources to engage, mobilise and participate in public life.

The technology which is most prominent in discussions about the digital divide is, of course, the Internet. Since its emergence in the 1980s, there is evidence to show that usage of the Internet in many countries is following a well-established pattern of technology diffusion. This pattern sees early adoption by a relatively small percentage of innovators and technophiles, succeeded by a surge in take up by a significant percentage of the population, with a 'tail' of the population who are late or non-adopters of the technology (Rogers 1995). Thus, in the UK for example, the number of households with access to the Internet increased almost sixfold from 2.3 million in September 1998 to 13.1 million in May 2005, (over half of all UK households –55%), with 60% (38.14 million) of adults in the UK saying that they had used the Internet somewhere in the previous three months (National Statistics 2005). Similarly, the number of North American adults going online grew by 100% between 2000 and 2005. Overall, approximately 68% of adult Americans (more than 2.2 million people) now use the Internet. But, as figure 3.2 shows, these levels of uptake in the UK and the US are not representative of everywhere else in the world.

While it is estimated that, in July 2005, there are almost a billion people online globally, this represents only 15% of the world's entire population (Internet World Statistics n.d.), and there are clear differences between nations. Most of the African countries, for example, have fewer than 10% of their population online, while in some countries the online population is approaching 90%. But even within Europe there are significant differences between the larger and more affluent countries where (depending on the source of the statistics) penetration may be more than 70%, and the smaller and less affluent countries, where penetration can be below 10%. There are also differences in access and use within nations, even those with the highest levels of Internet access. Computer and Internet use are divided along demographic and socioeconomic lines, with the youngest, most affluent and better educated most likely to enjoy the benefits of connection: *"the Internet, like cable TV, mobile phones and fax machines before it, connects the connected more than the peripheral"* (Norris 2001).

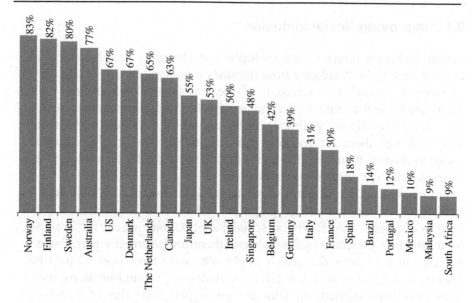

Fig. 3.2. Regular Internet Users (Accenture 2004).

A challenge for all in a democratic society is to ensure that it is not just the privileged few who enjoy the benefits of connection, but that the whole of the world's population can do so. Concerns about the digital divide have led to numerous initiatives to provide free or cheaper access to computers, software and the Internet. However, evidence also shows that the digital divide is not simply a consequence of whether or not people have access to digital technologies. Even when equipment and services are provided free of charge, there are many barriers to prevent people from making effective use of them. Cultural diversity, lack of relevant content, language and literacy are significant barriers to uptake (Warschauer 2003). Thus, the existing divide between materially rich and poor is now exacerbated by the related divide between the information rich and information poor. To stem the digital divide, therefore, requires not only improvements in access to the Internet, but also the provision of meaningful and appropriate content. The value of the Internet is determined by what people put on it and how people interact with it; thus, citizens with diverse needs and interests as yet not represented must be actively engaged and enabled to develop that content and stimulate interaction.

3.1.3 Improving Social Inclusion

Social exclusion refers to the multiple and changing factors which can cause people to be *"excluded from normal exchanges, practices and rights of modern society"* (Commission of the European Communities 1993). There are several factors which can contribute to social exclusion, such as economic, educational, political, health and ability, or geographical factors. Although there are concerns that 'digital divides' might exacerbate social exclusion, there are also hopes that the new digital technologies can be exploited to promote social inclusion.

Information and communications technologies overcome distances in both space and time, ignore geographical and political boundaries, and can help to overcome limitations on social participation caused, for example, by disability. Connected individuals can therefore potentially participate in a wide range of activities which might otherwise have been impossible, leading to a more inclusive society. A number of ground-breaking initiatives have been carried out with groups at particular risk of exclusion; some of these are discussed in more detail in Chapter 5. In the UK, for example, there have been projects such as 'Womenspeak' (a project using interactive ICT to link Parliamentarians and survivors of domestic violence) (Moran 2002), and a project to give Irish women travellers an online voice. Similar projects have been carried out with Asian women (Moran 2000).

A survey carried out for the US National Organisation on Disability in 2000 found that 48% of disabled people said that going online significantly increased their quality of life, compared to 27% of non-disabled people. In the UK, a study for the Leonard Cheshire Foundation (Knight et al. 2002) found that 54% of disabled people sampled considered Internet access essential, compared with only 6% in the general population. By contrast, a survey in the US found that 28% of non-users with disabilities said that their disability made it difficult or impossible for them to go online (Pew Internet And American Life Project 2003).

Ensuring accessibility to the Internet and to digital technologies more generally for disabled people is not only an important step towards promoting social inclusion, but it is now one which is increasingly required by legislation (viz. the 1995 Disability Discrimination Act in the UK and the 1990 Americans with Disabilities Act in the US). However there is ample evidence to suggest that designers and providers are struggling to meet the requirements of the legislation, and there is a long way to go to achieving the goal of universal accessibility. A study of 1,000 websites covering a wide range of services carried out by the Disability Rights Commission (2004) found that 81% failed to meet basic accessibility guidelines which have been produced by the industry itself – the World Wide Web consortium's Web Accessibility Initiative (W3C 2004).

In addition to the social and legislative drivers, there are also strong business drivers for more inclusive products and services. As Sir Christopher Frayling, Chairman of the Design Council and Rector of the Royal Society of Arts, clearly states *"the challenge of designing inclusively for the whole population is not just a matter of social urgency – it has become one of the defining business priorities of the age. The need has never been greater for products, services and environments to be developed in such a way that they reflect accurately the diverse demands of today's consumers"* (Frayling 2003).

Promoting social inclusion is, of course, more than just a matter of ensuring that designs do not exclude individuals or groups from access to technology. To achieve greater social inclusion requires that those who are currently marginalized in society are enabled to actively participate in the determination of both individual and life chances (Stewart 2000). In order to be able to influence the shape of future technologies, stakeholders (citizens) need to be actively engaged in the identification and articulation of their goals, needs and aspiration, and in the evaluation and validation of alternative options.

3.1.4 Promoting Democracy

There is a perception amongst politicians and governments in many countries that the population has become more and more *"disenchanted with the traditional institutions of representative government, detached from political parties, and disillusioned with older forms of civic engagement and participation"* (Norris et al. 1999). What Norris (2001) calls the *"cyber-optimists"* in society regard digital technologies as the panacea to many of the problems which underlie this apparent civic disengagement. E-democracy and its subsidiary e-government are two of the perceived lynchpins of the e-society. E-democracy can be defined as the use of ICTs and strategies by democratic actors (e.g. government, elected officials, the media, political organisations, citizens/voters) within political and governance processes of local communities, nations and the international stage (Clift 2004). In the UK, government policy on e-democracy has two tracks:

- firstly it is about encouraging people to take part in elections by giving them choices about how they cast their vote, including through the internet, either at home or at public venues, and by using mobile phones;

- but is it also about getting people to interact with Government between elections, allowing them to raise topics they want discussed, and influencing Government policy, including participating in on-line discussion fora.

The aim of the proposed policy is to take advantage of the new technologies' potential to encourage people to participate in the democratic process.

There are three stated objectives:

- facilitating participation in the democratic process: making it easier for people to collect public information, follow the political process, discuss and form groups on political issues, scrutinise government and vote in elections;
- broadening participation by opening up a range of new channels for democratic communication – this may enable involvement from people who in the past may have felt excluded from the democratic process or unable to participate;
- deepening participation by creating a closer link between citizens and their representatives (http://www.e-democracy.gov.uk).

This policy has given rise to two activity streams, concerned respectively with e-voting and with e-participation.

Voting systems are fundamental to the democratic process, and many governments are concerned about low or falling levels of turnout at elections.

photos from
Susan King Roth
"Disenfranchised by Design"
in IDJ, 1998

Fig. 3.3. Difficulties in using machines.

As a way of making voting easier and thereby encouraging turnout, many are exploring mechanisms for e-voting. Both the US and UK are currently trialling e-voting systems, but in addition to public concerns about the security of online votes, pilots and trials have highlighted a number of usability and accessibility problems of the different systems which have been tested. Fig. 3.3 shows one example of a usability problem. The figure shows a voter having difficulties with a machine clearly designed for a much taller user.

To explore the potential for e-participation, a number of pilot projects were set up in the UK. These pilots focused on three primary groups: councilors, council staff, citizens and communities. Councilors were offered e-petitioning services and online surgeries, in effect updating traditional techniques. Councils were provided with information on funding, and with guidance on tactics and strategies for implementing e-democracy in different types of authority. Tools and techniques were also provided to implement programmes and to assess progress against a baseline of national public opinion research. Interfaces with citizens and communities was mainly by websites and web portals offering information and access to forums for discussion and e-petitioning. They also included SMS broadcasting of local government activities, mobile phone games for young people and development of e-democracy icons to make websites more accessible to those with disabilities.

E-government services can enhance opportunities for citizens to debate with each other, to engage with their local services and councils, to access their political representatives and to hold them to account. They can also support councillors in their executive, scrutiny and representative roles (Office of the Deputy Prime Minister 2003). Many countries are investing heavily in e-government initiatives. One aim of such initiatives is to make government more accessible to citizens, but there are many examples where this objective is not being achieved. A survey in 2004 of interactive local council websites in the UK, for instance, found that of 23 websites which offered citizens the capability to carry out transactions with local authorities online, only one achieved a 'AAA' standard for accessibility, (the highest rating according to the International World Wide Web Consortium's Web Accessibility Initiative). Of the remainder, three achieved a single 'A' rating and the other 19 websites were deemed not to meet the W3 minimum accessibility criteria (Socitm 2004).

For new technologies to succeed in promoting democracy, serving the democratic process, and in avoiding 'disenfranchisement by design' (King Roth 1998), it is crucial that citizens are engaged in the planning and design of all aspects of e-voting and e-government. Although there is recognition of this principle, it is not necessarily being effectively applied in practice. While local authorities in the UK have been consulted by Government about the development of e-government strategies and systems, there is little evidence of systematic or widespread participation of other stakeholders, particularly citizens. This demonstrates the gap between UK Government aspirations for improving participation and social inclusion, and the activities which are actually taking place.

3.2 The Benefits of Citizen Engagement

The benefits of actively engaging citizens in designing the world around them are numerous and diverse in nature. This section reviews the wide ranging, and sometimes unplanned, benefits which derive from engaging citizens in different ways and in different roles in a variety of projects and initiatives. This includes emerging e-government and e-commerce applications as well as an array of products. Although emphasis will be placed in this book upon electronic systems and services, the benefits also apply to other domains such as product design and building design, where there is an equally strong case for developing products and facilities which are accessible to all and which meet the real needs of consumers and users.

3.2.1 Better Understanding of Needs and Requirements

From the citizens' perspective, the advantages of having a voice in shaping their environment and the nature of services and products can be profound and far-reaching. The experience of participation offers opportunities for individuals to articulate their hopes, fears, aspirations, problems and frustrations with their on-going life experiences. These reported perceptions, real life experiences and goals of individual stakeholders in society are often important and sometimes fundamental to the proper specification and verification of design or process requirements to be met by ICTs. Improved and validated requirements specifications lead to better design. At a later stage in the design lifecycle, resultant design prototypes, and simulations can be tested with relevant user groups, generating early feedback on citizen-consumer responses. Thus a significant benefit of citizen engagement is its impact on the design of the environment in which we live, on the manufactured products and on the raft of conventional and e-services we use to conduct our lives in the Information Society.

Feedback gained before a system is built can be used to make improvements which would be impossible or extremely expensive if flaws were to be discovered at a later stage of the design. For citizens/consumers there are the evident benefits associated with the outcomes of improved design. These advantages might include, for example, a better match between the citizen's needs and the services provided, improved usability, reliability and security.

For designers, developers and providers a major benefit of citizen engagement is that it provides them with insights and a sound and extensive knowledge base of citizen-consumer intelligence. Entering into genuine dialogue with citizens reveals the diverse objectives, aspirations and needs of different groups in society. This is valuable since most people find it difficult to imagine the possibilities outside their own experiences. Where there is a significant gap in understanding, developers tend to create products based on their own interpretation of the needs of others, thus often generating a solution which is less than satisfactory (Eisma et al. 2003).

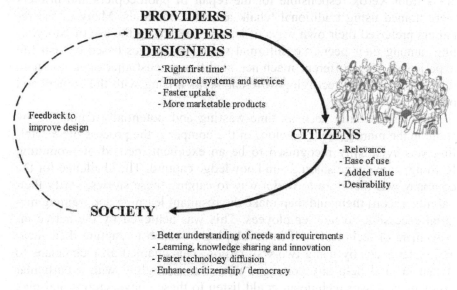

Fig. 3.4. Designing for a better society.

Eisma et al. (2003) give an instructive example of what can be discovered through engaging with citizens: "*we talked to a woman in her late sixties who had had a stroke which resulted in some functional impairment. We discussed her use of her mobile phone (Phillips C12 Savvy) and then showed her a more modern, smaller one (Motorola v66). Contrary to our preconceptions (that she would prefer her existing phone with its larger buttons) she did not comment on the size of the buttons, instead she remarked that she liked a small phone which would fit in her pocket, as she could not use a handbag (it slides down her paralyzed shoulder)*".

As Eisma et al. note, this insight challenges preconceptions about the kind of mobile phone which would be most appropriate for an older user with disabilities. The generic assumption that older people prefer larger control devices, like many other assumptions made about the design requirements of older people, requires validation with the users themselves.

3.2.2 Learning, Knowledge Sharing and Innovation

A well-documented and detailed account of how effective communities of practice evolved in Xerox from informal storytelling among technical staff provides rich evidence of the value of engagement (Seely Brown and Duguid 2000). The report details the history from the 1980s when technicians from Xerox responsible for the repair of photocopiers and printers were trained using traditional 'chalk and talk' methods. Many of the repairers preferred their own ways of learning including the use of 'storytelling' among their peers, i.e. informal verbal exchanges based on real life experiences with different machines at different customer sites, to share their knowledge of rectifying different faults arising with the copiers and printers.

Although initially seen as time-wasting and potentially damaging by some in the management echelons of the company, the process of storytelling was eventually recognised to be an excellent method of promoting learning, knowledge sharing and knowledge capture. The challenge for the company was therefore to find a way to capture these stories, verify their validity, record them and then make the resultant learning and training material accessible to new employees. This was achieved by the active involvement of technical staff in developing a system to capture their ideas and experiences by using two-way radios. This enabled all technicians to 'listen in' and help any colleague who was struggling with a particular problem. A newer technician could listen to these conversations and pick up tips and techniques that enabled them to become better repairers. The system was such a success that the stories were used to develop new training material for other technicians.

The technicians and employers improved the system by co-designing and developing "*Eureka*", a web-based system that enabled their ideas and stories to be validated and recorded in a way that would be readily understood by most of the target group. This was achieved by vetting ideas and stories through a peer review process using the (Eureka) web-based system to create and store examples of good practice in copier and printer repair. Widespread use and enthusiasm for the system has brought substantial financial benefits for the company. The system is reported to have saved

Xerox around $100 million dollars a year, and improved the learning curve of the technicians by 300%. Another example is given in Hepsø and Botnevik (2002) who describe the effect that storytelling and communities of practice have had in improving crane operations on North Sea oil platforms owned by Statoil – the Norwegian State Oil Company.

Considerable learning often takes place in the process of engagement itself and the citizens involved become more informed as users/consumers of ICT products, systems and services. As a consequence of this learning, knowledge of the technological possibilities grows. The importance of this for improving confidence and enabling participation has been highlighted by Eisma et al. (2003). In their research they concluded that *"older people are sometimes too much in awe of the technical knowledge of the developers, and it is important to make them aware of their (own) expertise, and how valuable their contribution is."* With this awareness and confidence grows the capacity and interest of stakeholders to explore and evaluate alternative options – and to suggest new options for consideration, or even quite new directions to explore.

This capability can be seen in a number of examples of older people being introduced to new technology. Inglis et al. (2002) after passing PDAs round to older people as part of a user-centred design process for memory aids, commented on the responsiveness the participants showed to the new technology. They also reported that younger, technically-aware users were able to ask for functionality, unlike the older generation which had experienced less exposure to developments in technology and were therefore unaware of the possibilities. This underlines the need to spend time and effort transferring knowledge to citizens to build capacity which will enable them to contribute to the design process (Inglis et al. 2002).

Eisma recalls talking to an older woman in one of the research focus groups used in their research. The elderly woman reacted to the description of every project very positively, wanting to get involved. When Eisma told her the methods they would be using were focus groups, hands on workshops, questionnaires, interviews, etc, the elderly woman responded: *"yes, an exchange of information... I have the experience of being an older person I can share with you and you have just told me about so many things I have never thought of before... we can both help one another"*. After an hour, this die-hard 'no computers for me' told Eisma that she was going to the 'learning flat' (an apartment equipped with ICTs) the next week to start using the computers *"as I would need it for using the messaging type thing you were talking about"*. Eisma said to her *"so, you're now interested?"* Her friend said *"that's because you've given her a reason"* (to start using a computer) (Eisma et al. 2003).

3.2.3 Faster Technology Diffusion

From the perspective of many providers of electronic services the return on investment in service delivery requires extensive uptake of the services by the public. Whether the providers are local councils implementing e-government or are e-commerce companies vying for business, they have in common the commercial imperative to attract citizens/consumers, sustain their interest in using the service and win repeat business. The critical success factors for achieving this citizen/customer commitment and loyalty are well-researched (Martin 1992; Skellett 1995; McIlroy and Barnett 2000; Kotorov 2003; Uncles et al. 2003; Lundkvist and Yakhlef 2004) and include such factors as perceived relevance of the services, accessibility, usability, good value for money, clear benefits and value from using the service. To meet each of these criteria successfully demands good knowledge and understanding of the needs of prospective consumers in society. Direct engagement with relevant individuals or groups is the richest, most revealing and valid source of knowledge about them. The compelling benefits for providers of engaging with citizens thus derive from understanding the interests, needs, wants, priorities and preferences of its targeted group and then providing services tailored to their characteristics. As with product designers, the economic benefit of 'getting it right first time' can make the crucial difference between a company prospering or failing. When services are well-matched to the life situation of their intended users the reliability of projections of take-up of new services is greatly increased. Enhanced predictive capabilities offer powerful commercial advantage in a highly competitive marketplace and therefore are a further and significant benefit of citizen engagement.

3.2.4 Enhanced Citizenship

There is a growing recognition on the part of many within the developed democracies that new relationships between citizens and institutions of governance must emerge if a crisis of democratic legitimacy and accountability is to be averted (Coleman and Gotze 2002). Increasing the participation and engagement of citizens is perceived to be a key feature of such new relationships, with benefits both for citizens themselves and for governments and their agencies. For example, in the United States, an organisation called America Speaks facilitates engagement processes including what it calls the "*21stCentury Town Meeting*". Its justification for these is that "*the growing power of special interests in all levels of governance has eroded a tradition of collaboration between decision makers and citizens.*

Barraged by organised issue campaigns and professional lobbyists, decision makers find it difficult to gauge how ordinary citizens feel about issues. In turn, "general interests" citizens feel disregarded and less inclined to participate in public life" (America Speaks n.d.).

The Canadian government has embraced citizen engagement as a means of achieving its goals of supporting open, honest, transparent and accountable government, by enabling citizens to participate in the policy development and decision-making processes. The Queensland government, in Australia, has recognised the value of engaging community members in decision-making processes, stating that *"engagement allows government to tap wider perspectives, sources of information, and potential solutions to improve decisions and services. It also provides the basis for productive relationships, improved dialogue and deliberation, and ultimately, better democracy"* (Queensland Government: Department of Communities 2004). It is suggested that participation *"makes people responsible for the decision-making process and their behaviour"*, which has a significant effect on ways they use their resources (UNESCAP n.d.).

In the UK, the Office of the Deputy Prime Minister and the Home Office produced in 2005 a consultation document entitled 'Citizen Engagement and Public Services: Why Neighbourhoods Matter'. The paper begins by explaining the relationship between public services and citizen engagement as follows: *"by enabling communities to help shape decisions on policies and services, we will support civil renewal and strengthen the legitimacy of the institutions of government. The more effectively communities are engaged in shaping services, the more likely it is that quality will be delivered. The more that communities understand the issues and limitations around decisions on services, the more realistic and sustainable those decisions are likely to be. Indeed, reform and modernization of the public services will not be accepted as legitimate unless it is based on citizens' support"* (ODPM 2005).

Another area in which citizen engagement has been acknowledged as crucial in the UK is in the development of the National Health Service. An initiative entitled 'Shifting the Balance of Power within the NHS' had the aim of promoting public participation in the control of the NHS. This initiative sought to move toward a model of increased partnership with objectives of creating partnerships with local communities, assessing the needs of patients and the public, developing the required resources to involve these groups, and ultimately to empower the patients by allowing them to participate in how services are designed, developed and directed (UK Department of Health 2001).

Involvement of a diverse range of stakeholders in a community has been identified as a key mechanism for public engagement in the United States.

Here the aim is that the community should be represented by all voices in order to reduce misunderstandings and a lack of trust on community issues. Public engagement discussions have enabled people to weigh up a variety of ideas and listen to each other in an attempt to build common understanding in their communities. Examples include: the San Jose Unified School District, where a new Department of Public Engagement was created with the specific purpose of organising community forums and other outreach. Other examples have led to more subtle, but equally significant, outcomes such as new trust and openness among different sectors of the community. For example, in Hattiesburg, Mississippi, a community forum on expectations for students led to new alliances between education advocates and clergy, which in turn proved important in planning a forum on race and education (Public Agenda 2003).

Moreover, from a democratic perspective, it is beneficial to have more citizens who understand potential choices and are informed about emerging opportunities and threats in the Information Society. Crises of public confidence in the way in which the UK Government handled BSE (Bovine Spongiform Encephalopathy, or 'mad cow disease') and anxieties about scientific developments such as GM (genetically modified) crops, led to the production of a new code of practice for scientific advisory committees in the UK. This document stressed the need for a more inclusive approach. A report from the House of Lords on 'science and society' stated that "*today's public expects not merely to know what is going on, but to be consulted; science is beginning to see the wisdom of this, and to move 'out of the laboratory and into the community' ...to engage in dialogue aimed at mutual understanding*" (Irwin 2001).

3.2.5 Sustainability

Information and communication technologies have much to offer community groups and not-for-profit organisations. Yet, as Merkel et al. (2005) point out, few non-profit organisations are likely to have paid IT staff; most rely on volunteers with widely different skills and who may only work with a group for a limited period of time. This situation creates a number of barriers to the effective use of technology. The people involved may not have the necessary skills to select and implement appropriate new technologies to help their organisation and to achieve their objectives. Alternatively, the organisation may have access to people with these skills who then move on, or who are only available part-time, with the consequence that there may not be skilled individuals available to use or maintain the system. The issue of sustainability under such circumstances has become a cause for concern. Merkel et al. suggest that *"sustainability in this context involves finding ways to support groups as they learn about technology, as they identify ways that technology can be used to address organizational and community level problems, and as they develop plans to take on projects involving technology"*. From experience working with community groups to promote IT adoption, they propose that the key to sustainability is to engage and empower the community members themselves so that they fully 'own' and take control of the planning, development, implementation and maintenance of ICTs (Merkel et al. 2005).

3.3 Conclusions

In conclusion, the principal benefits of citizen engagement in civic society are significant and far-reaching. Firstly, the systems, services and products which result from active and informed citizen engagement can succeed in meeting the real needs of citizens/users for an enhanced quality of life. Secondly, the increased uptake of new technologies and faster diffusion leads to economic benefits to providers and the possibilities of further enrichment in provision for the public. Such engagement can also be expected to improve the effectiveness and acceptability of information systems in the public sector. It may also help individuals to become active in their communities, thereby enhancing citizenship and the democratic process.

References

Accenture (2004) eGovernment Leadership: High performance, maximum value. The eGovernment Executive series. http://www.accenture.com

America Speaks (n.d) Homepage http://www.americaspeaks.org/

Clift S (2004) E-Government and Democracy – Representation and citizen engagement in the information age. http://publicus.net/e-government.

Coleman S, Gotze J (2002) Bowling Together: Online Public Engagement in Policy Deliberation, BT/Hansard Society. http://www.bowlingtogether.net/

Commission of the European Communities (1993) Social inclusion 2000 http://www.socialinclusion2000.co.uk/si.html

Disability Rights Commission (2004) The web: Access and inclusion for disabled people. The Stationary Office (TSO).

Ehn P, Kyng M (1994) A tool perspective on design of interactive computer support for skilled workers. Proceedings of the 7th Scandinavian Research Seminar on Systemeering, pp 211-242.

Eisma R, Dickinson A, Syme A, Goodman J, Mival O, Tiwari L (2003) Mutual inspiration in the development of new technology for older people. Proceedings of the INCLUDE 2003 Conference.

Frayling C cited in Clarkson PJ, Coleman R, Keates S, Lebbon C (2003) Inclusive design: design for the whole population, Springer-Verlag, London.

Hepsø V, Botnevik R (2002) Improved Crane Operations and Competence Development in a Community of Practice. In Proceedings of the Seventh Biennial Participatory Design Conference, ed. Binder T, Gregory J and Wagner I, Malmo, Sweden, 23rd-25th June 2002, CRSP, pp 63-73.

Inglis E, Szymkowiak A, Gregor P, Newell AF, Hine N, Wilson BA, Evans J (2002) Issues Surrounding the User-centred Development of a New Interactive Memory Aid. In Universal Access and Assistive Technology, ed Keates, Langdon, Clarkson, Robinson. Springer-Verlag, London, pp 171-178.

Institute for the Future (1997) The 1997 ten-year forecast. http://www.iftf.org.

Internet World Statistics (n.d.) www.internetworldstats.com

Irwin A (2001) Citizen Engagement in science and technology policy: a commentary on recent UK policy. PLA (Participatory Learning and Action) Notes, 2001, 40, pp 72-75.

King Roth S (1998) Disenfranchised by Design: voting systems and the election process. Information Design Journal, 9(1).

Kling R (1999) What is Social Informatics and Why Does it Matter? D-Lib Magazine. http://www.dlib.org/dlib/january99/kling/01kling.html

Knight J, Heaven C, Christie I (2002) Inclusive Citizenship. London: Leonard Cheshire.

Kotorov R (2003) Customer relationship management: strategic lessons and future directions. Business Process Management Journal, 9(5), pp 566-571.

Lundkvist A, Yakhlef A (2004) Customer involvement in new service development: a conversational approach. Managing Service Quality 14(2/3), pp 249-257.

Martin RA (1992) Creating, Maintaining and Reinforcing a Customer Service Culture. International Journal of Quality and Reliability Management, 9(1).

McIlroy A, Barnett S (2000) Building customer relationships: do discount cards work, Managing Service Quality, 10(6), pp 347-355.

Merkel CB, Clitherow M, Farooq U, Xiao L, Harvey Ganoe C, Carroll JM, Rosson MB (2005) Sustaining Computer Use and Learning in Community Computing Contexts: Making Technology Part of Who They are and What They Do, Journal of Community Informatics, 1(2).

Moran M (2000) Irish Traveller Movement. www.itmtrav.com/AR2000.doc

Moran M (2002) Womenspeak: E Democracy or He Democracy? A Fawcett Occasional Paper by Margaret Moran MP. http://www.thepolitician.org/politician/article_011.html

National Statistics (2005) National Statistics Omnibus Survey, May 2005. www.statistics.gov.uk/releases

Norris P, Curtice J, Sanders D, Scammell M, Semetko H (1999) On Message: Communicating the Campaign, Sage Publications Limited.

Norris P (2001) Digital Divide: civic engagement, information poverty and the Internet. Cambridge: Cambridge University Press.

Office of the Deputy Prime Minister (ODPM) (2003) Local e-Government: process evaluation of the implementation of electronic local government in England, CURDS, Newcastle upon Tyne.

Office of the Deputy Prime Minister (ODPM) (2005) Citizen Engagement and Public Services: Why Neighbourhoods Matter, p 7. http://www.odpm.gov.uk/ stellent/groups/odpm_localgov/documents/page/odpm_locgov_034880.pdf

Pew Internet And American Life Project (2003) The Ever-Shifting Internet Population: A new look at Internet access and the digital divide. http://www. pewInternet.org/reports/toc.asp?Report=88

Public Agenda (2003) http://www.publicagenda.org/pubengage/pubengage_questions. cfm

Queensland Government: Department of Communities (2004) Engaging Queenslanders: a guide to community engagement methods and techniques. Queensland: Australia.

Rogers EM (1995) Diffusion of Innovations. 4th Edition, The Free Press, New York.

Seely Brown J, Duguid P (2002) The Social Life of Information. Harvard Business School Press.

Skellett C (1995) Understanding and meeting the needs of our customers. Managing Service Quality, 5(4), pp 22-24.

Socitm (2004) Better Connected. Society of Information Technology Management, London, UK.

Stewart A (2000) Social Inclusion: an introduction. In P. Askonas and A. Stewart (eds) Social Inclusion: Possibilities and Tensions. London, Macmillan.

UK Department of Health (2001) Shifting the Balance of Power within the NHS. http://www.dh.gov.uk/assetRoot/04/07/65/22/04076522.pdf

UK Local e-democracy national project pilots: http://www.e-democracy.gov.uk/ pilots.

Uncles MD, Dowling GR, Hammond K (2003) Customer loyalty and customer loyalty programs. Journal of Consumer Marketing, 20(4), pp 294-316

UNESCAP (n.d.) Homepage. http://www.unescap.org/

W3C (2004) Web Accessibility Initiative (WAI) homepage. http://www.w3c.org/ wai

Warschauer M (2003). Technology and Social Inclusion - Rethinking the Digital Divide. MIT Press.

4 Citizen Engagement in Practice

The fast growing and increasingly widespread interest and global activity in citizen/stakeholder participation and engagement have spawned numerous experiments, pilots, initiatives and projects for a variety of purposes.

Despite the plethora of initiatives, however, documenting, reporting and evaluation of the varied exercises has not been systematic. Referring to pilot exercises in e-participation in countries using the Government Online International Network (GOL), Macintosh (2004) observed: "*although some governments and research centres have already undertaken a number of surveys in this area there is no standard way to describe the approach and to detail the outcomes.*"

Furthermore, while some initiatives have been evaluated by independent reviewers, most have not, and material which is in the public domain has often been produced by members of the project team, often the project champion. This sometimes makes it difficult to ascertain objectively the success of the exercises reported. There is variability in the amount of detail about what has been done, with whom, how, and to what effect. Yet to inform and guide effective citizen engagement initiatives worldwide requires the sharing of exactly this type of knowledge and good practice. It is especially important that governments can benefit fully from their investment in the many exploratory and innovative exercises in participation they have instigated. For this to happen detailed and clear analysis of the varied initiatives is required. We seek here to provide an enriched framework for such analysis.

4.1 Characteristics of Citizen Engagement Initiatives

In this book we have necessarily only been able to include a small sample of the numerous and highly diverse citizen engagement initiatives which are taking place across the globe. Given the relative lack of systematic reporting and analysis, we have selected cases which offer what we believe to be valuable insights into the practice and outcomes of citizen engagement. We have attempted to show the global extent of initiatives by taking examples from 10 different countries, and by choosing examples which are illustrative of the kinds of activities which are being undertaken. Regarding the many initiatives that aim to develop low cost, sustainable ICT (viz. "*the $100 laptop*" – Negroponte 2005) for the benefit of disadvantaged communities, we have included two examples (Nepal Wireless and Jhai Foundation). There are of course many other examples, but the aim here is to highlight citizen engagement/participation aspects. For this reason we have not included case studies of telecentres. Although these are a common approach to providing ICT at the community level, evaluative reports suggest that in general these appear to be introduced without taking due account of the needs of community members or aspects of the local context.

We have developed a framework to present the case material in a way which enables comparisons to be made and conclusions to be drawn. There are many ways of characterizing and classifying citizen engagement. One classification which has been widely used is the three stage model of levels of involvement (OECD 2001), which we have already outlined in Chapter 1. Another way in which citizen engagement has been classified in the literature is by the role of the technology. Macintosh et al. (2004), describe three different ways in which technology can support participation. The first is in an e-enabling role where the technology provides support for those who do not typically access the Internet. This means a wider audience can be reached (using a range of technologies to cater for the diverse technical and communicative skills of citizens). It also serves to provide participants with relevant and useful information in an accessible format. The second is e-engaging where a wider audience can be consulted to allow for deeper contributions and to support deliberative debate on policy issues. The third is e-empowering in which technology supports active participation and facilitates bottom-up generation of ideas to influence agendas. E-enabling and e-engaging provide for "*user access to information and reaction to government led initiatives.*" E-empowerment on the other hand sees citizens emerging as producers, rather than just consumers of policy: "*here there is recognition that there is a need to allow citizens to influence and participate in policy formulation*".

For our purposes, these two descriptors – level of involvement and use of technology - are useful but not central to our theme. Since the focus of this book is on citizen engagement, the classification by level of engagement was used to discard case studies where there was little or no reported engagement. Regarding the role of technology, the processes and mechanisms of participation are clearly important, but our interest is not so much in the way in which technology has been used as part of the engagement, rather in whether the engagement has had some influence on shaping either the technology, or the sociotechnical context.

Thus, the most important criterion to apply, given the theme of this book is the **purpose or focus** of the engagement process. By far the majority of published examples of citizen engagement initiatives relate to engagement in aspects of public planning or policy making. Some of the most inspiring examples demonstrate the empowerment of citizens to shape their own futures, to become *"makers and shapers"* rather than *"users and choosers"* (Cornwall and Gaventa (2000) cited in Lister 2004). There are also a number of examples where citizens have been involved in shaping some aspect or features of a technical system – typically, in creating or influencing a web site or web pages. Such examples are much narrower in scope, and are therefore likely to have limited impact or potential impact on citizens' lives and quality of life than, by contrast, initiatives which engage citizens in shaping their communities or developing national policies. Rather harder to find have been well-documented examples which combine both types of engagement, i.e. where citizens have been actively engaged in the creation of sociotechnical systems.

The stages in the policy making process and the ICT design process are actually very similar (Table 4.1). For the purposes of making comparisons across case studies in both domains we have therefore produced a combined model, as shown in Figure 4.1.

Table 4.1. Comparison of stages in policy making and ICT design process

Policy Making (OECD 2003)	ICT Design
Agenda setting	Concept specification
Analysis	Analysis of requirements
Formulation	Design & development of the system
Implementation	Implementation
Evaluation and monitoring	Evaluation and monitoring

Citizen engagement activities also vary according to a number of other dimensions. The issue of who is engaged is critical to understanding the nature of the process and in judging the effectiveness of the outcomes: what kinds of citizens were involved, how many, and how were they selected? Then there is the issue of duration – some initiatives are short term, lasting a few weeks or months; others are longer term initiatives which may last for several years. Regarding outputs and outcomes, the focus in published reports tends to be on notable successes whilst scant attention is generally paid to problems or shortcomings in the engagement process. Finally an important parameter relates to evaluation – has this been carried out, and if so, by whom? In particular are there defined criteria for assessing success and impact?

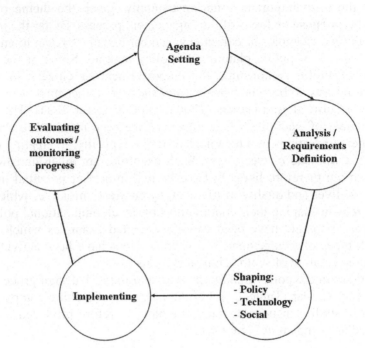

Fig. 4.1. Stages in policy/technology development.

4.2 A Framework for Analysis of Citizen Engagement Initiatives

The above factors have been used to create a framework for the description and analysis of the citizen engagement initiatives which we have selected for examination. Each case includes the following information, where it was available:

- the level of engagement (i.e. active participation);
- the objective of the engagement;
- the stage of decision-making in policy/technology development;
- who was engaged (how many citizens, from where and by whom);
- the mechanisms of engagement (including the role of technology);
- the duration of the initiative;
- the key outcomes;
- how the initiative was evaluated and by whom.

A total of 20 cases are examined in this chapter and chapter 5, illustrating citizen engagement/participation at a variety of different stages in decision making (see Fig. 4.2). Table 4.3 shows the distribution of the case studies by country. This chapter presents 13 of the cases. These have been divided into two categories (see Table 4.2): those which have a broad policy-making objective, and those which involve the shaping of technology, and/or its socio-economic context.

Table 4.2. Categorisation of Chapter 4 case studies (N = 13)

Citizen Engagement in Policy-Making	Citizen Engagement in shaping ICT and its socio-economic context
1 Netmums – UK	8 Bundestag website design – Germany
2 Matacawa Area Coordinating Council – USA	9 K-Net – Canada
3 Future Drug Research and Development Project – Denmark	10 Reflect ICTs – Uganda pilot
4 National Forum on Health – Canada	11 Reflect ICTs – India pilot
5 'America Speaks' – USA	12 Nepal Wireless – Nepal
6 Madrid Participa – Spain	13 Jhai Foundation – Laos
7 Chicago neighbourhood planning – USA	

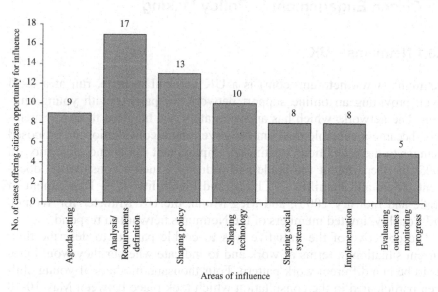

Fig. 4.2. Distribution of cases by stage of citizen influence.

The descriptions of the cases vary in length and level of detail. In part this simply reflects what is available in the public domain. More significantly there has tended to be greater coverage given to those cases where citizens have been engaged at several stages in the ICT development process.

Table 4.3. Distribution of case studies by country (N = 20)

Country	No of Cases
Canada	2
Denmark	1
Europe	
Germany	1
Spain	1
UK	8
India	1
Laos	1
Nepal	1
Uganda	1
USA	3

4.3 Citizen Engagement in Policy Making

4.3.1 Netmums – UK

Netmums (www.netmums.com) is a UK national website, run at a local level, providing an online support network for parents with young children. The network, which has approximately one hundred thousand members, became a valuable medium for government consultation on proposed changes to the regulations relating to employment rights and maternity. In 2005, the Department for Trade and Industry issued a consultation document: Work and Families – 'Choice and Flexibility' (UK Department of Trade and Industry 2005), and Meg Munn, the UK Minister for Women and Equality, invited members of the Netmums network to respond.

The objective of the initiative was to enable parents to describe their current situation in terms of work and to indicate whether they would prefer to be in a different work pattern. Four thousand mothers of young children participated in the consultation which took place between May 10-18 2005. The results contributed to the Government's deliberations on the issues and identified clear challenges for both Government and employers to address.

Meg Munn subsequently sent the following message to Netmums: *"thank you for your report on your recent survey, 'the Great Work Debate', which has fed into the DTI's Work and Families consultation on Choice and Flexibility. This helps to give us an insight into the day to day issues that parents are dealing with in their every day lives"*. A full report from the survey was then published on the Netmums site (netmums.com n.d.).

4.3.2 Macatawa Area Coordinating Council – USA

Emery and Purser (1996) describe how citizens participated in decision-making in the community of Macatawa, an area of south-west Michigan in the United States.

The Macatawa region experienced huge growth in population and industry in the 1990s. The rapid expansion led to traffic congestion, lack of services and a rise in juvenile crime. In response to concerns, the Macatawa Area Coordinating Council (MACC) (a local community development organisation) hosted a search conference to plan and create a common vision for a more desirable future for the area. Those invited to participate included mayors, the police, executives, local business owners, teachers, parents, clergy, housewives, social service agency directors, environmentalists, students and transportation engineers. The search conference approach encouraged a bottom-up planning process and the development of a vision statement. The conference group then identified eight strategic areas for action, and formulated action plans for community development initiatives. A key outcome was that those participating made public commitments to move the plans forward. The initiative led to positive benefits not only in terms of the physical aspects of the community, but also in terms of community cohesion. The former chairperson of the MACC *stated: "we walked into the conference as stakeholders, but we walked out as a unified community"* (Emery and Purser 1996).

4.3.3 Citizen Involvement in Future Drug Research and Development – Denmark

A project reported by Moldrup et al. (2000) was carried out in Denmark with the aim of engaging citizens in decision-making about the direction of future drug research and development, in order to help mitigate against social, economic and ethically undesirable consequences. This participative study was one of the first attempts to fully utilise Internet technology to collect and process citizen input in such a context. Specifically, the study aimed to find out:

- how citizens assessed the degree to which they have choice or can influence future directions in medical drug research;
- citizens' attitudes to drug research and development;
- how citizens would choose to influence decision-making on future drug research and development.

The study used the Delphi method, an iterative series of questionnaires, to reach a conclusion. A 'snowball' process was used to reach potential respondents. All people with the last name Andersen, and also all females with the first name Mette in the Danish email catalogue from www.jubii.dk, were contacted by email to ask for their participation in answering an initial questionnaire. These initial contacts were also asked to forward the email to families and friends to request their participation. As a result, 417 people were sent a second questionnaire and 377 replies were received, giving a response rate of 90.4%. The data were collected by email during January-February 1999, and were processed online by Infopoll in Canada.

The results showed that citizens wanted more autonomy and influence in making decisions about their own health, and that they perceived that the power of health professionals, e.g. GPs, to make decisions on their behalf was declining. Respondents also wanted more involvement from patient organisations, representative citizen groups and ethics committees as a part of the decision-making process concerning future drug research and development.

The researchers concluded that the demographics of the respondents generally matched Danish demographics, although the number of respondents aged 18-50 was higher than for Danish society as a whole. They obtained an unexpectedly high response rate from women, unskilled workers and people aged 50-59. However because the survey was undertaken by email, the researchers cautioned that the results could not be extrapolated with confidence to the population as a whole (Moldrup et al. 2000).

4.3.4 The National Forum on Health – Canada

This case describes a major national consultation on healthcare policy and provision in Canada. It was highly participative in nature and involved one thousand three hundred Canadians selected to be broadly representative of the diversity of Canada's size, demographics, economic activities and ethnicity. Thirty-four different communities took part. The consultation sought to engage a variety of communities often not included, such as homeless people, street kids, new Canadians, low-income mothers, senior citizens and First Nations. Study circles or discussion groups were used as the mechanism for engagement. Seventy one of these took place. The duration of the consultation was about six months.

The consultation was initially proposed in 1994 when there was growing public concern regarding the perceived threat to long-established healthcare policy and principles. The Federal Government announced that it would engage in extensive dialogue in relation to health and health care in Canada by setting up a national Forum for this purpose. The stated mandate of the Forum was *"to involve and inform Canadians and to advise the federal government on innovative ways to improve our health system and the health of Canada's people"* (Wyman et al. 1999). Public opinion showed that many Canadians welcomed such involvement although there was some strongly expressed opposition and negative criticism. Twenty-four members were recruited to the Forum, *"including economists, health policy analysts, physicians, health care providers, lawyers, academics, business people and community activists. These individuals were all held in high esteem, and their collective credibility silenced much of the anti-Forum sentiment in the initial months of their tenure"* (Wyman et al. 1999). Funding of $12 million was provided for the Forum to carry out its mandate over four years and report back to the Prime Minister.

The initial work of the Forum defined objectives and established the framework for dialogue structured around four areas: **values**; **striking the balance**; **determinants of health**; and **evidence-based decision-making**. In addition to carrying out reviews and research themselves, members of the Forum launched a major citizen engagement exercise to involve individual Canadians, organized groups and key stakeholders. The Forum decided to use a 'study circles' approach to support the engagement process. The approach uses structured, facilitated and in-depth discussions to promote mutual understanding and knowledge sharing, to encourage people to consider each other's viewpoints in a non- confrontational manner. This decision was based on the premise that citizens have a responsibility not just to give their views on important matters of policy but to be informed on issues relevant to policy making. Accordingly, a way of developing the capacity of citizens to contribute effectively in complex policy deliberations was needed. The study circles or discussion groups afford citizens the opportunity to engage in exploration of complex policy issues. Prior to participating in a study circle, interested individuals were asked to register in advance and to commit to approximately nine hours of time, over two to three sessions.

A workbook titled *"Let's Talk"* was developed to help participants to prepare. This contained statistical data, written information and some preliminary analysis of that information, related to the four broad themes initially outlined by the Forum.

The consultation took place in two phases.

Phase 1 was a scoping study to identify the views of Canadians regarding the present and future direction of health and health care issues. Its objectives were:

- to engage Canadians in a dialogue on health and health care and on the changes and improvements needed at the national level; and
- to examine issues as they relate to the health of Canadians.

Phase 2 was to *"ground test"* the directions of the Forum before these directions were articulated into recommendations. Its objectives were:

- to seek views on the Forum's proposed directions and options; and
- to solicit advice on approaches to implementation.

By the end of Phase 1, seventy-one study circles had been expertly facilitated, and in April 1996 key stakeholders were invited to a conference in Toronto. The conference brought together representatives of local, regional, provincial and national organizations with a specific interest in health and health care. More than 200 people attended the conference and participated in professionally facilitated groups to discuss the Forum's four key issues:

- how to allocate and organize resources in health and health care;
- how to move from research to action on the determinants of health;
- how to encourage evidence-based analysis and research in decision-making about health and health care; and
- how to identify the values Canadians hold about health and health care and ensure these values influence decisions.

In Phase 2, feedback on proposed directions and options was sought by Forum members from the wider constituency. Plans for return validation meetings with study circles had to be abandoned when the time-frame for the Forum to do its work was reduced significantly. Nevertheless Forum members remained committed to testing their strategic directions with the public and the second consultation phase achieved this through a telephone survey and two regional conferences in Vancouver and Montreal held during a six-week period in the fall of 1996. These conferences brought more than 200 citizens and stakeholders together with no explicit weighting of public and professional views. A background document, *"Advancing the*

Dialogue on Health and Health Care", was sent to all participants in the community study circles, to conference attendees, to individuals and groups who had expressed interest to the Secretariat and other federal departments, to stakeholders such as the Canadian Medical Association, unions, and community-based organizations.

These events were instrumental in identifying where members of the two groups agreed or disagreed with the interpretations and views of the Forum members.

The conferences and telephone interviews (the latter were held both with study circle participants and randomly selected members of the public) verified that the Forum had done a good job of capturing and responding to the concerns, opinions and suggestions of Canadians. Forum members also reviewed the findings of the consultation and found a strong degree of consensus between the views of the public and stakeholders in both phases of consultation. On February 4, 1997, the Forum presented its findings to the Prime Minister. The report, *"Canada Health Action: Building on the Legacy"*, was well received by health care consumers, practitioners, and administrators alike.

Regarding outcomes from the consultation, the government did, in fact, begin to act on a number of these key recommendations. Work was initiated in the areas of pharmacare, home care and the determinants of health, directions firmly rooted in the work of the Forum. In addition, the public consultations illustrated that:

- Canadians are willing to commit a considerable amount of time to policy discussions that have meaning and value to them;
- study circle participants were willing to prepare for discussions;
- participants were willing to modify their views as the discussions continued. For example, participants' sense of imminent decline of the health system was significantly reduced after the discussion;
- participants felt ownership for the directions proposed by the National Forum on Health;
- participants realized that they had a role to play in implementing the directions and ensuring government action;
- the deliberative technique used in the study circles was successful in generating informed and constructive directions for policy change.

As a further outcome, in September 1999, the Annual Conference of Federal-Provincial-Territorial Ministers of Health produced a firm commitment to joint action and collaboration on a number of key health issues (Wyman et al. 1999).

4.3.5 'America Speaks' – USA

'America Speaks' is an organisation which was established in 1995 in the USA to facilitate the involvement of citizens with decision makers in processes that affect their lives http://www.americaspeaks.org. The organisation was founded by Carolyn Lukensmeyer, now president of 'America Speaks', who had formerly been active in public service for 10 years. In 1994, motivated by concern that citizens were being shut out of policy-making processes, she travelled the USA to explore how citizens had organised themselves effectively, made an impact on local policy concerns and sustained their engagement over time.

In January 1995, armed with the results of her findings, she brought together 50 elected representatives, journalists, community activists, organisational developmental consultants and foundation representatives to work out how best to be able to involve citizens in policy making. The meeting evolved a concept of large-scale citizen forums, which could be used in national dialogue on key public policy issues. These forums, known as 21st Century Town Meetings, involve hundreds of thousands of people in meetings where they can discuss and deliberate on issues. Participants are recruited across all demographic groups. Up to five thousand people at a time may be invited to such a forum, meeting around tables in groups of 10-12 to share ideas and opinions. Each table is assigned a facilitator skilled in small group dynamics who ensures that the group stays focused on the topic under discussion and follows a democratic process. Ideas are recorded on a laptop on each table, connected by wireless to a central console of computers managed by a Theme Team, whose responsibility is to collate and record the deliberations of the forum. Each participant can vote on an issue using a polling keypad. Decision makers take part in table discussions, observe the process, and respond to input by answering questions at the end of the meeting. A preliminary report on the day's meeting is distributed to participants before they leave.

Since 1997, 'America Speaks' has conducted forty-five 21st Century Town Meetings in 31 states around the U.S. and in the District of Columbia. Projects have included helping the District of Columbia and New York to target changes in budgetary policies needed to improve fiscal status. Since 1999, 10,000 citizens of Washington D.C. have held Citizen Summits every two years to help develop the city's budget and strategic plan.

In 1999, funded by the Pew Charitable Trusts, 'America Speaks' engaged a broad cross-section of Americans in a national dialogue about Social Security reform and urged Congress to support legislation that reflected citizen preferences.

'Listening to the City' was a project in New York in 2002, which sought the views of citizens on the development of the World Trade Centre site after the 9/11 bombings. The outcome significantly impacted the rebuilding process and site design, and changed the decision-making climate.

The Deliberative Democracy Consortium was created in 2002 as a result of initiative from 'America Speaks' to design and experiment with innovative methods of citizen engagement. (http://www.deliberative-democracy.net/) One project researched the development of online tools and services to promote citizen engagement online (America Speaks n.d.).

4.3.6 Madrid Participa – Spain

The City of Madrid launched the Madrid Participa e-consultation initiative in 2004 as part of its aim to bring government closer to citizens through the use of new ICTs. The broad objectives of the initiative were to promote citizen engagement in local governance, to promote the use of ICTs as tools for engagement, to strengthen neighbourhood associations, and to help bridge the digital divide. Specifically, the e-consultation initiative aimed to reach a large number of citizens and to trial a number of different voting channels (Barrett and Reniu 2004).

The first e-consultation, to test citizens' responses to new ways of participating, took place in the Centre district of Madrid between 28-30 June 2004. A website (www.madridparticipa.org) was constructed to provide information to citizens about the e-consultation and to collect votes as part of the consultation itself. Six polling stations were set up where citizens could register to participate in the e-consultation. These polling stations also had computers connected to the Internet which citizens could use for voting, and volunteers were available to teach citizens how to use the technology (Barrett and Reniu 2004).

Once citizens had registered for the consultation, they could vote electronically through the Internet either at the polling centres or independently. Prior to the Madrid Participa initiative, the City had already established twenty-one public Internet access centres, primarily in markets, neighbourhood association offices and centres for the elderly, for those who did not have personal access to these technologies. Citizens could also choose to vote via mobile phones with Java or SMS messaging. Secure voting software was made available. The e-consultation covered questions about improvements in public infrastructure, quality of life issues and revitalization activities (Cervelló 2006).

Before the e-consultation took place, a communication exercise was carried out to inform and engage citizens, and volunteers and other local government officials were prepared and trained. Personalised letters explaining the purpose and the methodology of the e-consultation were sent to all those 136,337 people in the centre of Madrid who were entitled to take part. This proved to be the most effective method for recruiting citizens to take part in the e-consultation. Media support for the exercise was widespread and very positive (Barrett and Reniu 2004).

A total of 882 voters (0.65% of the electoral roll for the district) took part in the first e-consultation. Of the voting means available to them, 53% voted electronically in one of the polling sites, 32% voted remotely via the Internet, 3% used mobile phones with Java, and 9.5% used SMS messaging. Half of the respondents approved of electronic means to participate in consultation and in binding elections. Just 15% said that they would be reluctant to use electronic tools for voting in binding elections. Overall, most who took part were very positive about the effort to engage them in discussion, but were critical of the questions asked in the e-consultation and the options for responses. People were concerned about the need for advanced security for e-polling (Cervelló 2006).

A sociological evaluation of the exercise showed that the demographic profile of respondents compared with the population as a whole lacked people in the 16-24 age group and amongst those aged over 70. While EU and Latin American immigrants took part, Asian and African immigrants, of whom there are significant communities within the area, had a participation rate of virtually zero.

Although the response rate was low, the City of Madrid was encouraged to undertake three further e-consultations during 2005. The participatory web portal has been re-designed, and the initiative has promoted awareness of the City's public access Internet centres and helped people to learn to use ICTs. The City council believes that in future participation rates can be improved with an aggressive communications campaign and with a more efficient registration process.

4.3.7 Chicago Neighbourhood Planning – USA

This pioneering case describes active engagement of a group of citizens facilitated by use of ICT in a planning initiative in Pilsen, Chicago. Pilsen is a largely Mexican-American community of approximately 50,000 people (1999 figures) adjacent to the University of Illinois in Chicago (UIC). At the time of the case study (1999) the expansion of the UIC had encroached on housing and businesses in the district and had also resulted in the closure of large, well-publicized community programmes. This situation had led to overall distrust of the university by local residents. The university and community leaders alike recognized the need to improve the relationship and rebuild trust. When community leaders identified a need to redevelop the main commercial core of the Pilsen district (18th Street) as an attractive commercial area and to address problems such as urban decay and crime, they saw an opportunity to bring all stakeholders together, including university staff and local residents, in a participatory planning and design initiative (Al-Kodmany 1999).

A planning team was formed comprising 25 community residents, including representatives of the 18th Street Commission, and two planners, two architects and an artist from the university. The university's highest priority for the engagement was to build community trust. The team's objectives included:

- creating a mutually respectful partnership with Pilsen residents;
- preserving the history of the neighbourhood;
- providing a broader understanding and context of urban issues;
- exploring effective visual communication methods.

The process began by exploring current conditions in the neighborhood. The university team members soon realized however, that the techniques they were using to present information to residents (mainly slide images presented by projector in a fixed sequence) were not promoting meaningful public participation. This technique did not allow participants to visualize new developments in context, and participants became focused on small details of existing sites, rather than *"applying their community knowledge and expertise to develop overall strategies and solutions"* (Al-Kodmany 1999). The UIC team therefore sought a visualization environment which would promote full citizen engagement. To do this they embarked on building an interactive geographical information system (GIS) image database. Existing maps, photographs, tabular detail, and text information about the Pilsen district were used to create thematic layers relating to, for example, demographics, transportation, housing and property, economics, history, and crime statistics. The GIS provided critical contextual information but this needed to be supplemented by a way of creating and manipulating visual representations of new ideas. This facility was provided by a graphics artist, trained to draw urban scenes, using an electronic sketchboard which was linked to the GIS. The artist captured participants' wishes and concerns and produced rapid sketches that could be evaluated and annotated. Participants were also able to draw their own visualizations on the sketchboard.

These two tools were used during the course of a series of planning workshops; two screens enabled the presentation of the GIS images and the artist's sketches to provide 'before and after' scenarios. The tools enabled participants to visualize aspects of the community easily, helped to generate new requirements, and to evaluate and build consensus about solutions. In a final development, photo-manipulation was used to create realistic visualizations of new ideas for the neighborhood which had been developed and explored using the other tools.

While the technology at the time was more limited than current visualization software, this case study is an example of how technology can assist people to envision their future environment. The technology was used to augment participants' imagination and local knowledge to help them to define their needs, identify solutions to problems and in such ways shape desirable digital futures. This technology-enabled engagement represented a considerable departure from the established ways of doing things. Traditionally, planners and architects have built models, which they follow up with presentation to an audience. The GIS capability made it possible for community residents to be invited not just to give their responses to proposals presented to them, but to offer their own suggestions for redevelopment throughout the planning process. As an example of a specific design benefit arising from the contributions of residents, discussion and visualization had revealed that existing sidewalks (pavements) were totally inadequate for pedestrian use, and that the elderly and disabled had particular problems moving around the neighbourhood. As a result, sidewalks became a priority in the redevelopment proposals. Another example related to the proposed landscaping. When the artist drew in large trees lining the main highway, one resident pointed out that the underlying sewer system was a vaulted structure which would not be able to support the trees. Shrubs and small plants were therefore substituted.

The exercise was successful in promoting participative engagement by the community. The findings of the study confirm conclusions by other authors about public participation and the evolving role of the planner as an *"enabler"* or *"facilitator"*, rather than simply as a *"provider"* of services (Al-Kodmany 1999).

4.4 Citizen Engagement in Aspects of ICT Design

The seven examples of citizen participation/engagement presented in 4.3, are illustrative of the varied ways in which people are involved and engaged in informing decision-making and policy. In the examples reported, while ICT has been important as an enabler, the focus of attention has not been explicitly on the design of ICT. For this next section we sought published examples of citizen participation/engagement explicitly in the design and shaping of ICT. Although we found many such examples, the scope of citizen involvement has tended to be rather limited. For instance, there are many cases where citizens have been given the opportunity to design web pages, or to specify their needs of a website. We have included just one example of this type of engagement in favour of describing cases where the engagement has a broader focus, addressing ICT in the context of social and community needs and contributing in some way towards desirable digital futures.

4.4.1 Bundestag Website Design – Germany

This case provides an example of a consultative exercise carried out with citizens by the Bundestag – the German parliament. The objective of the consultation was to inform design of the national government website. The respondents were self-selecting. Their names were sourced from four mailing lists containing names of people who were interested in the work of the parliament and who wished to receive regular e-mails informing them about new developments. This gave an address pool of approximately twenty thousand individuals.

The project used ICT for online consultation to find out what information, functionalities and content offerings citizens of the German Bundestag would like to see provided. *"The aim was to gain better knowledge of the desires and criticisms expressed by users of the Bundestag's website so as to be able to optimise the site's content based on this information"* (Fühles-Ubach 2005).

The process used open ended questions. Two phases of development were used, with feedback of findings from the first round given to participants who then had the opportunity to participate in response to these. There were 493 participants in the first phase and 345 in the second phase. At the end of the project, 242 participants responded to a short questionnaire evaluating the whole participatory process itself (Fühles-Ubach 2005).

This process of citizen engagement was regarded by the Bundestag as highly successful, and resulted in numerous new suggestions from citizens that could not have been identified by the previously-used methods of simple questionnaire surveys. *"The intention with these methods is to prompt the target groups concerned into an active dialogue which then also helps shape the planning and implementation of processes in whose progress they are interested or even involved"* (Fühles-Ubach 2005).

Findings from the process of citizen engagement were that:

- women and young people were under represented in the process;
- the over 65's were well represented;
- participants were interested not only in content but also in user friendliness;
- participants were eager to see if they had been listened to and had had an impact on what was done;
- almost half the responses were submitted in the first two days of the project with only a slight increase resulting from reminder emails. They thus suggest that a reminder should be sent after only 4–5 days, allowing data collection to be carried out over 2 not 3 weeks (Fühles-Ubach 2005).

4.4.2 K-Net (The Kuhkenah Network) – Canada

This is a case study of a participative, broadly-based programme underway in geographically remote communities in Canada. The Keewaytinook Okimakanak (KO) First Nation communities are part of the Nishnawbe Aski Nation, located in north-western Ontario across an area roughly the same size as France. The total population of the area served is about twenty five thousand, most of whom are aboriginal people living in communities of about three to nine hundred inhabitants. For most of these, the only year-round access into or out of their area is by small airplane, although most have a few weeks of winter road access. Hospital and high school access, for example, have traditionally required air travel, although most homes are within walking distance of local services and administration buildings (Beaton 2005). Demographically, nearly half of the community members are under the age of 20; there is a high percentage of unemployment (36%) among adults, and high school completion rates are low. However the communities are located in resource rich areas; forestry and mining are expanding and tourism is an economically important activity. The programme centres around K-Net (the Kuhkenah Network of Smart First Nations) – a telecommunications network that provides broadband connectivity to communities in the region, with associated support services. The ICT facilities have been harnessed by communities to deliver improvements in local health, education, and economic development.

The initiative began in 1993/4 when local education directors identified the need to equip schools in the area with computers and greater access to information. At the time, telecommunications services to the region were poor, with some communities having no telephones and others only having a single phone to serve all residents. In response, the Keewaytinook Okimakanak tribal council began mobilizing local and federal funding.

As a result they were able to establish K-Net (the Kuhkenah Network – Kukehnah being an Oji-Cree term for *everyone, everywhere)* to provide an electronic bulletin board service, offer training and acquire computers for each KO First Nation. The first communities on the network (which at that time did not have telephones) were given access to the Internet and instant messaging. Federal resources were then successfully leveraged to get some of the communities connected to the phone for the first time. By 1999, the programme had fulfilled the original objectives of providing regional tele-communications connectivity (bandwidth), training, promoting awareness, linking the technological needs of the communities with various funding and development programmes to facilitate communication (Ramirez et al. 2004).

In 2000 the programme organisers bid to the Canadian Government for funds to become a Smart Communities Demonstration Project. The com-petition required the winners to demonstrate both community engagement and 'smart results'. In other words, the sponsors *"wanted to ensure that services were developed with the communities, not for them"* (Ramirez et al. 2004). K-Net succeeded in the competition to become Canada's only Aboriginal Smart Community Demonstration Project. This brought grant funding of $5 million between 2000 and 2004, which had to be matched with $5 million from other sources, including private businesses, to enable an expansion of the programme's activities.

A series of facilitated workshops was held in communities across the region to engage community members in defining their own requirements and priorities for expansion. As a consequence, two important develop-ments emerged. One is the online Keewaytinook Internet High School (http://kihs.knet.ca/). Chiefs and community elders could see that the use of computers and Internet communications would make life far more inter-esting for their young people, as well as providing them with new skills. The establishment of the online High School has enabled young people from grade 11 upwards to stay within the support of their families and communities, rather than flying out to board at High Schools, whilst also giving them the opportunity to contact young people in other communities. From September 2005, online schooling has also been available for grades 9 and 10. The school is authorised to give credits leading to the Ontario Secondary School Diploma. The online High School is seen as a critical benefit to community, not only in providing an attractive educational facil-ity which can encourage young people to complete their high school edu-cation, but also in retaining young people within the community at a time when they are maturing and could lose a sense of belonging by having to board away from home. The K-Net technologies also of course allow people of all ages in the community to educate themselves through participating in government programmes, university courses and other education and training activities (Beaton 2005).

A second priority area for development was health services. A Keewaytinook Okimakanak Telehealth project was initiated which delivers a variety of telemedicine applications. There are now telehealth workstations in each remote, fly-in community. These have diagnostic tools, a document camera for transmitting X-rays for diagnosis, a patient microphone, a video monitor, and a videoconference unit for consultations and telepsychiatry sessions. Community members have been trained to be telehealth co-ordinators, and can link patients with medical experts in hospitals in urban centres. The Telehealth facilities have proved cost-effective, and have delivered several benefits both to community members and to health professionals. They have helped to reduce the need to travel by air for health consultations, and have helped health professionals to deliver a more responsive and targeted service. Through the communications facilities and high speed access to information, healthcare workers have been able to share best practice, improve their own learning and understanding of health problems, and build up support networks among other professionals.

The K-Net network has also focused on providing opportunities and support for economic development. A unique aspect of the network is that it is wholly-owned by First Nations communities. Each community provides local support personnel, sets service rates and determines local billings. Job opportunities have been created in e-centres, by the Internet High School, and by the Telehealth programme. Indirect financial benefit has also come to the communities, e.g. as a result of providing accommodation to the people coming into the region to undertake some of the new jobs. The infrastructure is also providing some income generating opportunities by making traditional arts and crafts available to a world market (see: http://arts.knet.ca). Savings are being made in the cost of telecommunications, and as a result of the reduced need to travel out of the community for education and health facilities.

The broadband facilities have enabled the community members to communicate more easily both with other community members, with family members who have moved away, and with the rest of the world. This has had benefits in reducing the sense of isolation felt by community members which has been an important factor in encouraging migration of young people out of the community. The facilities have also enabled people to contribute local and culturally relevant content, including native language resources, which helps both to preserve the unique identity of the KO First Nations community and to share it to promote understanding. For example, K-Net hosts a forum called Turning Point, "*a dynamic and respectful meeting place for First Nations, Metis, Inuit and diverse non-Aboriginal peoples"* which enables aboriginal and non-aboriginal people of Canada to have open and direct communication with each other (http://www.turning-point.ca).

Sustainability, balance and respect are important values to the KO First Nations people which have influenced the way in which K-Net has developed. The involvement and commitment of the tribal chiefs and leaders has been instrumental in the success of K-Net. Evolution of the network and its services takes place through careful negotiation and recognised consultations. Each community is expected to provide funding and resources for use of the network. The initiative has delivered a wide range of benefits to the communities and to individuals, and it has also been influential in providing a model of good practice of community ICT development, and in influencing federal telecommunications policy within Canada (Ramirez et al. 2004).

4.4.3 Reflect ICTs Project – Pilots in Uganda and India

We have selected two pilots for analysis from the *Reflect* ICTs project carried out by ActionAid, a Non-Governmental Organisation (NGO) which operates internationally. ActionAid is explicitly committed to improving the life chances of the poorest people in the world. This project has been sponsoring participative programmes of information gathering and assessment in Uganda, Burundi and India (Beardon 2005). The project focuses on poor people, recognizing that they are particularly likely to be women, the very old and very young, and internally displaced individuals. These people have the least access to reliable and timely information which would help them to increase their life chances and quality of life.

Unusually for participation projects, the documentation published by ActionAid provides extensive description of the participative processes. This includes a clear statement of the principles and approach underpinning the project. *"New technology needs to be rooted in the existing, and new technologies need to make sense in terms of people's own coping strategies. In terms of ICT4D* (ICT projects for development in Africa), *this means applying new technologies to meet people's expressed needs and to tie in with their existing motivations, not an end in itself."* The stated aim of the project as a whole is *"not to provide ICTs to people. It is to build people's capacity to identify and articulate their information needs, to consult experts and information providers, to hold people accountable, to make demands, to be able to access, share and act on information in the long term"* (Beardon 2005).

These pilot projects are particularly relevant to this book as they show (i) examples of building capacity for engagement in planning and decision-making, (ii) the importance of appropriate learning opportunities, and (iii) the key role of tools for supporting learning which are designed to the suit the characteristics of the people involved. This is especially important and challenging when seeking to engage people who lack basic literacy skills in design and decision-making. As the *Reflect* ICTs project appears to offer many lessons and good practice in successful engagement with people who are severely disadvantaged in many respects – including education, economic status and social position, we believe it worth reporting on two of the pilots here. We have therefore selected pilots in Uganda and India for analysis and discussion.

In the participative process used in all the pilots in the *Reflect* ICTs project, facilitators recruited from the community were trained by the *Reflect* organisation and supported by the pilot team. Groups, or circles, of people in villages were set up according to participatory principles, to discuss local issues and develop action plans. The role of the facilitator was to support each group. A tool was developed to help the groups think about and discuss a range of topics. This consisted of five resource sheets, covering respectively the *Value of information; What makes information useful; Documenting local knowledge; Accessing information* and *Identifying information gaps.* The facilitators for each group, supported by the pilot teams, led the articulation and analysis of communication issues identified by participants.

(i) Reflect ICTs Project – Uganda Pilot

The pilot is located in the Kabarole district near the border with the Democratic Republic of Congo. It involves *Reflect* groups and six school-based youth groups. Most people in the community are subsistence farmers, living in absolute poverty. Their lack of information is seen as a major barrier to improving their lives. For example, without knowledge of the prices at which produce is sold at market, people sell their goods at half the market price. The result of the *Reflect* circle analysis of communication patterns, information flows and needs showed that the most widely used means of communication were talking, meeting and drumming. These were also considered to be the most useful ways of communicating. Radio was available but less affordable and although video was seen as desirable it was less accessible. Analyses of information needs revealed the priorities of group participants, listed in Table 4.4.

Table 4.4. *Reflect* ICTS Uganda Pilot: Prioritised information needs by gender and age

Group	Information Need
Men	- Where to access credit
	- Markets for their produce
	- Job opportunities
	- Modern farming practices
	- Land ownership rights
Women	- Where to access credit
	- Agriculture
	- Health, particularly HIV, antenatal, reproductive
	- Education opportunities for girls
	- Cooking
	- Women's rights: dowry; children; poverty
Girls	- Education opportunities for girls
	- Reproductive health/HIV/AIDS
	- Women's rights
	- Job opportunities
Boys	- Business/job opportunities
	- Education
	- Agriculture
	- Health: HIV/AIDS, condom use

Based on the information needs identified in the *Reflect* circles, plans were developed in an iterative process in teams which included local participants, ActionAid staff, and members of partner organisations. In the next phase of the project, pilot teams were able to analyse, discuss and debate ICT issues and devise a plan founded upon the stated communication preferences, while the second phase was for the implementation of the plan. As a result of this information needs analysis and action planning by citizens, Uganda now has a central information resource centre. *"This is a central place for information to be stored and shared and provides a one-stop centre for sharing information between partners, including communities, facilitators, local government and traditional information providers. Equipment includes internet-connected computers, digital cameras and world space receivers. Air time is also being purchased for radio programmes. The centre will also develop a databank of traditional medicines and their applications, act as a training centre, and undertake pro-poor advocacy with information providers and policy makers on the development and information needs of poor people"* (Beardon 2005).

(ii) Reflect ICTs Project – India Pilot

The *Reflect* ICTs pilot in India was located in Balangir in Orissa, (Eastern India). Major contributing factors to the extreme poverty in the region are the alternating droughts and floods which occur with increasing frequency. In addition, a complex array of social, economic and political factors (including a strict and active caste system) impact on the quality of life experienced by most of the population. The poor do not participate in local decision-making and lack access to information which would enable them to improve their lives.

Following the same process described in the Ugandan pilot, information needs were identified in the *Reflect* circles. The needs identified related to sustaining the basic livelihoods of the participants – as listed in Table 4.5.

Table 4.5. *Reflect* ICTs India Pilot: Prioritised information needs

Information Need
- Citizens rights
- Available benefits
- Schemes to ensure food security
- Agricultural practices
- Water conservation
- Seasonal employment opportunities
- Local governance

Documented records of the pilot report that, as a result of participation in the first stage of the pilot, people have become more aware of their rights – e.g. the benefits and services to which they are entitled. The communications system under development in the second phase of the project is informed by the information needs analysis conducted in the *Reflect* circles. The emerging system is being designed to strengthen existing communication patterns through the preferred channels explicitly specified by the participants. It is therefore developing as a sociotechnical system, rather than simply a technical system. This means, for example, that the system will offer facilitators support and information in recognition of their acknowledged status as trusted and reliable sources of information. The system has been designed to provide a wide range of information using electronic media, including video, audio and television and paper-based records. These will be located at district level for use by participants of all *Reflect* circles on request. Where it is available (e.g. in the offices of some partner organisations) the Internet will be an additional resource to feed information into the system. Local village resource centres will house materials generated locally and developed by *Reflect* groups (newspapers and letters, posters leaflets and booklets, cassettes, pictures and so on). In addition a radio set would be available for each circle. Plans are in place to monitor the system on the basis of usage and application of information (i.e. not just by the simple availability of information). Indicators elaborated by participants in the *Reflect* circles include: numbers of landless families; migrants and preventable deaths; development funding; literacy; and participation in decision making. Thus there is built-in evaluation of the pilots, based on criteria defined by the participants in the pilot. Monitoring and evaluation have been planned both of the systems themselves and of the *Reflect* ICTs project more widely (Beardon 2005).

4.4.4 Nepal Wireless

The case reported here is a participative project which was the brainchild of a single individual, Mahabir Pun, a computer engineer who had studied for a Master's degree in Education in the USA. When he returned to his native Nangi, a mountainous village in Nepal, he resolved to set up a computer network which would provide computers and Internet connection to Nangi and its neighbours. On the website http://nepalwireless.net/, Pun explains that he realised that he would need to bring computers to the villagers to show them exactly what they could do with ICT (Pun n.d.).

When his school in Nangi received a gift of computer parts from an Australian school in 1997, Pun assembled computers in wooden boxes to equip classrooms. He tried to obtain a phone connection, which could be used to connect to the Internet. The villagers got a radio phone but the line was not clear. The cost of a satellite phone was beyond their means. Pun wrote to the BBC reporting his experiences and his story was published in 2001. As a result of the publicity, Pun received help and support from around the world and learnt of 802.11b wireless technology, which could be used to connect computers in a network and to the Internet. Two foreign volunteers came to Nangi to help set things up, and more people followed. A small pilot scheme ran successfully in September 2002. Pun appears to have engaged people through demonstrating the potential of ICTs – by developing their awareness of the capabilities, helping them to articulate their needs and to recognise potential uses which will benefit them.

Subsequently, the network has been extended to seven villages. The villages are connected by wi-fi, although shortages of powered wireless devices and poor weather conditions mean the connections are not constant. The original relay station set up at the top of a tall tree, 10,800 feet above sea level, and consisting of a TV dish antenna and one litre measuring can, is still working (Since1968.com 2004).

Following the success of the trial, an American, Mark Michalski, helped Pun to write a proposal for a grant from the Donald Strauss Foundation to extend the network with more rugged and up to date equipment. The project's website is hosted on the server of one of the original volunteers, Jonni Lehitranta, in Finland.

"Although there is a shortage of power at the schools, relay stations, and proxy server station, the villagers still can send and receive their messages through NetMeeting or through e-mails using our POP server located in Finland," reported Pun (Since1968.com 2004).

Nangi and Paudwar villages use the networks to communicate with their yak herders and camping grounds in the mountains. The herders use the Internet to buy and sell livestock and share veterinary tips as well as staying in touch with their families. Children in two high schools use email to write to each other and to pen-pals abroad.

The educational programme is now supported by a non-profit organisation in the USA known as the Himanchal Education Foundation. Not only does the Foundation support education, it is also promoting income-generating schemes such as handicrafts, farm animal-rearing, fish farming and tourism resorts (Himanchal Education Foundation 2005).

The villages are generally subsistence communities, relying on their own animals and vegetable cultivation. The only income has been from men joining the military, but this may change as children acquire ICT and other skills.

Both Nepal Wireless and the Himanchal Education Foundation rely heavily on volunteer support and commitment. Mahabir Pun has been the driving force, operating in a pragmatic way and taking account of complex political circumstances. There are no reported evaluations of the project in the public domain as yet. The considerable interest in the international community suggests there are worthwhile achievements to report.

4.4.5 Jhai Foundation – Laos

The Jhai Foundation is an organisation that works with the people of Laos. The purpose of engagement was to create various ICT applications that support community economic and social development. Broadly-based participation of many stakeholders characterises the initiative. The foundation has a board of directors consisting of people with varying backgrounds and skills (e.g. employment specialist, computer company executive, lawyer, information technology professor, social worker etc.), an advisory board including a *"project management engineer and development specialist, an investment banker, three highly trained nurses, a veterinarian programme director, a farmer, computer experts, a psychologist, three medical doctors, two priests, business executives, and a former senior executive of Applied Materials"* (The Jhai Foundation n.d.). The foundation has a number of active projects in which local people can choose to participate on the basis of their preferences and skills. The participants in the projects are volunteers and any project can have up to 225 volunteers per week. Volunteers come from many domains and walks of life. The Jhai Foundation website lists amongst the volunteers *"farmers, attorneys, business people, accountants, graphic designers, website designers, database management experts, construction workers, computer programme trainers, agricultural experts, small business developers, coffee tasters, coffee industry experts, clerical workers, bankers, warehousemen, procurement specialists, doctors, nurses, hospital administrators, food industry technologists, weavers, engineers, telecommunication specialists, well-diggers, teachers, and non-profit management experts. The ethnicity of the volunteers are typically ¼ Laotians, ¼ Lao-Americans, and ¼ are veterans of the Vietnam war"* (The Jhai Foundation n.d.).

The projects supported by the foundation initiative include coffee growing, education, information technology and economic development. The information technology project in particular has introduced computers into the schools on Laos, created four Internet learning centres to teach both adults and children, and has plans to establish 20 more. Regarding the first learning centre, the Foundation reports: *"the whole community feels it owns it. It teaches both kids and adults. And it is initiating a collaborative, project-based learning project that is unique in the world. Its project is to collaborate with schools in similar latitudes and in the U.S. to discover ways to experiment with local organic cash crops for local and international markets. From the beginning kids make money, their parents find ways to keep their kids home, and the school gets new community resources – parents who are farmers, agriculture extension agents – that they never had before"* (The Jhai Foundation n.d.).

Overall, the foundation has helped 25 villages improve their social and economic well-being, helped villages create many new businesses and moved 10 tons of medical supplies. The projects produce high impact because their communities own them. *"We always hire locally, if possible, and help fund contracts, signed by local people, with local experts...Jhai helps create change that is sustainable, because it is locally conceived and implemented to be that way, with minimal interference and direction from outsiders. And we always try to start slow, making sure everyone is on board, building momentum as we go"* (Jhai Foundation n.d.).

The perceived benefits are significant for the individuals and communities involved. It appears that the Jhai Foundation demonstrates considerable good practice in engagement/participation, giving rise to positive outcomes and significant benefits for the individuals and communities involved. The Foundation has received a *"Best Practices"* award from the United Nations Secretariat, e-ASEAN, and UNESCO (Bangkok) (Jhai Foundation n.d.).

4.5 Conclusions

The cases considered in this chapter reveal a wide variety of practice in existing citizen engagement and participation projects. There is great diversity in every respect, from the objectives of the engagement (analysing information needs, improving services, and informing/influencing government policy) to the nature of the impact of the various initiatives. Initiatives take place in both developed and developing countries, and involve a wide range of people differing on numerous attributes, including levels of education, trades and professions, social position and economic standing, background and experience. The exponential growth of interest, research and experience in these topics is demonstrated by the scale of an international conference on Engaging Communities held in August 2005. The conference attracted 400 papers and delegates from 26 countries. When these are published, the content of the papers will represent a rich resource and will merit analysis on the basis of the framework developed in this book.

Although the processes of citizen participation are often not fully documented, the progress and successes reported by the projects described here could not have been achieved without the active cooperation and support of participants. Despite the immense diversity of the cases examined, common themes emerge. The next chapter continues with the reporting of case material, this time with a specific focus upon the engagement of citizens who are regarded as marginalized or in danger of social exclusion. Key issues and implications arising from all of the 20 examples are analysed in Chapter 6 to reveal the generic processes and benefits of citizen engagement.

References

Al-Kodmany K (1999) Using visualization techniques for enhancing public participation in planning and design: process, implementation and evaluation. Landscape and Urban Planning, 45. Elsevier, pp 37-45.
America Speaks (n.d). Home Page. http://www.americaspeaks.org/.

Barrat I and Reniu JM (2004) Electronic Democracy and Citizen Participation. http://www.scytl.com/pdf/madrid_participa_sociological_report.pdf

Beardon H (2005) ICT for development: empowerment or exploitation. Learning from the Reflect ICTs project. ActionAid, London.

Beaton B (2004) The K-Net Story: Community ICT Development Work. The Journal of Community Informatics. 1(1), pp. 5-6.

Cervelló G (2006) Madrid Participa. http://www.e-democracy.gov.uk/knowledgepool/ default.htm?mode=18pk_document-285

Cornwall A, Gaventa G (2000) From users to choosers to makers and shapers. IDS Bulletin, 31 (4), 50-62.

e-democracy.gov (n.d.) Homepage. http://www.e-democracy.gov.uk

Emery M, Purser RE (1996) The Search Conference: A Powerful Method for Planning Organizational Change and Community Action. Jossey-Bass, San Francisco.

Fühles-Ubach S (2005) How would you like it to be? – Results and project development from the first multi-phase online survey (online consultation) on the future of the Bundestag's website content. http://www.dialoguebydesign.net/docs/ Report_BT_OnlineKonsultation-english.pdf

Himanchal Education Foundation (2005) Homepage. http://www.himanchal.org

Jhai Foundation (n.d.) Homepage. www.jhai.org/

K-Net (n.d.) Homepage. http://knet.ca/

Keewaytinook Okimakanak Telehealth (2005) Interim Report http://telehealth.knet.ca/ modules.php?op=modload&name=News&file=article&sid=142&mode=thread& order=0&thold=0&POSTNUKESID=ed0e16286fcf7000635e817461057f9c

Lister R (2004) Poverty. Polity Press, Cambridge.

Macatawa Area Coordinating Council www.planning.dot.gov/Documents/CaseStudy/ Macatawa/macatawa4.html and http://134.215.205.97/default.asp

Macintosh A (2004) Characterizing E-Participation in Policy Making. In: Proceedings of the 37th Hawaii International Conference on System Sciences, 2004. IEEE.

Macintosh A, Masters Z, Smith E (2004) Young People and e-Democracy: Creating a Culture of Participation. Springer.

Madrid Participa (n.d.) www.madridparticipa.org

Moldrup C, Morgall JM, Almarsdottir AB (2000) Citizen involvement in future drug R and D: a Danish Delphi Study. Foresight, 2(5) pp 497-506.

Negroponte N (2005) Sub-$100 laptop design unveiled. http://news.bbc.co.uk/1/hi/ technology/4292854.stm

Nepalwireless (n.d.) Homepage. www.nepalwireless.net

Netmums.com (n.d.) The great work debate. www.netmums.com/cpg/whatmatters/ greatworkdebate.htm

Organisation for Economic Co-operation and Development (2001) Citizens as Partners: Information, consultation and public participation in policy-making.

Organisation for Economic Co-operation and Development (2003) OECD Policy Brief: Engaging Citizens Online for Better Policy-Making. March 2003.

Pun M (n.d.) The beginning. Nepal Wireless. http://www.nepalwirelss.net/story01.php

Ramirez R, Aitken H, Jamieson R, Richardson D (2004) Harnessing ICTs: A Canadian First Nations Experience. K-Net.

Since1968.com (n.d.) Mahabir Pun Nepal Wireless Interview. http://www.since1968.com/ article/so/nepal-wireless

UK Department of Trade and Industry (2005) Work and families – choice and flexibility. A consultation document. http://www.dti.gov.uk/er/choice_flexibility _consultation.pdf

Wyman M, Shulman D, Ham L (1999) Learning to Engage: Experiences with Civic Engagement in Canada, Canadian Policy Research Networks http://www.cprn.com/en/doc.cfm?doc=87

5 Giving a Voice to the 'Hard to Hear'

In making the case for citizen engagement, Chapter 3 has already raised the issue of the digital divide and the potential for new digital technologies to exacerbate social exclusion. The need to engage with all citizens in order to design ICTs which can be used successfully by the general public has been emphasised repeatedly. Many of those at risk of exclusion may for a variety of different reasons, be 'hard to hear' by planners, policy makers and designers. These groups include, for example, the elderly, the disabled, young people, ethnic minorities, those on low incomes, the homeless or itinerant groups. Many governments have stated their concerns and objectives to extend the benefits of ICT to all citizens, including those regarded as coming from such marginalised groups. Certainly in the UK, the 'hard to reach' or the 'hard to hear' are attracting increasing attention, in fact rather more than other citizens. The Digital Inclusion Panel was set up by UK Government in 2004, bringing together stakeholders from the public, private and voluntary sectors. The aim was to identify groups most at risk of digital exclusion, identify future actions that might encourage digital take-up, and to make recommendations about how industry, government and the voluntary sector can work together to drive a 'digitally United Kingdom'. There have been many other initiatives supported by other government departments in the UK such as the Home Computing Initiative (HCI), which encourages employers to loan PCs for home/flexible working. A number of community-led initiatives (e.g. Access to Broadband Campaign, Community Broadband Network) also address social exclusion issues, including geographic isolation. There are thought to be around 400 such community projects with varying degrees of sophistication and impact.

Internationally a vast number of initiatives, projects and programmes of varying size, scale and scope are addressing similar issues. Although substantial resources and efforts are being invested in promoting social inclusion, documentation of the processes involved, the approaches and methods used and their effectiveness in increasing levels of inclusion is in short supply. This chapter is intended to inform the proliferating projects and programmes which have a mission to engage with the 'hard to hear'.

Assuming that the powerful drivers that now exist for technological change will continue to exert an inexorable influence for greater citizen engagement, the challenge of determining who to engage and how to engage them looms large. Chapter 4 has provided glimpses of 'how to engage' by describing a small sample of the many successful citizen engagement activities which are being undertaken across the globe – and later chapters will provide more guidance.

We begin by outlining the special characteristics of the 'hard to hear' which are relevant to their engagement. Examples of some groundbreaking projects and initiatives which have been used to engage successfully with such groups will then be described and discussed.

5.1 Why are Some Citizens 'Hard to Hear'?

There are two main reasons which can prevent some citizens from engagement. The first is that they have simply not been identified as being legitimate stakeholders in a particular initiative. As a consequence, designers, developers and policy makers have not made efforts to communicate with them and involve them in decision making. The second is that the citizens themselves may lack (or perceive that they lack) the motivation, confidence or resources – whether time, knowledge or skills – needed in order to engage in an initiative. Identification of those citizens who are at risk from exclusion for either of these reasons is therefore a crucial first step in seeking to engage them.

There is an old adage which says *"what the eye doesn't see, the heart doesn't grieve over."* In other words, if you are not aware of something, then you are not going to concern yourself with it. In the first instance to give citizens a voice therefore, government, business, as well as ICT developers and designers must *"see them"*, and recognise the diversity that exists. It can be difficult to recognise just how many different kinds of citizens there are. There is certainly evidence that designers tend to design for people like themselves – small wonder, therefore, that many of the hi-tech gadgets which are on the market appeal so strongly to the young, the affluent, the male. Norman (2000) points out that designers, who, in practice are often engineers or managers, *"tend to feel that they are humans, therefore they can design something for other humans just as well as the trained interface expert."* Cooper (1999) puts it in a typically succinct way: *"programmers aren't evil. They work hard to make their software easy to use. Unfortunately, their frame of reference is themselves, so they only make it easy to use for other software engineers, not for normal human beings."*

Norman reinforces the point that designers are not typical users. *"They become so expert in using the object they have designed that they cannot believe that anyone else might have problems; only interaction and testing with actual users throughout the design process can forestall that"* (Norman 2000). Of course, it is not just designers who have difficulty appreciating the extent of diversity in society – most of us share that characteristic – including key role-holders in government agencies, local authorities etc.

Certain groups of stakeholders become excluded from adequate provision in terms of systems, services and products. This is because they have not been identified as a group with specific characteristics which may need special consideration. This may arise as a result of over-generalisation, e.g. there is recognition in many circles of the need to design for 'the elderly', or 'the disabled' and yet people in these categories will have a hugely diverse range of characteristics. For example, two important differentiators regarding adoption of the Internet by older people appear, from recent research (Olphert et al. 2005) to be income and social support. Clearly those who are well-off will not necessarily face the same problems as those who are poor; similarly those who are part of a strong social support network of family and friends will not necessarily face the same problems as those who are isolated.

Another adage says *"there are none so deaf as those who do not want to hear"*. This can mean that although some categories of citizens have a legitimate 'stake' in a proposed development – and therefore a right to be heard – they may sometimes be ignored by other leading and influential stakeholders who fear delays, loss of power or control, or increased costs through having to engage with others.

Further there are people who choose on a regular basis to engage in consultations and other participative exercises but they may not be representative of the wider community. Research by Jagodzinski and Forde (2005) endorses the finding that those who make their views known are not often representative of the wider community: *"…in talking to people in Devon we have often heard the view that the existing mechanisms, such as community forums in Town Halls and so on, are dominated by articulate and outspoken people who have the confidence, the time and the transport to stand up in public and voice their opinions. This can lead to a sense of disenfranchisement and exclusion from decision-making amongst the majority"*. Issues relating to motivation and selection of participants will be discussed in more detail in Chapter 9.

5.2 Citizens at Risk from Social Exclusion

There is no standard definition of social exclusion. The British Government's own definition of social exclusion is that it is: "*a shorthand term for what can happen when people or areas suffer from a combination of linked problems such as unemployment, poor skills, low incomes, unfair discrimination, poor housing, high crime, bad health and family breakdown*" (Office of the Deputy Prime Minister 2004).

Essentially, those who are socially excluded "*have little access to power and decision-making bodies and little chance of influencing decisions or policies that affect them*" (Combat Poverty n.d.). This definition continues: they have "*little chance of bettering their standard of living*", reflecting a focus on social and economic disadvantage as being causative factors. Thus much work on social inclusion addresses low-income and poverty as key factors. For example the s2net (The Social and Sector based E-learning enhanced by Professional Open and Distance Learning Networks) project, which aimed to use e-learning in vocational training to help prevent old and new forms of social exclusion, concluded that "*unemployment is the most obvious, immediate, statistically valid factor of exclusion*" (s2net Project 2003). Someone with a well-paid job, a good social network and high social status, for example, a manager or professional, is therefore likely to be the most socially included. At the other end of the spectrum, the unemployed who lack a social network or social status, and the homeless tend to be the most excluded. In between, ethnic groups such as immigrants, who do have paid work but may suffer low social status in their new country of domicile, would count among the socially excluded.

The s2net project (2003) identifies the following groups as being at particular risk of exclusion:

- young people in general. Young people can face social exclusion because they have no power or influence (e.g. can't vote);
- immigrants, refugees and asylum seekers. Visa problems can exclude access to work or voluntary work;
- people with disabilities;
- homeless people;
- elderly people. Older people can face social exclusion due to isolation from their families and fear of going out;
- the unemployed;
- people on low income/benefits;

- prisoners and first-time offenders;
- travellers;
- people living in rural areas (where social exclusion can arise due to a lack of transport, employment opportunities and facilities);
- people who do not have access to information and knowledge;
- people from disadvantaged, crime-ridden areas and background;
- geographically isolated communities;
- single parents;
- minority groups (e.g. ethnic minority groups, people of different religions);
- carers;
- people suffering mental and/or physical illness;
- women.

It is recognized that social exclusion is a multi-dimensional phenomenon. Janie Percy-Smith (ed) (2000) identifies seven dimensions of social exclusion: economic, social, political, neighbourhood, individual, spatial and group, and highlights their interactive nature (see Fig. 5.1). Many individuals will experience a combination of such factors which could exacerbate the difficulties of engagement. On the other hand, individuals with fewer of these attributes are likely to be easier to engage.

Among the various barriers which exist to prevent increasing Internet use, language and website content have begun to receive attention. For example at the United Nations' World Summit on the Information Society (WSIS) in Geneva in 2003 UN Secretary General Kofi Anan noted that 70 percent of all websites are in English. Peter Armstrong, Director of Oneworld.net, a website for development issues, comments: *"if a person comes up to the terminal and there is nothing there in their language that is relevant to their lives, then why should they bother?"* (Boyd 2003).

There are numerous initiatives which are seeking to redress the imbalance in content and language of the internet. The K-net project (described in Chapter 4) has developed and provided own-language resources for the indigenous communities it serves.

Another example is DireqLearn, a South African organisation. DireqLearn customizes educational tools for hundreds of schools in Namibia, Nigeria and South Africa. The idea, says DireqLearn's Leonard Tleane, is to give students the knowledge they want, in a language that they can understand (Boyd 2003).

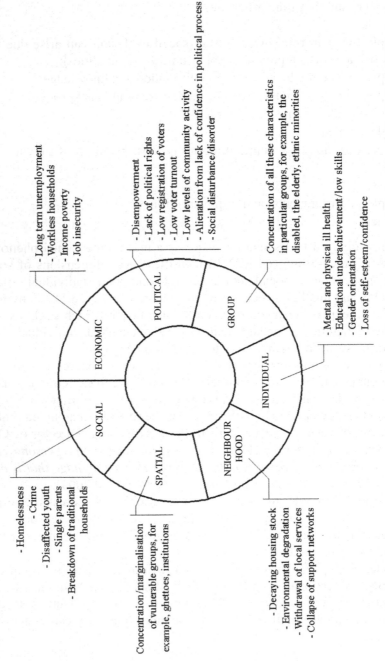

Fig. 5.1. Interactive nature of dimensions of Social Exclusion (adapted from J Percy-Smith (ed) 2000).

5.3 Case Studies

Numerous case studies document the huge range of initiatives taking place internationally to bridge the 'digital divide'. Many of these aim to provide access to new digital technologies (mainly the Internet) to those who have not previously had it. Through providing access to high speed communications and to information resources, such projects empower people to have more control over aspects of their own lives. This enables individuals and communities to participate in decision making that affects them. It would be possible to write an entire book on these exciting developments alone. However the impact that such projects have on the shaping of new technologies is less well documented. Since this is the focus of this book, we have tried to select case studies which are related to new technology (again, mainly the Internet). However several of the case studies have been included because they represent good practice in engaging with specific 'hard to reach' groups rather than because they have a specific technology shaping objective. Given the strong focus of activity on this topic at present, the majority of the cases in this chapter are drawn from the UK.

Table 5.1. Case studies of ICTs use in Hard-to-Hear categories

Name of project	Hard-to-hear category
UTOPIA	Older people aged over 60
Surrey 50+ website	Older people aged over 50
'Logged Off' – Carnegie Young People Initiative	Young people
Online Surgeries for Young People	Young people
LOCOMOTION	Elderly, disabled people
WomenSpeak	Women suffering domestic violence
Jamie's Big Voice	The homeless

5.3.1 UTOPIA – UK

In 2002 the Department of Computing at the University of Dundee set up the UTOPIA (2004) project (Usable Technology for Older People: Inclusive and Appropriate) with the following objectives:

- to develop effective methods to involve people aged 60 and over early in the development of ICT products;
- to provide tools to industry which would assist in the development of ICTs for older people.

The project involved two cohorts of participants. One group comprised older people (aged 60 and over). The second grouping included representatives of Scottish industry. The goal of the project was to provide design tools to enable older people to use ICTs effectively. In the project, researchers sought to explore in detail what was different about older people in their relationship with technology, compared to younger age groups (Eisma et al. 2004).

The approach used by the researchers to recruit participants was to contact organisations concerned with older people throughout Scotland by mail and by telephone. Organisations contacted included charities such as Help the Aged and Age Concern, as well as community centres, libraries, educational institutions offering classes for the elderly, sheltered housing, residential homes, church groups and social groups such as 'Over 50' clubs, stroke clubs, etc. Once contact was established, the researchers maintained their relationships with groups by sending out newsletters, making personal visits and sometimes by making small contributions (such as a tin of biscuits for a Christmas raffle).

Both qualitative and quantitative data were obtained through questionnaires, interviews, focus groups and workshops in which ICT products were handed round to members for them to use and comment on. The researchers note that it was not always easy to keep a group focused on a subject of discussion, because the opportunity to socialise in such groups was more important to members than meeting researchers' objectives for the group.

The researchers discovered that assumptions about older people's design needs are not always correct. For instance, efforts to make technology less complex do not always lead to increased adoption amongst older people. So although televisions with built-in CD-ROM and DVD drives are manufactured with the aim of making it easier for people to play CDs and DVDs than if they have to use separate equipment for each task, older people do not necessarily use these facilities. Older people are more likely than younger people to fear using new technology, and lack trust in systems. They are more anxious to 'get it right' than try to develop speed. They need more reassurance that they will be able to operate new technology 'correctly', and are more likely to take a step-by-step approach to understanding controls. Older people are also less likely to understand concepts, visual language and interface metaphors on ICTs than younger people.

The researchers confirmed previous findings that *"traditional requirements gathering methods are also problematic when used with older people e.g. in questionnaires, older people are more likely to use 'don't know' options and need a higher threshold of certainty before they will select options useful to the researcher"* (Park and Schwarz 2000). The most successful techniques of engagement were workshops in which devices were passed around, enabling people to experiment with them and to make comments on their use. These sessions frequently changed the older people's perceptions about the products to much more positive outlooks.

Based on the data collected in the project, researchers developed guidelines and advice to industry on what to consider in designing ICTs for older people. These findings and the guideline tools were disseminated at two workshops held for representatives from Scottish industry. Participants who attended these workshops were more likely than respondents from industry as a whole to say that they considered older people in design. Despite this, however, these participants were generally not aware of the diversity of the over 60 age group. The most effective tool to communicate with industry regarding the requirements of older people was found to be video recordings of technology use by older people. For example, one representative from a mobile phone company borrowed a video presented at the workshop which showed an older lady who had had a stroke talking about using mobile phones and computers. The video was distributed throughout senior management in the mobile phone company to create wider awareness of the issues.

5.3.2 The Surrey 50+ Website – UK

As part of the UK Government's Local e-Democracy programme, Surrey County Council undertook a pilot project to engage older people. A primary aim of the project was to create a website targeted at people over 50, which would enable the active engagement of older people in developing public services and support better government for older people. A further objective was to promote the use of ICTs amongst the over-50s through online participation and opportunities for learning about technology. The project ran for six months from September 2004 to March 2005. A local councilor took on the role of champion of the project (Surrey 50+ n.d.).

Participation in developing the website was sought from older members of the local community. Other relevant stakeholders such as Age Concern and Housing Associations were also involved. To publicize the project and encourage participation, letters were sent to the 1000 members of the existing 'Over 50' network, presentations were made to local councilors, and advertisements placed on key websites, in local papers and other publications. Eight training sessions were then held in local libraries.

The technology used for the project was an open source content management package called APLAWS, which had been designed specifically for local authority use in England. It was adapted to build a web portal specifically aimed at the over 50 age group. The software was also adapted specifically to offer usability for older people, conforming to level AA of the W3C Web Accessibility Initiative for website standards. For example, readers can change the font size if they wish to see script at a larger size (Allen 2005).

The portal offers news, forums and questionnaires, and links to other websites and organisations considered to be of interest or help to the over 50s. The most interactive parts of the website are the forums, on which individuals can pose questions for councilors and council staff to answer. Topics under discussion include Employment, Education, Environment, Leisure, Housing, Health Care, Discrimination, Social Care, Transport, Community Safety and Benefits. Online registered members of the over 50 network now receive updates on council news via email and/or SMS text alerts if they choose. Older people without computers are able to access the website from centres, some of which are sponsored by the charity Age Concern (Surrey 50+ n.d.).

Another open source package, AWSTATS, was used to monitor use of the website. Almost 2000 people had visited the portal between September 2004 and March 2005. Review of the forums suggests that although they are not used heavily, there is a continual feed of questions. Discussions are not long since particular questions are usually answered by a council official. This suggests that in-depth discussion does not yet take place online. Although the pilot project has ended, the web portal continues to offer a local online resource with information considered to be of use and interest to older people. Users of the website did express an interest in using it for voting on issues but this facility is not yet available. The county council considers that the project has succeeded in raising awareness and usage of ICT amongst older people. The project has also helped the county council meet its targets for delivering local authority services electronically (i.e. by web, telephone contact centres, digital TV, mobile phones etc.) by 2005/2006.

The project report concluded that the period allowed for developing the portal had not been long enough. Neither was the content management system ideal in that it was not compatible with Microsoft products, which are generally far better known and familiar to staff tasked with updating the website and monitoring project management. This meant time was needed to learn new operating procedures.

5.3.3 'Logged Off' – Political Disaffection Amongst Young People – UK

'Logged Off' was a project commissioned by the Carnegie Trust to establish whether new technologies could encourage greater participation in political life of young people (aged from 13-18). Previous studies showed that young people are becoming increasingly disengaged from participating in mainstream politics. This is exemplified by the finding that for the local government elections in 2002, total voter turnout was only 40%, with the lowest turnout of all occurring in the 18-25 year age group.

The Carnegie Trust sponsors research and educational programmes to enable young people to feel that they have more control over their lives and to take action. For this project, the Trust carried out quantitative research involving young people between the ages of 13 and 18. The Carnegie Young People Initiative established contact with young people through its Participation Workers Network for England. Participation workers set up events on a regional basis, working closely with the Clubs for Young People Initiative. The research was carried out through face to face interviews. A special website was set up asking participants to comment on a range of websites, and to search for political information and opportunities to interact. Participants were able to read comments made by their peers and respond to different points of view. Researchers sought to establish how young people reacted to information presented on the website, how they interacted with websites, and whether the content of the sites changed their views (Carnegie Young People Initiative 2003).

In its final report on the research, the Trust was able to recommend that in the short term:

- the Government should commit itself to develop effective strategies, including the use of ICTs, to engage young people;
- the Government should fund development of a toolkit which would enable anyone with interest in engaging young people's political engagement to develop a successful ICT strategy;
- the Government should establish NET:ENGAGE throughout UK – a network of young people who could evaluate ICT initiatives aimed at engaging young people;
- all government websites should include at least one page aimed specifically at young people;
- in order to achieve this, government should run an annual, national competition inviting young people to design these web pages;
- the Government should extend its examples of producing versions of consultation designed specifically for young people;

- the Government should fund the creation of a citizenship portal;
- the extent to which young people have used ICT to engage with politics, decision-making and civic society should be reflected in their National Record of Achievement;
- the Connexions Smartcard should be used to reward young people who use ICTs as a means of political engagement;
- the location of free ICT facilities should reflect the environments that young people like, which might involve giving young people free access to technology in cinemas, shopping malls, leisure centres and youth shelters (Howland and Bethell n.d.).

Medium term recommendations focused on wider issues of developing interactive TV and mobile phones as media for engagement. The computer industry was charged with making the Internet safer for young people.

5.3.4 Online Surgeries for Young People – UK

Another pilot project undertaken as part of the UK Government's Local e-Democracy programme focused on engaging young people in the parliamentary and political process. The project, undertaken by the Royal Borough of Kingston-upon-Thames, involved a series of six 'online surgeries' in which young people were able to discuss issues with elected representatives in their local authority. The aim was to make young people more aware of political structures and processes within England (Local e-Democracy National Project n.d.).

The project was sponsored by the Office of the Deputy Prime Minister with the help of The Hansard Society. The Hansard Society had identified that young people were capable of identifying political issues and that they would be enthusiastic about setting an agenda for debate in online surgeries (The Royal Borough of Kingston upon Thames n.d.).

The organizers wrote to selected schools to invite their participation. The project was also publicized in the local press in October 2004 and January 2005. All local councillors, MPs and Greater London Assembly members received emails asking for their support and participation, and Heads of schools and citizenship teachers received personalized briefing letters. Six surgeries were then organized.

In preparation for the surgeries, year 10 and 11 students attended workshops given by the Hansard Society and the council. In the workshops preliminary information about the status and work of local councillors and MPs was provided. Ideas to discuss during the surgeries were elicited in the 'brainstorming'. Students were handed questionnaires to answer both prior to and after the surgeries. On the day of the surgeries, students gathered round computers, registered online for a chat room and posed their questions. These were forwarded to Hansard Society staff in their offices, who articulated the questions within the chat environment and forwarded the questions to an appropriate political representative. The student and the representative then held one-to-one discussions on topics including graffiti, drugs, voting, Iraq and careers. Each surgery had at least one local councillor and one MP or Greater London Assembly member available to consult. In total over 60 young people and ten political representatives took part in the online surgeries (Hansard Society 2005a).

It became evident that the surgeries made it possible for young people to discuss topics that they probably would not have discussed in person with politicians. This was especially the case for those who were not very vocal in class or who did not like working in groups. Expressed willingness to vote in future and to have a say in the way that the country was run increased significantly between the initial expression of views before the surgeries and those expressed afterwards. Students reported that they had learnt much more about the work of political representatives as a result of participating in the surgeries. Teachers felt that the experience engaged the students much more in politics and citizenship courses and were keen that more surgeries should take place in future (Hansard Society 2005a).

Overall, the Hansard Society concluded that online surgeries were just one of the measures that could be used to engage citizens as a whole. The Royal Borough of Kingston council feels that it now has a much stronger relationship with schools. Recommendations for the future were that a longer lead time should be allowed to 'book' politicians, especially MPs, to take part, and that preliminary workshops for students should be more interactive.

5.3.5 LOCOMOTION – Disabled and Elderly Citizens – UK/Germany

LOCOMOTION is the acronym for a project to develop location-based mobile phones applications for independent living of disabled and elderly citizens. This research project was set up and administered from the Department of Medical Physics and Clinical Engineering at Barnsley District Hospital. The aims of the project were: (i) to explore the potential for combining mobile phone technology and GPS technology to provide facilities and services which would enable vulnerable people to be more independent in their homes and to give confidence in travelling; and (ii) provide peace of mind to their families and reduce the burden on professional carers (Locomotion 2004).

The target users of the project were older people, the elderly with dementia, people with learning disabilities and professional carers. Members of the target group were recruited in the UK and in Germany to participate in interviews and focus groups to identify requirements for products and services. Participants were subsequently actively engaged in the physical design of a product, development of mobile alarm services and a website interface (Hawley 2004a).

Two prototype products were developed. The first consisted of a standard mobile phone with location awareness using GPS (accurate to 50 metres), which enabled members of the target groups and their carers to identify their locations, and help them to find their way to unfamiliar destinations. The other was a mobile tracking device with a single 'panic button' that puts users in contact with a call centre.

Trials with 40 volunteers generated a positive response from the test users, none of whom had ever used mobile phones before but all of whom noted the utility of the system. It was found to be especially useful for people suffering from diseases such as Alzheimer's or those whose health may be impaired but who wish to continue living independently. Users also saw further advantages, for example using the location awareness system to find the nearest pharmacy or hospital.

Professor Hawley from Barnsley District General Hospital (leading the UK trials) explained "there are people who have found it beneficial", adding that this was due to the engagement of "potential users, and obtaining their opinions and ideas first" (Hawley 2004).

This case makes clear the importance of the role of intended users in designing ICTs for their use – and the value of their contributions. The example shows this to be especially critical where users are vulnerable and where the design has to meet the needs of two or more interacting parties – as occurs routinely in a care situation.

5.3.6 WomenSpeak – Women Suffering Domestic Violence – UK

WomenSpeak was an Internet-based consultation project involving survivors of domestic violence, coordinated by Women's Aid and The Hansard Society. The project was supported by The All Party Parliamentary Group on Domestic Violence. Survivors talked directly to MPs about their experiences and set out the agenda for "what women want" to ameliorate their situation (Women's aid 2000).

The objective of the project was to enable women suffering domestic violence to communicate directly with parliamentarians to convey the true nature of the issues involved.

Participants in this project were women in the UK suffering domestic violence. They came from a variety of social backgrounds, including different ethnic and minority populations. Respondents represented a variety of social backgrounds from across the UK, although 22.4% were from Greater London. The project was gender neutral but almost 100% of contributions came from women.

ICT was used as a means to facilitate the goal of enhancing communication for these women. The organizers set up a secure website which women could use to communicate with MPs. The website needed to be secure, so that abusive partners could not detect what the women were doing. Security procedures involved the women ringing the moderator to be allocated a username and password to gain access to the secure site. To achieve robust security only specified moderators and women in women's aid or outreach groups could provide these details.

Many women needed training to enable them to interact online, as well as means of safe, secure access, often in community centres and schools. Announced by e-Minister Patricia Hewitt early in March 2000, the interactive discussion continued throughout that month.

Flyers were sent out to women's aid refuges, women's and disability groups and outreach organisations five months in advance of the consultation. The time lead was essential in order to ensure that the widest range of experience could be heard. Media coverage was targeted to contact women who might never have contacted a refuge or agency dealing with domestic violence. In total 204 women were registered for the consultation, of whom 199 participated by logging on to the website. Several of these women came from ethnic (Bangladeshi) and minority (Irish travellers) groups.

At first sceptical about politicians, many women valued the opportunity of being able to talk to legislators as a result of the exercise. Initially, *"only 5.2% of respondents were members of a political party. 62.7% had voted in the last election, compared with 71.3% nationally. Only 17.9% thought that their MP did take an interest in the issue of domestic violence"* (Margaret Moran, MP for Luton South), (Moran 2000).

An important outcome of this exercise was that women were able to demonstrate the diversity of their circumstances, report their experiences of responses from the police, the judiciary, and lack of provision in state aid and support structures. They were also able to suggest mechanisms to overcome these problems. As a result, these experiences of survivors have been used to inform debate on issues such as health services, child contact and housing. There were a number of outcomes:

- priority was established for re-housing survivors of domestic violence in the Homelessness Bill;
- the one-year immigration rule which forced women entering the UK to remain with a violent partner or be deported has been changed;
- the Children Act will take into account harm caused to a child of witnessing domestic violence;
- the need for sustainable funding for domestic violence projects has influenced the Comprehensive Spending Review;
- the UK government has formed a ministerial group on domestic violence, to coordinate policies and to develop a comprehensive strategy to tackle the problem.

Another important outcome of engagement in this project is that many women who took part have been able to find and develop social support networks. For example, a group of Bangladeshi women in Luton have set up their own online community through Bury Park community centre. The project has been a model for other e-democracy initiatives, such as U-Speak launched by the Social Security Select Committee.

5.3.7 Jamie's Big Voice – The Homeless – UK

Homeless people are entitled to vote in the UK, and yet the voices of these vulnerable and excluded people are rarely heard during elections. In the run-up to the UK General Election in May 2005, the charity 'Crisis' was concerned that the issue of homelessness was not being addressed by the political parties. They sought novel ways of drawing attention to the plight of the homeless and approached the Hansard Society to explore the possibilities of using online technology to raise awareness and to stimulate discussion and debate with the media, parliamentary candidates, and the general electorate.

A blog (weblog) was identified as a potentially useful medium. Jamie McCoy, formerly a homeless drug addict and now a writer and poet, was identified as an eminently suitable author - on the basis of his personal history (which is well-documented in the sources referenced below) and his compelling and provocative writing style. His blog, available at http://www.jamiesbigvoice.com, was launched in April 2005 amidst considerable publicity. Before the blog began, the Hansard Society reviewed different platforms. The free blogging service "Blogger" was chosen, partly because as a free service it would help to keep down the costs of the project, and partly because it was easy to use by a novice. The Hansard Society configured the site, and also provided Jamie with training and technical support, but the content and 'voice' are Jamie's own. (Jamie has since developed the site himself). Prior to the launch, the Hansard Society undertook an extensive campaign to publicize the site and generate interest. The site was monitored by both news broadcasters (the BBC, CNN) and influential newspapers (the Guardian, the Independent, the Times and the FT). Jamie wrote daily contributions commenting on a wide range of topics including homelessness, and conveying the experiences and opinions of other homeless people whom he interviewed. Since the election in May 2005, Jamie has continued to write his blog, attracting considerable on-going interest (Jamie's Big Voice 2005).

This case study provides a highly accessible example of ICT-enabled 'one-to-many' communication which conveys grassroots opinion and first-hand reports of real-life experiences of adversity. Blogs are uniquely empowering of marginalized individuals who find themselves developing their own capabilities and new social networks while informing others and engaging in wider, sometimes global, society. Writing his blog has given Jamie confidence to comment on social and political issues. He has become more aware of resources online and in the community. However, the benefits of giving him an online 'voice' extend beyond the individual level. At the time of the Hansard Society's report of the project in 2005, there had been more than 5000 'hits' on Jamie's website. Readers included homeless people themselves, and some were surprised to find that homeless people were entitled to vote despite not having a fixed address. Communicating personal experiences in this way serves to promote wider understanding of social problems, provide insights, engage others and, potentially, to inform policy-making.

Mark Flannagan, Director of Communications and Campaigning for Crisis, comments on the value of blogs: "*Jamie's Big Voice is an example of a phenomenon that should spread to every organization to tell it like it really is. Let a thousand blogs bloom. Each one will capture one perspective of what it is really like to live with a long-term chronic health condition, to live as a single mum, be concerned about the destruction of our planet or to be homeless*" (The Hansard Society 2005).

5.4 Conclusions

A stated objective for this chapter is to inform new initiatives and projects intended to engage with the 'hard to hear'. To this end, the most important conclusion to emerge from the reported case studies is that engaging with the 'hard to hear' can indeed be done very successfully – with the right engagement strategies. The compelling evidence is that while some categories of citizens may be perceived as hard to reach, and therefore hard to hear, nevertheless even the hardest to reach and the hardest to hear – such as vulnerable women – can not only be reached but also involved and engaged successfully. It is equally clear from the case material that appropriate engagement strategies which overcome barriers, build trust, promote learning and give incentives for further engagement are the key to achieving rewarding and positive outcomes. In each of the cases discussed, an appropriate strategy appears to have entailed a process (not always pre-planned) which was demanding of time, patience, skill and the application of appropriate tools and techniques. Further, in the case of extremely vulnerable groups, these strategies appear to have had an implicit code of conduct embedded in them to ensure that due attention was paid to safeguarding the security and well-being of the individuals concerned. This included making a commitment to acting upon the information elicited responsibly and with extreme caution. It is clear that for vulnerable groups, the engagement process can be difficult and painful for the participants, especially those who may be divulging information about themselves and their situation for the first time. To reduce their exclusion, their trust must be won and then sustained as positive change is brought about. To help to grow trust there may well be a case for arriving at an agreed code of conduct very explicitly and for articulating it clearly.

It is evident that there are many lessons to be learned from current practice in participation and engagement which would help to avoid repeating damaging mistakes, would improve practice and enhance the success rates of initiatives undertaken to reduce social exclusion. However, for clear lessons to be drawn requires systematic reporting and evaluation of projects and initiatives.

The case descriptions presented in this chapter demonstrate the exciting possibilities and the lasting benefits for individuals and for society which can result from engaging with the 'hard to hear' One significant and characteristic benefit is the empowerment which enables citizens to make a direct contribution to shaping their own lives and those of others in similar circumstances. Jamie's Big Voice, the Carnegie Youth Panel, and the e-democracy pilot projects in Kingston (the Over 50's website and the online surgeries for young people) are examples where specific groups have been given a voice, facilitated through the use of ICT. There are examples of contributions to the design of policies (e.g. with the Womenspeak example), systems and services (e.g. LOCOMOTION) and products (e.g. UTOPIA). Here, the engagement of citizens from specific groups has led to design solutions which meet the needs of a wide range of citizens, and thereby help to promote social inclusion and avoid 'exclusion by design'. As Newell points out, however, we are all 'extraordinary' users sometimes and in some circumstances. Designs which accommodate 'extraordinary' users will therefore be useful and usable by 'ordinary' users in 'extraordinary' circumstances (Newell 2000).

Another conclusion with a lesson to be drawn for future practice is that better documentation of initiatives would add significant value through building knowledge of good practice in citizen engagement. Many project reports record their successes in reaching out to engage the 'hard to hear', but in most cases do not give details about the process. For example, details of how they set about identifying their targets, selecting participants, getting them involved and keeping them engaged are often missing, and yet these are the very steps which often prove to be the stumbling blocks in efforts to engage those citizens at risk of social exclusion.

Good practice in citizen engagement processes which can inform other initiatives is reported in a number of the cases. For example, the UTOPIA project showed the superiority of using video recordings of actual user experiences of technology (compared with verbal or written reports) in persuading key stakeholders of the merit and importance of user-centred design. In some other cases, the methodologies adopted are innovative, tailored to deal with the needs of specific stakeholder groups. In other cases, the methodology is a standard one, but care has been taken to identify and engage specific stakeholder groups. Thus both the UTOPIA and the Carnegie Youth Panel projects have established citizen panels which enable relationships to be built up with citizens over time and the engagement process to become more familiar and sustainable. We will return to discuss these and other mechanisms for promoting and sustaining citizen engagement in Chapter 9.

Finally, and perhaps most importantly of all, the significance of capacity building and the necessary know-how emerges from the cases examined. There is an abundance of evidence which shows that to develop an understanding of the potential of ICT to improve their lives is a major challenge for the many people who have little or no familiarity with these technologies. A key conclusion to emerge from these findings is that adequate time and good opportunities for people to learn and to develop understanding must be factored into project planning. Without this provision, people cannot readily develop new ways of thinking and new ways of doing things. This leaves them at risk of exclusion, particularly 'digital exclusion'.

In summary, engaging the 'hard to hear' appears to be as rewarding as it is demanding and while there is good practice in evidence, the codification and dissemination of it has lagged behind. It is hoped that this book will prove to be a stimulus both for improved documentation of existing practices and for innovation in citizen engagement strategies and processes.

References

Allen J (2005) 50+ website. An engagement website for people aged 50+ in Surrey project report. http://www.e-democracy.gov.uk/knowledgepool/default.htm?mode=1&pk_document=367

Boyd C (2003) Local content key for digitally divided. BBC. http://news.bbc.co.uk/1/hi/technology/3314171.stm.

Carnegie Institute Young People Initiative (2003) Logged Off http://www.carnegieuktrust.org.uk/cypi/our_work/research/e-participation

Combat Poverty (n.d.) Glossary of Poverty and Social Inclusion terms. http://www.cpa.ie/facts_jargon.html

Cooper A (1999) The Inmates are Running the Asylum. SAMS Publishing, Indianapolis, Indiana.

Eisma R, Dickinson A, Goodman J, Syme A, Tiwari L, Newell AF (2004) Early User Involvement in the development of information technology-related products for older people. International Journal Universal Access in the Information Society. Vol.3. No.2. Springer Verlag. pp 131-140.

Hansard Society (2005) Weblogs – a powerful voice for campaigns? http://www.hansardsociety.org.uk/programmes/e-democracy/Weblogs

Hansard Society (2005a) Online Surgeries for Young People http://www. hansardsociety.org.uk/node/view/475

Hawley M (2004) http://www.fastuk.org/organisation_details.php?Ref=1173. Dept of Medical Physics and Clinical Engineering – Barnsley Hospital NHS Foundation Trust.

Hawley M (2004a) Presentation on New Approaches and Technologies for Prevention and Rehabilitation for monitoring the health of elderly patients. http://www.whiterose.ac.uk/events/ageing/files/slides/hawley.pdf

Howland L, Bethell M (2002) Logged Off – How ICT can connect young people and politics? Demos, 2002. http://www.demos.co.uk/loggedoff_pdf_media_public.aspx

Jagodzinski P, Forde J (2005) Putting rural communities online: an ethnographic view. Presented at: 2nd International Conference of the Community Informatics Research Network, 22nd-27th August 2005: Cape Town, South Africa.

Jamies Big Voice (2005) jamie's big voice http://jamiesbigvoice.blogspot.com/

Local e-Democracy National Project (n.d.) Online surgeries for young people. http://www.e-democracy.gov.uk/pilots/onlinesurgery.htm

Locomotion (2004) Project details http://www.fastuk.org/project_details.php?Ref=683

McCoy J (2005) Jamie's Big Voice. http://www.jamiesbigvoice.blogspot.com/

Moran M (2002) Womenspeak: E-Democracy or He-Democracy? http://www.egovmonitor.com/features/moran01.html

Newell AF, Gregor P (2000) Designing for Extra-ordinary People and Situations. CSERIAC Gateway (Crew System Ergonomics Information Analysis Center), pp 12-13.

Norman DA (2000) The Design of Everyday Things. MIT Press, London/New York.

Norris P (2001) Digital Divide: Civic Engagement, Information Poverty and the Internet. Cambridge University Press, Cambridge.

Office of the Deputy Prime Minister (2004) Tackling Social Exclusion: Taking stock and looking to the future, emerging findings. http://www.socialexclusion.gov.uk/downloaddoc.asp?id=13

Olphert CW (2005) Towards Digital Inclusion – Engaging Older People in the Digital World. Submitted to the Conference 'Accessible Design In the Digital World', Dundee, August 2005.

Park D, Schwartz N (eds) (2000) Cognitive aging: a primer. Psychology Press, Taylor and Francis Group, Hove, UK.

Percy-Smith J (ed) (2000). Social inclusion. Open University Press, Buckingham.

Royal Borough of Kingston (2005) Online surgeries for young people http://www.e-democracy.gov.uk/casestudies?mode=1&pk_document=346

S2net Project (2003) Social inclusion/exclusion. http://www.europace.org/s2net/docs/wp6/Social Inclusion Statement.doc

Surrey County Council 50+ (2005) Surrey 50+ http://www.surrey50plus.org.uk/ccm/portal/

UTOPIA (Usable Technology for Older People: Inclusive and Appropriate) (2004) Publications page last updated 6th April. http://www.computing.dundee.ac.uk/projects/UTOPIA/Publications.asp

Womens aid (2000) Womenspeak. http://www.womensaid.org.uk/page.asp?section=00010001000900080001000s

6 Modelling Citizen Engagement

The case studies presented in Chapters 4 and 5 have revealed the exciting possibilities for shaping society and transforming lives through engaging citizens as contributors to the decision-making process. Partly as a consequence of their diversity on very many parameters, the case descriptions reveal crucial data relating to numerous aspects of the citizen participation/engagement experience. In this chapter, we seek to use the data from this rich pool of documented experience to characterize and to model effective citizen engagement.

6.1 Dimensions of Citizen Engagement

The analytical framework for the case studies described in Chapter 4 identified some of the key dimensions which characterize citizen participation/engagement exercises. Our analysis of the cases has revealed a number of additional dimensions. These are crucial both to understanding the dynamics of the process and to the planning of effective, successful citizen engagement strategies. These additional parameters are:

- **initiator** (who are the initiators of the participation/engagement i.e. institutions or citizens);
- **structure** (pre-planned/formal or spontaneous/amorphous);
- **focus** (specific or broad);
- **scale** (size of the exercise, i.e. small group – local community – region – nation – world);
- **impact** (individual – local – national – global);
- **citizen influence** (extent of opportunity to influence the design decision-making process).

Each of the above are discussed below.

6.1.1 Initiator

Many of the well-documented and widely-publicised exercises described in Chapters 4 and 5 have been initiated by local, regional and national government institutions. In many cases there are individuals who spontaneously become project 'champions' or are formally designated as such. The objectives of such initiatives are usually aimed at implementing government agendas on issues such as enhanced civic participation, implementation of electronic service delivery, and reducing social exclusion. Typically the focus is determined by government, and projects are set up which are funded for periods ranging from a few months to two or three years. These exercises serve, variously, as demonstrators, as test-beds for ideas, as small-scale pilots to assess viability of the innovation, or to inform the roll-out of a particular policy, ICT system or service on a larger regional or national basis.

The common characteristics of institution-led engagement initiatives are that the institutions provide the funding and define the high level objectives. For example, the government-led exercises described in this book essentially seek to examine the impact and potential role of specific ICT applications on citizen behaviour and attitudes. Thus in the UK, 22 local e-Democracy pilots explored the impact of webcasts, blogs, text alerts, e-panels, e-consultation, committee information systems, online surgeries etc. (Local e-Democracy National Project Case Studies 2005). Non-governmental organizations (NGOs) also lead exercises and projects to explore the use of ICTs to engage with citizens – particularly those who are 'hard to hear' or those at risk of social exclusion.

Another, very different, kind of institution-led citizen participation is seen in the programmes introduced by NGOs such as ActionAid, voluntary organizations and formal or informal citizen groups. In some cases, the organisation or entity promoting the exercise has specific political aims, which are not necessarily party political ends. As reported in Chapter 5, Crisis, a charity for the homeless, supported Jamie McCoy's blog (weblog) to voice opinions from an under-represented group, because it sought to influence politicians from all parties to improve provision for the homeless (Hansard Society 2005).

Funding and other resources, e.g. for education and training, are in most of these cases provided by an institution – governmental or otherwise, although the focus and direction of specific projects may be determined and carried out by citizens themselves to some degree. For example, the Canadian National Forum on Health, initiated by government, required participants to be well briefed prior to participating in the Forum and resources were provided to achieve the necessary learning and understanding of the issues. Subsequently participants were free to exercise their judgement and discretion in contributing their own ideas on healthcare priorities (Wyman et al. 1999). Table 6.1 lists the case studies by initiator.

Table 6.1. Initiators of the case studies

Initiated By	
Institutions	Citizens
Online surgeries for young people, UK	Nepal Wireless, Nepal
Surrey 50+ website, UK	Jhai Foundation, Laos
Bundestag website design, Germany	K-Net, Canada
Madrid Participa, Spain	
Macatawa project, USA	
America Speaks, USA	
Reflect ICTs India and Uganda	
UTOPIA project, UK	
National Forum on Health, Canada	
'Logged-Off' Project, UK	
LOCOMOTION, UK	
Netmums, UK	
WomenSpeak, UK	
Future drug research and development, Denmark	
Participative design in neighbourhood planning, Chicago, USA	
Jamie's Big Voice, UK	

6.1.2 Structure

There is wide variation in the structure of participation/engagement initiatives. This ranges from the formalized and organised (e.g. in exercises initiated and supported by institutions) to informal and largely reactive initiatives led by concerned individuals or groups. Most of the initiatives described in Chapters 4 and 5 have explicitly sought the participation/engagement of citizens in a formal way in pursuit of some more or less closely defined objectives. However there are some examples where citizen engagement has arisen in a spontaneous way in response to a perceived need. For instance, the K-Net, Jhai Foundation and Nepal Wireless initiatives began as what might be termed 'grass-roots' initiatives, where individuals or groups of individuals set out with specific objectives which then inspired and motivated other individuals to engage and participate. Such examples make very clear that the structures associated with participation and engagement evolve and change in a highly dynamic way. Often a highly motivated individual or small group engenders a process which begins in a loosely structured and informal way. As momentum builds up and action becomes more focused, the engagement process may become more formalized and institutionalized.

At one extreme, highly amorphous structures are occurring spontaneously. There are indications that ICT is fostering and enabling citizen engagement in exciting and innovative ways. One dramatic example of an emerging phenomenon is afforded by the SEA-EAT initiative which arose following the December 2004 Tsunami disaster: *"The December 26, 2004 tsunami that hit the communities encircling the Indian Ocean will be remembered as one of the world's worst natural disasters. It may also well be remembered as one of the earliest successful uses of the entire continuum of Internet and other communications tools to respond, to help, to grieve"* (Smith et al. 2005). Individuals across the globe created SEA-EAT (the South – East Asia Earthquake and Tsunami weblog) within 12 hours of the initial earthquake to coordinate the news, information and reactions that were dominating web space. Many different forms of digital technologies were used including blogs which served as the earliest reporting mechanisms of the disaster. The SEA-EAT blog was used to quickly respond to the outpouring of support and grief, by providing news, information and contacts. An online blog recording eye witness accounts was also published by the mainstream press. The facility to make donations online resulted in contributions from individual Americans matching the $350 million pledge of the US Government within ten days of the disaster; total online donations worldwide reached $750 million by January 10th. The disaster also led to the creation of 'wikis' (a web application that allows users to add content, as on an Internet forum, but also allows anyone to edit the content – see en.wikipedia.org/wiki/WIKI) to document the event for posterity. Mobile phones and 'short message service' (SMS) or text messaging also played a part and were used by citizen journalists to report on the aftermath of the tsunami from places without Internet infrastructure (Smith et al. 2005).

Contributions to the SEA-EAT blog about the tsunami and its impact were tailing off when a devastating earthquake took place in Kashmir on 8th October 2005. Within 24 hours, another blog had been set up with similar objectives and functions as the tsunami-help blog.

In terms of the technologies used, blogging and contributions to wikis are perhaps the most transforming new technologies in giving citizens their own voice. An important factor in their appeal may well be the fact that at present, access to these technologies is a free resource. In the case of blogs, sustainability depends primarily on the commitment of the blogger. Their use relies on the efforts, commitment and enthusiasm of the contributors.

Relevance to the 'user' is a given as individuals and groups themselves decide on the purpose, focus and content of their communications.

Although apparently increasing, the scale of spontaneous citizen action is hard to quantify and not always highly visible. However, it is an influential force in society that can only become stronger as more people become aware of the possibilities. A striking contrast with e-government programs is the fact that energy and motivation of citizens to engage in these activities is evident in abundance – there is no need for extensive persuasion or high profile public relations campaigns to secure their involvement and commitment.

6.1.3 Focus

The case studies described here also show significant variation in terms of their focus. As we have already mentioned in Section 6.1.1, the focus of projects in most cases is defined by the initiator, although the extent of definition may be very specific or very broad.

Examples which have both a very specific and 'narrow' focus include the Surrey Over 50's website, and the Bundestag website. Initiatives which have a specific but potentially broad-ranging focus include Netmums and WomenSpeak, which sought to elicit the experiences and attitudes of a particular group in order to inform Government thinking and, potentially, policy making. Others have an even broader focus. For example, the Macatawa project, the Chicago neighbourhood planning project, the Jhai Foundation and the K-Net projects all had broad aims related to the improvement and regeneration of a particular community.

In deeply impoverished communities in the developing countries, we have seen that the focus of initiatives is more likely to be upon improving basic living conditions through a variety of technologies, including ICTs, to enable economic activity, health care and education. In western nations, initiatives are often focused upon the needs of excluded or marginalized groups. The focus in these cases is upon capacity building in the community.

In several of the cases, the specific issue on which the initiative focuses may in fact be somewhat secondary to a more general aim of engaging citizens in some way. For instance, 'Logged Off' (cited in the previous chapter) which was initiated by the Carnegie Foundation. This research exercise was conducted to explore the potential for ICTs to engage young people more effectively in political issues, the processes of public decision making and civil society (Howland and Bethell 2002).

The way in which the focus of an initiative or project is defined will have implications for the appropriate scale of citizen engagement, but perhaps more importantly it will have implications for the extent of impact and influence which citizens can have over decision making, as described in the following sections.

6.1.4 Scale

Another dimension we have identified for classifying participation/engagement is its scale. The proportions of citizens in a community who are engaged and the kinds of citizens involved in participatory exercises vary widely. Some initiatives, such as 'America Speaks' in the USA seek wide engagement of large communities to be broadly representative. (http://www.americaspeaks.org). 'America Speaks' therefore aims to involve as many people as possible in 'town hall forums' to deliberate on issues and make their views known to decision-makers. Fifty thousand people or more may be involved in these exercises. At the other end of the continuum, far narrower small scale engagement is sought for specific purposes. For instance, as part of the drive for greater social inclusion in the UK, there has been a focus of attention and investment of effort on reaching those who would not normally participate. Examples described in Chapter 5 are Jamie's Big Voice, the voice of one man speaking on behalf of the homeless in UK, or the young people who took part in the online surgeries as part of a UK e-democracy pilot project (Being Heard 2005). Care must however be taken in extrapolating from results gained from a small sample to the population as a whole.

6.1.5 Impact

The striking variation in breadth of focus and scale of the various citizen participation/engagement exercises analysed has already been discussed. Projects also differ in terms of the significance of their impact on citizens, some dealing with issues of central importance to citizens, and others with more peripheral aspects. An example of peripheral impact, the German Bundestag consultation reported in Chapter 4 was a participative exercise launched specifically to improve the design of the Bundestag website (Fühles-Ubach 2005).

Citizens with a particular interest in the operation of the parliament were recruited to inform the exercise. While significant to the group concerned, typically the impact of such specifically focussed projects on the lives of most citizens is marginal and does little to enhance democracy or the quality of life more widely in society. Examples of exercises with wider significance and scale of impact include the Netmums consultation exercise which had the potential for major impact on employment practices throughout the UK (Netmums.com n.d.).

In the Netmums consultation, parents of young children were given a voice to make known their values and requirements in relation to employment and maternity rights via the Netmums network. Their views informed the deliberations of Government on the issues and informed national policy as well as identifying clear challenges for both the government and for employers in the UK.

The findings from the twenty cases examined show the varied impact of participation/engagement on the lives of citizens. The most pervasive far-reaching effects are seen where whole communities are transformed through participation/engagement exercises, e.g. the *Reflect* ICTs projects in India and Uganda, the K-Net project, the Macatawa and Chicago participative neighbourhood planning initiatives. This does not however mean that involving only a small number of people in the engagement process limits impact. For instance, gaining understanding of complex and very serious social issues such as domestic violence has been a most significant outcome of the WomenSpeak initiative with the potential for major positive impact on society, although only a small number of participants were involved.

6.1.6 Citizen Influence

The number of stages at which citizens have influence in the decision making process is another important parameter of participation/engagement. Each of the case studies described in this book was examined to identify which aspects of decision-making in the planning/design process were in fact open to citizen influence (see Table 6.2). The table shows that, in most cases, citizens were afforded the opportunity to engage in only a sub-set of the planning, design and development stages of any given project. Most of the exercises address only one or two elements of the complete decision making process. Thus, for example, the Bundestag website project invited the participation of a self-selected group of citizens in just one stage of the decision-making cycle – the analysis and requirements definition stage. The specific objective of the project was to better meet the information needs of citizens regarding the functioning of parliament. From the documented reports, the exercise was well-received by its target audience and successful. Certainly, the design outcome is likely to have achieved a good match with the needs of the enthusiastic and engaged citizens recruited for

Table 6.2. Opportunity for Citizen influence by case (N = 20)

Stage Case Study	Agenda Setting	Analysis/ Requirements Definition	Shaping Policy	Shaping Technology	Shaping Social System	Implementation	Evaluating outcomes/ monitoring progress
Bundestag Website, Germany		✓	✓				
Macatawa Project, USA	✓	✓	✓		✓		
America Speaks, USA		✓	✓			✓	
Madrid Participa, Spain		✓	✓	✓	✓		✓
Future drug R&D, Denmark			✓				
Reflect ICTs Uganda, India	✓	✓	✓	✓	✓	✓	✓
K-Net, Canada	✓	✓	✓	✓	✓	✓	✓
National Forum on Health, Canada	✓	?	✓				
Participative neighbourhood planning, USA		✓	✓		✓		
'Logged-off', UK		✓		✓			✓
LOCOMOTION UK		✓	✓	✓			
WomenSpeak, UK	✓	✓					
UTOPIA, UK		✓	✓	✓			
Online Surgeries for Young People, UK			✓				
Surrey 50+ website, UK		✓					
Jamie's Big Voice, UK	✓	✓	?			✓	
Netmums, UK	✓						
Nepal Wireless, Nepal		✓	✓	✓	✓	✓	
Jhai Foundation, Laos	✓	✓				✓	?

the venture. However the number of stages in which citizens are involved is not of itself an indicator of the importance of the engagement nor of the likely success of participation/engagement exercises. This is clear from the Netmums case where citizens were only involved in one stage of the pol-icy-making process. However, because it was the crucial agenda-setting stage, their contributions had the potential to influence everything that sub-sequently happened, as a result of clarifying for members of the working party the critical aspects and issues to address in their deliberations.

It seems that only in a minority of cases are citizens given the opportu-nity to be part of every stage of decision-making. Only three of the 13 cases described in Chapter 4 (namely, the two *Reflect* ICTs pilots (Beardon 2005) and K-Net (Beaton 2004)) gave citizens the opportunity to be part of the whole spectrum of decision-making, from setting the agenda to choos-ing or developing ICT solutions and 'owning' the subsequent implementa-tions. Such experiences enable citizens to develop an holistic view of the technological, social and policy aspects of developments which relate to them, empowering them to shape decisions on design and policy – and progress towards desirable digital futures. In other words, building the ca-pacity of citizens to participate and engage effectively. Confining partici-pation to specific decision-making stages of any development limits the understanding, the learning and the sense of ownership citizens have re-garding the eventual outcome.

6.2 Modelling Citizen Engagement

Using a framework based on concepts from systems theory, we have ana-lysed the case studies described in Chapters 4 and 5 to identify the inputs, outputs and the intervening transformations involved in participation/ engagement projects. Based on the results, a descriptive model of effective citizen engagement has been developed, as shown in Fig. 6.1. In this model, the diverse characteristics, knowledge and experience of citizens are identified as the inputs to a transformation process. Supported by rele-vant tools, and with appropriate leadership and facilitation, this leads not only to the generation of *outputs* (i.e. artifacts such as problem definitions, requirements specifications, action plans or policy statements), but also to the generation of a range of *outcomes* (e.g. raised awareness, greater con-fidence, empowerment). These are in some respects less tangible than the outputs but profoundly significant in enabling people to influence and shape decisions, thereby contributing to the creation of desirable digital fu-tures.

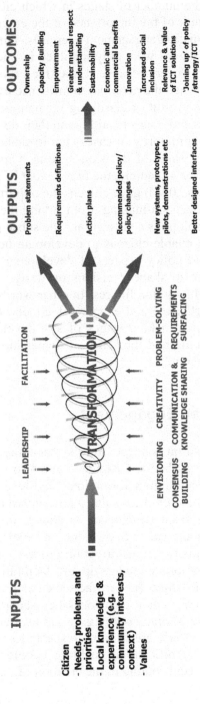

Fig. 6.1. A model of Citizen Engagement.

6.2.1 Citizen Input

Citizens bring inputs of many different kinds to participation and engagement exercises. These inputs include deep knowledge of their own personal circumstances, needs and problems – in other words, they offer rich and detailed understanding born out of first-hand experiences. Such knowledge cannot be provided in its fullness by intermediaries or external agencies.

The understanding of the complexities and nuances relating to the parameters of our lives derives from our experience of day-to-day living. Citizens' inputs may be highly specific and sometimes unique, relating to their own needs and requirements, explicit and tacit knowledge on local context, on community interests, and crucially, on priorities and values.

Established methods typically used in ICT development do not adequately elicit and articulate these. All of these inputs are of profound importance in informing the shape of a digital future that will be perceived as relevant and desirable by its citizens. Examples of some of the inputs which citizens have brought to the various exercises reported in Chapters 4 and 5 are discussed below.

Knowledge and understanding of needs, problems and priorities

The UTOPIA project was able to generate guidance for ICT designers about older people's needs and how to accommodate them. This was achieved through in-depth engagement with a wide range of older citizens. Video footage of interactions with older people was then used to help convey understanding of the problems to the designers (UTOPIA 2004).

WomenSpeak, an online interactive project, enabled women who had suffered domestic violence to make essential inputs to the formulation of policy and of an action plan. They shared with concerned politicians their experiences and their ideas regarding their priorities for action in this area. Their perspectives and analysis of the issues gave unique insights and understanding of a very sensitive subject to the politicians addressing this issue (Moran 2002).

The Canadian National Forum on Health and the Macatawa cases provide examples where citizens contributed to prioritizing actions. In these cases eventual implementation of plans reflects the stated priorities of citizens and therefore acceptance and positive support of the changes is more likely to follow.

Local knowledge and experience (e.g. of community interests, context)

The crucial significance of context (whether geographical, cultural, economic, social and political or other factors) for the development of effective interventions is very clear from all the cases considered.

The aim of the Macatawa case study, for example, was to improve quality of life and living conditions in their community. A wide range of citizens of the Macatawa area contributed their local knowledge and experience of citizenship in the community to identify and specify problems in their community and region, and then developed action plans to address these. Similarly, local knowledge and first hand experience of villagers participating in the *Reflect* ICTs projects enabled them to specify their individual information needs and requirements and to share their knowledge of what technologies would or would not be useful – and above all practicable and affordable for them.

Values

Understanding what we, as citizens, really value is fundamental to informing design decisions and shaping digital futures which we perceive to be desirable. Values are often so deeply embedded in a culture that they are not easily articulated. To explicitly gain inputs regarding values can be of enormous significance to the projects and programmes seeking to make beneficial and acceptable changes in communities. The documented study of developments in the K-Net project provides us with powerful evidence of this. The activities and conduct of the indigenous peoples represented by the Keewaytinook Okimakanak are permeated by their deeply held belief in the importance of respect, for each other, for their community, for other peoples, for the environment and the need for sustainability. As a result of developing engagement processes which manifested respect, community members became engaged in the initiative and worked to identify and develop new applications of ICT which would serve their communities and which in turn would embody the values of respect towards citizens.

6.2.2 Transformations

In development projects of all kinds where citizens are active participants, inputs are synthesised into outputs through transforming experiences of collaboration, communication, shared learning and envisioning. These transformation processes are fuelled by harnessing human imagination, creativity and problem-solving capacities of the participants.

Characteristically, a key part of the transformation process is knowledge sharing across many divides (including those of domain, context and life experience, frames of reference, personal and professional goals and objectives, attitudes, perceptions). This can lead to identification of shared problems and formulation of problem statements which form the basis of agreement on potential solutions. The learning which takes place as ideas develop and as knowledge is shared helps citizens to use their imagination, to dream their dreams, to envision desirable futures and to engage in creative problem solving. Insights stem from bringing together people with a diverse range of skills and expertise and from different backgrounds working to a common purpose. Consensus on or even differences about goals may only become clear during the process of working together. Evaluating possible solutions may be a valuable part of building shared understanding, identifying potential problems and the creation of new, improved solutions.

The case studies provide evidence of the contributions generated through a transformation process. The *Reflect* ICTs Project illustrates the value of using creative approaches to build peoples' capacity to identify and articulate their information needs and, as a consequence, to increase their access to information. This led to the confidence of the participants being increased, and enabled them to develop the capacity to be aware of, and to speak up for their rights.

Although not formally documented as a case study, another positive example of utilising citizen creativity comes from the Hansard Society's experience in launching a national competition to design a web site for young people by young people. The project 'Being Heard' aimed to encourage youth participation in the policy and decision-making process of Government and used the creative skills of the young people themselves. The website itself provides a place to increase young people's awareness and participation in politics. This is achieved through the provision of information and a forum for them to voice their opinions and consult with decision-makers (Being Heard 2005).

The excitement of the transformation process for the participants grows as outputs begin to develop and outcomes can be anticipated. The feelings are vividly described by Al-Kodmany, in his description of the initiative in Chicago's Pilsen neighbourhood, USA, in which a combination of new technologies was used to engage citizens in the planning process for the regeneration of their neighbourhood. The use of technology provided citizens: "*...with a wealth of maps and visual data that helped orient the participants, identify problems and facilitate consensus*", "*...empowerment to plan and design for the future of their community.*" One resident of the neighbourhood exclaimed "*...as we saw ideas begin to take shape before* *our eyes we could feel the excitement rise. The pulse begins to beat a bit faster!"* (Al-Kodmany 1999).

Similarly, in the Macatawa area project, the transformation process generated a strong sense of enthusiasm to deliberate and decide on priority areas for action. Those involved in transforming their individual and collective contributions into action plans, committed to continued involvement in the projects they had been instrumental in defining and planning.

The case studies also revealed a very considerable array of tools and techniques which are available and in use worldwide to support and promote the processes. This aspect will be discussed further in Chapter 9 'Strategies for Citizen Engagement (ii) – Tools and Techniques'.

6.2.3 Outputs and Outcomes: Components of Desirable Futures

The transformation process which occurs in effective citizen engagement exercises delivers explicit, tangible outputs (see Table 6.3). Examples include:

- carefully formulated problem statements (informed by sharing experiences and knowledge of different stakeholders);
- analyses and specifications of information needs;
- agreed priorities for action;
- action plans.

Outputs

The effective shaping of requirements which results from the transformation processes serve to produce tangible outputs in the form of requirements specifications. For example, forums run by America Speaks always produce a preliminary report at the end of each deliberation, which can be taken away by participants at the end of the day. In turn, such documented outputs inform technical design decisions, increasing the relevance and value of solutions (as for example in the K-Net project). The Canadian National Forum on Health initiative resulted in an action plan formed on the basis of consensus among the participants on the healthcare priorities for the nation.

Tangible outputs such as these inform decision making and policy making which can then result in developments of ongoing benefit to individuals and communities. One such result is the establishment of a central information resource centre in a community in Uganda. This profoundly significant development came about as a result of the information needs analysis and action planning by the citizens involved in the *Reflect* ICTs project processes. Through similar transforming processes, the communities in North Western Ontario represented by the Keewaytinook Okimakanak have succeeded in making telecommunications facilities available to citizens. These include new telehealth facilities and a virtual high school. As reported in Chapter 4, the Internet High School enables young teenagers to stay with their families and engage with their communities rather than having to travel far afield and risk losing their roots. Similarly, the telehealth project makes substantial savings by enabling patients to have virtual consultations with doctors and other health professionals rather than having to travel hundreds of miles for appointments. Desirable digital futures seem to be evolving for this community.

Outcomes

From the case studies, we can also identify numerous examples of other kinds of outcomes. These are sometimes less tangible than the outputs cited above but nevertheless important. Examples of such outcomes are shown in Table 6.3.

Table 6.3. Examples of outcomes from Citizen Engagement processes

- Increased relevance and value of solutions generated
- Ownership of solutions
- Capacity building
- Empowerment
- Mutual respect and understanding
- Increased economic and commercial activity
- Increased innovation
- Increased social inclusion and community cohesion
- Joining up of policy, strategy and ICT
- Sustainability

An outcome which is less immediately visible but equally important in terms of its long-term benefit, value and influence is the sense of ownership experienced by participants. The Jhai Foundation has several active projects in which local people can choose to participate on the basis of their preferences and skills. Cultivation and sale of local coffee (Jhai Coffee) on a fair-trade basis has promoted economic development throughout the area assisted by the Jhai Foundation (www.jhai.org/).

The projects report high impact and attribute this to the fact that their communities own them. Similarly the philosophy and methodology of participation in the *Reflect* ICTs project regards the community as a whole as the basic unit for the engagement process. This approach has meant that whole village communities have been involved in problem formulation and discussion and in agreeing on priorities for action. At the other end of the technological spectrum, participants in the 'America Speaks' project are provided with electronic polling equipment and can debate issues round the table face-to-face with decision makers.

Another outcome identified from the analysis of the case material is capacity building – which is the change and development which takes place in individuals and thus in their communities as they participate in projects, learning new skills of many kinds and growing in confidence as a result. For example, a participative *Reflect* ICTs pilot in India (Beardon 2005) reports that the main objective of participating villagers has been to acquire information relevant to their needs. The pilot helped them to work out who has the information, where the information is and how much of it is relevant. Radio has been the most popular tool for information acquisition and advocacy. This has enabled the villagers to articulate proposals for expressing their needs and demands. Using ICTs to collect, store and analyse information is the next phase planned for the projects. Such capacity building provides the foundation for empowerment – in this case, enabling marginalized groups to become aware of their rights and to access information they need in order to improve their lives. Promoting learning and the development of skills and capabilities in this way are explicit objectives of the *Reflect* ICTs projects led by ActionAid. This institution regards capacity building as the key to achieving improvements in the quality of life of very poor communities. Investment in capacity building appears to far exceed expenditure on electronic resources, including ICTs.

A further outcome from the citizen engagement process is mutual respect and understanding between different groups. As an illustration of this, in consultations, K-Net received many requests for provision of a forum where aboriginal and non-aboriginal peoples across Canada could share information and discuss their views so that a respectful view of the aboriginal way of life could be promoted. Consequently, K-Net established 'Turning Point', which offers cyber-space for aboriginal and non-aboriginal people in Canada to have open and direct communication with each other (see: http://www.turning-point.ca/).

Other beneficial outcomes identified in several of the case study reports relate to major improvements in the effectiveness of economic and commercial activity. These have resulted from citizens communicating their needs, e.g. for information on prices at the markets where they sell commodities. A valued outcome of particular significance in some very poor communities is a direct result of having access to ICTs which enable people to monitor market prices and judge when they are likely to achieve a favourable return on the sale of their goods. They can therefore make an informed decision about going to market (e.g. in the Nepal Wireless and Jhai Foundation cases). Such tangible benefits of using technology stimulate the enthusiasm of users to find further ways of exploiting the ICT capabilities. This engagement has led to the creation of virtual outlets which use the Internet to develop opportunities to trade in new markets. In the Jhai Foundation case this means that local coffee produced in Laos is now marketed and sold across the globe. In Nepal, yak farmers in very remote areas now use electronic communications to buy and sell animals. Such successes have given added impetus to initiatives to develop low cost ICTs, affordable to poor communities.

Improvements in community relations are also evident in increased social inclusion and community cohesion, as is illustrated in the communities which host the Jhai Foundation and the Macatawa Area Coordinating Council respectively.

'America Speaks' and the Canadian National Forum on Health are two examples from the case studies of initiatives that currently affect policies directly, achieving the joining up of policy, strategy and the use of ICTs. These programmes have brought together physically both policy-shapers and citizens, and used ICTs to facilitate their deliberations and decision-making. This approach has been adopted in the UK for consultations over the National Health Service that were held in four pilot locations between September-October 2005. One thousand people took part in an NHS consultation at the Birmingham International Convention Centre at the end of October 2005 adopting a similar approach to that of 'America Speaks' (BBC 2005).

The full potential of ICTs as a key enabler of citizen engagement has yet to be fully demonstrated, and in many studies, e.g. Madrid Participa, electronic methods are seen as just one of the means available to citizens to be involved in democracy.

Sustainability of the results of the initiatives depends on a number of variables, including **adequate funding**, the commitment and **support of community leaders**, the availability and reliability of **technological equipment and expertise** and, most importantly, **a political and cultural environment which supports participation**. Informed understanding of the capability of the technology and acceptance of the rights of citizens to pursue appropriate means of improving their daily lives are also key factors in sustainability. Some of the initiatives described in the case studies have taken explicit steps to become sustainable. For example, K-Net is owned and managed by the local community. Although external funding has contributed to the success of the initiative, it is able to generate its own income by charging users (including the Canadian Government) for its services. Other initiatives such as Nepal Wireless, and the Jhai Foundation are working to generate income for communities through promoting the sale of local produce and handicrafts or encouraging tourism.

It is important to emphasize that the transformational processes which led to the outcomes described did not simply occur spontaneously – rather, leadership and facilitation were frequently crucial catalysts for action and for sustaining momentum in the projects. In several of the case studies, it is evident that one particular individual or small group has championed the cause and put in considerable personal effort to achieve success for the initiatives e.g. in setting up online surgeries for young people to engage with elected councillors and local council staff in Kingston, UK, in establishing 'America Speaks' to engage communities in debate and planning in the US, and in setting up schemes to support increased ICT-enabled commercial activity e.g. Nepal Wireless, and Jhai Foundation. K-Net is notable for the leadership of local chiefs and their clear vision of future ICT-enabled possibilities for their communities.

6.3 Conclusions

In this chapter we have presented a multi-dimensional model of citizen engagement, which reveals the richness and complexity of the process and the many benefits to be gained. This model extends current perspectives for analyzing citizen engagement which have tended to focus on the level of participation and/or the way in which technology is used in the process. It identifies a range of characteristics which not only enable a more comprehensive description of citizen engagement/participation initiatives but also offers powerful insights into the conditions for success of such initiatives.

It is evident that successes in civic participation – whether in impoverished communities in the developing world or in leading developed nations – are underpinned by the development of skills and capabilities of the participants. Therefore a key message for governments internationally who are concerned to promote participation and engagement of their citizens in democratic process and in civic society, is that investment in capacity building is the crucial route to empowering citizens to improve all aspects of their quality of life. The use of ICT is a powerful enabler in achieving this but will not of itself deliver more than limited and transient change. Significant and more lasting change and improvement comes through e-enabled new opportunities for economic activity, through understanding local governance, and learning how to have influence and exercise democratic rights. These outcomes empower people as stakeholders in society to have some influence over decisions made on their behalf and in shaping their futures.

Thus, the model provides a strong foundation to inform the direction and formulation of citizen participation/engagement exercises and initiatives. It also provides improved criteria for systematic monitoring and evaluation of their effectiveness. Above all we hope that clearer identification of the processes, benefits, and far-reaching rewards emerging from practice on an international basis, serves to inspire widespread citizen engagement in society.

In the next chapter, we explore the barriers which have prevented widespread adoption of a participative approach to the design of ICT systems and services, and propose an integrated conceptual framework for ICT design.

References

Al-Kodmany K (1999) Using visualization techniques for enhancing public participation in planning and design: process, implementation and evaluation. Landscape and Urban Planning, 45. Elsevier, pp 37-45.

America Speaks (n.d) Home Page. http://www.americaspeaks.org/.

Barrat I, Reniu JM (2004) Electronic Democracy and Citizen Participation.

BBC (2005) Patients take part in NHS debate http://news.bbc.co.uk/1/hi/health/4388294.stm

BBC (2004) Wi-fi lifeline for Nepal's farmers   http://news.bbc.co.uk/1/hi/technology/3744075.stm

Beardon H (2005) ICT for development: empowerment or exploitation. Learning from the Reflect ICTs project. ActionAid, London.

Beaton B (2004) The K-Net Story: Community ICT Development Work. The Journal of Community Informatics. 1(1), pp 5-6.

Being Heard (2005) You have the right to be heard. http://www.beingheard.org.uk/content/default.asp?page=52_1&id=226&topicid=48sectionId=n1_1

Carnegie Foundation (2005) Young people, the Internet and democratic citizenship – Making the connection. http://www.carnegieuktrust.org.uk/cypi/our_work/research/e-participation

e-Democracy (2005) Homepage http://www.e-democracy.gov.uk

Emery M, Purser RE (1996) The Search Conference: A Powerful Method for Planning Organizational Change and Community Action. Jossey-Bass, San Francisco.

Fühles-Ubach S (2005) How would you like it to be? – Results and project development from the first multi-phase online survey (online consultation) on the future of the Bundestag's website content. Available from: http://www.dialoguebydesign.net/docs/Report_BT_OnlineKonsultation-english.pdf

Hansard Society (2005) Weblogs – a powerful voice for campaigns? http://www.hansardsociety.org.uk/programmes/e-democracy/Weblogs

Howland L, Bethell M (2002) "Logged Off – How can ICT Connect Young People and Politics?" Demos, 2002. http://www.demos.co.uk/loggedoff_pdf_media_public.aspx

Jhai Foundation (n.d.) Homepage www.jhai.org/

Local e-Democracy National Project Case Studies (2005) Project case studies http://www.e-democracy.gov.uk/casestudies/casestudy.htm

Local e-Democracy National Project (2005) E-methods for public engagement: helping local authorities to communicate with citizens. http://www.e-democracy.gov.uk/knowledgepool/default.htm?mode=1&pk_document=458

Moldrup C, Morgall JM, Almarsdottir AB (2000) Citizen involvement in future drug R and D: a Danish Delphi Study. Foresight, 2 (5), pp 497-506.

Moran M (2002) WomenSpeak: E-democracy or he-democracy? http://www.egovmonitor.com/features/moran01.html

Netmums.com (n.d.) The great work debate. www.netmums.com/cpg/whatmatters/greatworkdebate.htm

Smith J, Kearns M, Fine A (2005) Power to the Edges: Trends and Opportunities in Online Civic Engagement. Available at: http://www.comminit.com/trends/ctrends2005/trends-259.html

UTOPIA (Usable Technology for Older People: Inclusive and Appropriate) (2004) Publications page. http://www.computing.dundee.ac.uk/projects/UTOPIA/Publications.asp

Wyman M et al. (1999) Learning to Engage: Experiences with Civic Engagement in Canada, Canadian Policy Research Networks http://www.cprn.com/en/doc.cfm?doc=87.

7 Citizen Engagement in ICT Design: The Challenge

Citizen participation and engagement are recognized increasingly as essential to a mature democracy. They are also highly desirable from a design and decision making perspective in delivering the relevant and valued outcomes described in the previous chapters. This argues for citizen engagement to become a mainstream activity in the development of ICTs (as is already the case in many policy and planning decisions in civic society). There are however, continuing barriers to progress in the ICT design domain. It appears that the learning and understanding of the role citizens can play and the significance of their engagement has not transferred effectively to the ICT professionals and practitioners responsible for the countless projects implementing 'e-everything' across society. In this chapter, we review some of the powerful deterrents to this transfer of knowledge and propose a constructive approach to overcoming these.

7.1 Barriers to Citizen Engagement in ICT Development

The list below identifies some of the most significant barriers to citizen engagement in ICT development projects:

- technical focus of ICT developments;
- limited practice of participatory design;
- role conflicts and role boundaries;
- knowledge silos;
- lack of appropriate skills;
- high perceived costs.

7.1.1 Technical Focus of ICT Developments

A major barrier to effective citizen engagement in ICT developments is the focus on technical systems rather than sociotechnical systems. Reference has already been made in Chapter 2 to the high failure rate of large scale information systems implementation projects over past decades, many in the public sector. Failures and shortfall in performance compared with promised delivery are often associated with design approaches drawing on the engineering model, which concentrate mostly (sometimes, entirely) on developing and delivering a functioning technical system. This means that little or no account is taken of the social system with which the technical system is inevitably linked. Nor is there recognition of the need to design the technical and social systems in parallel to achieve an optimized, effective sociotechnical system. There is therefore no perceived need to engage with members of those social systems during the development process. The consequence of such an approach is that the technical system may be entirely sound in terms of the software engineering. The design of the user interface may also be sound. Nevertheless, the system delivered for use is unlikely to be readily assimilated by the intended users for a variety of reasons. It is likely that there will be a poor fit with key aspects of the human and organizational systems (e.g. existing ways of working, information needs and communication patterns). The impact of this is often seen in slow adoption, even rejection, of the ICT system.

7.1.2 Limited Practice of Participatory Design

A second barrier is the limited use of participatory approaches to the design of ICT systems. As we note in Chapter 2, this has partly occurred for historical reasons. When computers were the preserve of experts in the laboratory, their design was a matter of programming and engineering. Since computers were both designed by and used by programmers and engineers, there was no need to involve anyone else in the process. As computers moved into the workplace, systems designers came to recognize that the wider range of users have different needs, and many accept that the best way to identify these is to engage directly with users. But, while user-centred design and inclusive design approaches are being promoted and encouraged within the ICT development industry, they are not yet part of mainstream ICT design activity. For example, most standard 'waterfall' type models of existing ICT design methods only allow for involvement of particular groups of users or role holders at specific and fairly limited stages of the design process. This is very different from engaging freely and widely with a range of user/citizen stakeholders and empowering them to inform design decisions throughout the process. For these stakeholders to enjoy real influence, they need to be actively engaged in envisioning the possibilities, identifying and understanding the technical options, and exploring alternative sociotechnical solutions.

As also noted in Chapter 2, participatory design has been developed and applied predominantly in Scandinavia. However despite the efforts of pioneering advocates and practitioners such as Mumford (1983), Muller (2002) and Cabana (1995), this approach has not been widely adopted in other countries. One likely reason for this is that participatory design fits well with the strong democratic culture of the Scandinavian countries, and in particular, with their commitment to industrial democracy which is formalized in legislation. By contrast, a truly participatory approach does not fit easily into cultures (whether national or organisational) which do not share the values or fully embrace the democratic principles that it embodies.

7.1.3 Role Conflicts and Role Boundaries

A further barrier to citizen engagement is created by traditional views about design and the role of designers. Mumford (1991) was among the first to identify that the way in which ICT design is approached leads to problems relating to role boundaries between the different professionals involved. However the problem is not confined to the ICT design domain. Designers in all domains have traditionally regarded it as their prerogative to formulate design solutions and then to implement them. Giving responsibility to others (e.g. to the end users of their designs) is a cause for concern for some, partly because it could threaten their capacity to innovate and partly because it could result in design solutions which are sub-optimal from a technical standpoint (even if the users prefer them). As Norman (2000) points out, most professional designers have spent a long time getting trained in their discipline, and are usually aware of the pitfalls. However, as Norman also points out, *"most design is not done by professional designers, it is done by engineers, programmers and managers."* Each of these roles has not only a different set of professional skills, but also different goals and responsibilities, which are likely to conflict with those of each other, let alone those of the end-users. For example, *"designers must please their clients, and the clients may not be the users"* (Norman 2000). With so much scope for conflict within design projects it is hardly surprising that some designers do not want to engage with a wider group of unknown people whose influence upon the project will at least be unpredictable.

There is, however, evidence of a modest degree of change in this relationship. For example, in the product design domain, some designers are embracing the notion of co-design (e.g. Gyi et al. 2005) in which potential future users are given an opportunity to exercise their creativity, albeit in the context of a controlled and limited brief.

Seely Brown and Duguid (2002) make an important point about designers' roles in the contemporary, digital world: *"issues about the breadth or narrowness of design are not, we should stress, issues for designers alone. Increasingly we all live in a heavily designed world and need to understand both the strengths and limitations of the designs offered to us. In particular, we all need to be able to deal with the hype that accompanies new technological design. In the digital world, moreover, many of the distinctions between designers and users are becoming blurred. We are all, to some extent, designers now. Many questions about design are thus becoming questions for us all."*

In contemporary society, citizens are making, and expect to make, decisions about their lives that are effectively design decisions. The technologies which brought us mass production made a wide range of goods and services accessible to a greater number of consumers, but with high standardization and limitations on choice (to quote the phrase attributed to Henry Ford – a car in any colour as long as it is black!) Developments in manufacturing mean that it is now both possible and economically feasible to create products to a more personal specification. In many aspects of consumers' lives there is scope for, and recognition of the demand for, personalization. With digital technologies such as the personal MP3 player and the personal video recorder (PVR), users are taking control of their own listening and viewing, creating their own playlists and TV schedules; our PC desktops can be personalized, as can the ring tones on our mobile phones. Many people create their own web pages and weblogs for a variety of professional and personal reasons. In all sorts of ways, many people are having a significant influence on the way their immediate environment and possessions look or behave: aspects which, in the past, would have been likely to be the territory of someone with the title 'designer'.

As citizen/consumer power and confidence grows, the traditional roles and power of designers becomes less appropriate. Instead, designers in the 21st century now have the opportunity to develop the tools and techniques to inform, inspire and enable citizens to influence the shape of future technologies. There is also an emerging role for a significant cohort of professionals to meet the fast-growing need to engage citizens, including the young, the old, the disabled and those marginalized by beliefs, ethnicity or life-style, in the articulation of their goals, needs, priorities and aspirations in the context of ICT systems development. It is likely that hybrid skills drawn from the social science community, human-computer interaction specialists, and the public planning domain, among others, will be needed to fulfill these challenging new roles.

7.1.4 Knowledge Silos

A knowledge gulf appears to exist between the ICT domain, and the public policy making and planning domains. In the latter, the development and application of 'social science' knowledge about human behaviour is the norm. In the former, the emphasis still tends to be on the creating and application of engineering and physical science knowledge. This is in spite of the fact that a significant body of knowledge exists about the relationship between people and ICT. Since the 1970s, the rapid development and proliferation of computer systems has been accompanied by a proliferation of research across a wide range of disciplines. Cognitive psychologists and ergonomists have been investigating the design of interfaces, software and hardware in order to make computers easier and more effective to use by the non-specialist user. In parallel, industrial psychologists and sociologists have been examining the impact of the new technology upon work, jobs, social networks and society. At the same time, business consultants and management scientists have investigated the financial and organisational costs and benefits of computerisation.

From these many endeavours, a vast but disparate body of knowledge concerning the relationship between people and technology and issues of uptake of ICT has developed. This body of knowledge continues to grow in abundance although, if anything, it is becoming even more fragmented. As technology has developed and spread across many different domains, pockets of specialist knowledge have built up within those domains, and new domains have arisen, for example: health informatics, ICT in the construction sector, games and entertainment applications, domotics and transport technology, (as evidenced by the spawning of ever more academic journals devoted to each of these areas of knowledge). While the importance of understanding and meeting the needs of stakeholders – especially the users – is a common theme in the literature and practice across almost all of these domains, there is little sharing of knowledge between them. Klein (2005) comments, "*engineers read what engineers have written, social scientists read what social scientists have written; when a social scientist publishes a paper in an engineering journal as I (Klein) have occasionally done, it reaches neither database*". The existence of such 'knowledge silos' means that knowledge and good practice developed in one domain is not routinely or easily shared to the benefit of others. In particular, ignoring social science knowledge condemns ICT developments to repeat the mistakes of the past.

7.1.5 Lack of Appropriate Skills

Mumford (1991) also suggests that an important barrier to involving potential users in ICT design is a lack of appropriate skills. There is certainly evidence that lack of expertise in the processes of engagement limits success despite the presence of interest and commitment. For example, endorsing Mumford's view that *"people don't know how to organize participation"* (1991), a recent study of the implementation of local e-Government in the UK found that local council staff reported real disappointment with the poor responses to consultation exercises run specifically to engage with young people (Damodaran et al. 2004). It appears that even where there is some expressed commitment to participation, this can be thwarted by a failure to adopt appropriate methods and behaviours. One reported study found that fewer than 40% of local authorities in the UK government had consulted or engaged local stakeholders in the planning and implementation of e-Government (Office of the Deputy Prime Minister 2003). This is despite the fact that improving democracy and empowering citizens is one of the stated objectives of the UK Government's local e-Government policy.

Considerable learning will be essential for key personnel, such as local government staff, if they are to accept and adopt a participative approach in their work roles. The repertoire of skills necessary to achieve participation is extensive. It includes social and facilitation skills, as well as knowledge of methods for stakeholder identification, communication, decision-making, requirements elicitation and methods for engaging different groups of citizens appropriately and effectively.

The current lack of understanding and skills in how to achieve more successful participation does not reflect a dearth of such knowledge and a 'need for more research'. On the contrary, there is a growing abundance of such knowledge both at a national level and internationally which derives from case studies and pilots. As we will discuss in Chapter 9, there are also numerous tools and techniques which have been developed to support citizen engagement and participatory design. However, these are often not well promulgated, especially outside the domain in which they have been developed, although the processes which they support are often fundamental to the effectiveness of many human and organizational activities.

The real limitation lies in the fragmentation of the knowledge base, noted above, and the widespread lack of awareness of this body of knowledge and its importance. As a consequence there is little investment in disseminating knowledge of participatory approaches, methods and tools and making this accessible to those who most need it. This is particularly true for many practitioners engaged in developing and delivering ICT systems and services for the public. One costly consequence is the wastage associated with 'reinventing the wheel'. Many conscientious members of staff in local councils and elsewhere are doing their best to engage the public without the benefit of a framework and appropriate tools and techniques to support them.

7.1.6 High Perceived Costs

While some of the barriers identified above relate to lack of awareness about the need for, or the appropriate processes for citizen engagement, a barrier for those who are contemplating citizen engagement can be the perception that it is a costly exercise. There is evidence that this perception does indeed discourage designers from pursuing user involvement in ICT developments (e.g. Sims 2003).

There is no doubt that effective citizen engagement is likely to be time-consuming and expensive. For example, recruiting people to participate in trials of products or systems, or in consultation exercises, requires careful design of the trial or exercise, careful selection of the sample of people to be involved, detailed consultation with a range of stakeholders to set up the processes and so on. Achieving longer term participation in a citizen panel is even more difficult. Accessing certain 'hard to hear' groups (e.g. the disabled, the elderly, young people etc.) in society presents particular challenges which have been explored in some depth in Chapter 5. To address the difficulties successfully demands both expertise and experience relevant to each group and, desirably, a 'champion' from within the participating group. However if care is taken to develop good relations with user groups, then unseen advantages can be achieved. Eisma et al. (2004) report: *"one lady (a project participant) was very pleased to speak on behalf of older users at a seminar for Scottish Industry...another user volunteered to administer one of the project's questionnaires to her contacts"*.

The resource implications of such engagement activities are considerable. Earlier discussion noted the need for people with the relevant skills to undertake the engagement process, and also for cultural and structural changes in organisations to promote and accommodate engagement. Additionally, as mentioned earlier, there will be new and different roles and functions to define. For instance, it may be important to blend the traditional skills of the designer with some of those of the market researcher or customer service staff. New policies and procedures to ensure that engagement becomes a routine part of planning and design projects will also be necessary. These and other such changes take time, and rely on careful planning, implementation and stakeholder involvement to be successful.

Thus, mainstreaming or institutionalizing citizen engagement processes in the public and private sector is a challenge of considerable proportions in terms of the resource requirements. As we have shown, however, to compensate for this investment, citizen engagement also brings huge dividends.

For organisations to take on the significant challenges and associated costs identified above requires awareness of both the 'carrots' and 'sticks'. This means knowing the likely rewards of engaging with citizens as well as the costs and negative consequences of failing to do this. It appears that few have a balanced view of this equation. In both the public and private sector, those charged with developing services or products appear to be far more aware of the high costs of engaging citizens (e.g. the time-consuming nature of consultation, focus groups, surveys etc.) than of the costs of failing to engage citizens. Despite the fact that the consequences or costs of the latter are well-documented, this reality does not seem to be widely recognized. This is reflected, for example, in the limited resources available to local government to fund relevant citizen engagement processes. It would be difficult for local government to justify the investment since the costs of citizen engagement are relatively easy to calculate and visible while the value of the benefits are harder to quantify. Although often profoundly important, the benefits are less tangible and some may take a long time to accrue. This makes it harder to justify expenditure on 'soft issues' of engaging with citizens and acts as a powerful deterrent to engagement processes becoming institutionalized as a routine part of ICT development projects.

7.2 Changing the Focus of ICT Development

In summary, the current position with regard to ICT design is that, while the benefits of user participation/citizen engagement are partially recognized, there are a number of barriers which prevent widespread adoption of this approach and realization of the consequent benefits. We propose that, if ICT design is to lead to the creation of desirable digital futures, there is a need for a significant shift in focus for the mainstream of current ICT design practice. The parameters of this shift are discussed below.

7.2.1 Parameters of the Shift

In Table 7.1 below we highlight the features of current approaches to ICT design and compare these with the features of an approach which we believe will deliver desirable digital futures.

Table 7.1. Comparison of features of current and desirable design approaches for ICT

Current State	Desirable Future State
Technical focus of ICT developments	Design focus is on the whole (socio-technical) system
Limited practice of participatory design and low levels of stakeholder influence	Participatory approaches become the norm; stakeholder empowerment
Traditional design roles	New hybrid roles
Knowledge silos	Knowledge and best practice widely disseminated
Lack of skills for citizen engagement in ICT developments	Widespread skills for participation and engagement
High perceived costs of engagement	Balanced cost/benefit analyses
IT departments 'own' the ICT system	Users 'own' the system

The belief that ICT design practice needs to change is not in itself a new conclusion. As we have already said in Chapter 3, there are many others – both practitioners and academics/theorists working in related fields, who have reached similar conclusions. Many authors from different backgrounds – such as Norman (2000), Cooper (1999), Seely Brown and Duguid (2000), Nardi and O'Day (1999), to name but a few influential and fairly recent examples – have produced provocative and powerful books based on a profound conviction that conventional approaches to design are failing to deliver the technologies we want.

The ongoing interest in design and in 'better' design has led, over the years, to the development of many theories, associated methods and design approaches, although most have had at best limited impact. Rather than identifying yet another 'new' design method, we believe that the key to designing desirable digital futures lies in embracing and integrating a wider range of design principles. Four approaches in particular seem to us to provide the necessary theoretical and methodological building blocks to underpin the required shift in design focus:

- **Sociotechnical systems theory** and **information ecologies**, which recognize the interdependency which exists between technology and society, and the co-evolutionary nature of the way in which these two elements develop and mutually shape each other.

- **Participatory** and **inclusive** design approaches.

Together these four approaches offer a conceptual and methodological framework to support the construction of strategies for engagement and participation and their implementation. Such an integrated approach would offer opportunities for empowering a wide range of citizens and engaging them in the shaping of sociotechnical systems, within the context of local information ecologies. In addition to the four constituents identified, there is an important role for the application of **change management** principles to achieve the required shift in design practice. In the following sections we shall describe the contributions of all five approaches in more detail.

7.2.2 A Sociotechnical Approach to Design

Sociotechnical theory originated from the work of Eric Trist and Ken Bamforth, researchers at the renowned Tavistock Institute for Human Relations, during the 1950s and 1960s (Trist and Bamforth 1951). Their study of coal mining in County Durham, UK, revealed that groups of miners working the same coal seam and using identical technology, had developed two quite distinct ways of working. This work led to the development of sociotechnical theory, which reflects the fact that all systems consist of social and organizational elements as well as technical elements, which are interdependent. This means for example, that if one component of a system is disturbed or changed, there will be ramifications throughout the system, often in unexpected ways and with outcomes that were not predicted. Sociotechnical theory emphasizes that successful systems require the simultaneous configuration of both 'technical' and 'organizational and social' aspects of the system. In this respect it shares features with 'open systems' theory (Von Bertalanffy 1976) which was developing at around the same time, and which has also had some influence on approaches to ICT design.

Lisl Klein (Klein and Eason 1991) points out that the basic premise of sociotechnical theory was not in itself new, since Marx had revealed the interdependence between the social and the technical. However, the Tavistock researchers both gave a name to the theory and took it down from the macrosocietal level to the work system level, where it can be more easily applied. Here, in the context of citizen engagement, we propose adapting some of these key concepts of sociotechnical theory for application to wider society, beyond the workplace – returning them to their origins as macrosocietal constructs.

Berniker (1992) asserts that *"in the half century since the Durham coal mine experiences, sociotechnical systems (STS) analysis practice has evolved into an effective technique for the design of innovative work*

organizations." Albert Cherns formulated nine principles of sociotechnical systems design (1976), which represent "*the classic formulation of the
body of experience and knowledge about work group design that has been
accumulated over the years*". These nine principles are shown in Table 7.2.

Table 7.2. A summary of Cherns' nine principles of sociotechnical design (1976)

Principle	Summary
Compatibility	The processes of design should be compatible with desired design outcomes (i.e. they should be highly participative).
Minimal critical specification	Methods of working and design must express the essential requirements.
Sociotechnical criterion	Control is local and should be given to the immediate work team – the aim is to make supervision minimal.
Multi-function	Individual and groups need a range of tasks. Organisational boundaries should not be drawn to impede the sharing of information, learning and knowledge.
Boundary location	Information should support those who need to take action.
Information flow	Those who need resources should have access to, and authority over them; roles should be multi-functional and multi-skilled. Information flow should avoid intermediaries where possible.
Support congruence	Other systems supporting the focal group should be congruent in their design.
Design and human values	Transitional arrangements between an existing and a new system should be planned and designed in their own right.
Incompletion	Redesign is iterative and continuous and requires review and evaluation.

These principles were drawn from the experience of a number of consultants and researchers in a variety of settings, and are intended as
guidelines to, rather than prescriptions for, design practice. The original
principles have been reviewed and revised both by Cherns himself and by
others (e.g. by Clegg, 2000) but they have stood the test of time in many
respects in terms of their relevance to the design of desirable digital futures. For example, applying the principle of minimum critical specification to large ICT developments would build in the flexibility essential to
cope with the complex and changing nature of social systems. As we have
already pointed out, human systems are subject to continuous change: they
change while you are analyzing them, they change while you are building

them, they continue to change after you have delivered them. Political will changes, consumer values change, societal needs change. In this sense, all systems are but pilots – all systems change all the time! Furthermore, human systems – unlike bridges, ships or airplanes, are too complex for complete analysis and are not amenable to a fixed design specification. Rather than resenting change and attempting *"complete and consistent"* specifications, therefore, we should embrace the dynamics of inevitable change and involve stakeholders in an evolutionary, incremental design process.

Framing the creation of a sociotechnical system as the primary design objective of ICT development helps to make explicit the way in which the citizen relates to the technical components of the system. Using e-government as an example, each of us as members of the public will have hopes, expectations, aspirations and fears about the technical systems with which government wishes us to interact. For us to readily embrace, or at least accept, a given system or service, first we need to know it exists, then what it offers and finally that it has some utility and relevance for us. Delivering an outcome which satisfies these criteria requires the ICT development team to understand what we regard as useful and relevant and to make their design decisions accordingly. The only real source of such knowledge is ourselves as citizens. Creating ICT design outputs which meet our needs therefore requires techniques to be in place to elicit our aspirations and needs. These techniques need to used as an integral part of the design and development process.

A report commissioned by the Office of the Deputy Prime Minister (ODPM) from the Centre for Urban and Regional Development Studies, University of Newcastle upon Tyne includes the observation that the ICT development process underway for e-Government is not participatory in nature although the formally stated objectives for e-government in the UK include reducing social exclusion and promoting democracy (Office of the Deputy Prime Minister 2003). (This certainly does not comply with Cherns' first principle of compatibility). Appropriate participative/consultative exercises with the public to check design assumptions, for example, would have revealed at the outset important perceptions, hopes, fears and expectations regarding electronic service delivery of local government services. Using this information to inform design decisions might well have avoided some of the causes of slow adoption. It is paradoxical that the design processes used to develop ICT systems intended explicitly to promote participation of the public have not themselves been participatory in nature – and it is clearly time to change this situation.

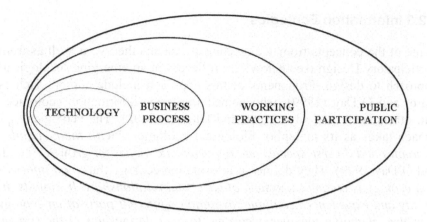

Fig. 7.1. Examples of elements of a sociotechnical system for e-Government (Office of the Deputy Prime Minister 2003).

It is evident from the discussion above, that local e-government should be seen as a sociotechnical system (see Fig. 7.1). The UK Government's strategy for e-government is a central part of its agenda to reform and modernise all public services. In 2000 it set itself the ambitious target of making all its services (at both national and local level) available online by the end of 2005. For this to genuinely lead to improvements in participation of citizens in the democratic process and to a reduction in social exclusion, democratic principles need to inform the process of designing e-government systems. Embedding democratic and participatory design principles into all local government processes, with clear relationships between services and initiatives and the e-government agenda is fundamental to success. In such a model, the key goal for e-government should be successful ICT systems which lead to increased participation and social inclusion, with all key stakeholders, including designers and citizens, voluntary and governmental agencies and business, sharing responsibility for achieving the objective.

Canada provides an example of world-leading success with its Government On-Line (GOL) strategy. It is instructive to note that this is underpinned by *"fundamental e-Government principles of clear vision, user involvement, good targets and departmental and jurisdictional integration"* (Accenture 2004). Sociotechnical aspects of the Canadian strategy include the re-design of governance and management systems to accommodate new models of service delivery and the requirements of users.

7.2.3 Information Ecologies

Some of the concepts from sociotechnical systems theory, as well as from Participatory Design (see below) are reflected in an emerging 'ecological' approach to design. Proponents of this approach include authors such as Nardi and O'Day (1999), who coined the term 'information ecologies', and others such as Seely Brown and Duguid (2002). The ecological approach takes as its metaphor biological ecologies, *"with their complex dynamics and diverse species and opportunistic niches for growth"* (Nardi and O'Day 1999). They define an information ecology thus: *"an information ecology is a complex system of parts and relationships. It exhibits diversity and experiences continual evolution. Different parts of an ecology coevolve, changing together according to the relationships in the system. Several keystone species necessary to the survival of the ecology are present. Information ecologies have a sense of locality"* (Nardi and O'Day 1999).

Thus, the approach shares with sociotechnical systems theory the focus on human activities that are served by the technology, rather than on technology itself (Nardi and O'Day 1999), and the recognition that there are strong interdependencies between different parts of a system. It also shares the belief that the value systems of stakeholders must be taken into account in achieving acceptable, effective systems – and that a participatory design approach – a *"collective, ongoing construction of enduring information ecologies"* is the way to achieve this. (Nardi and O'Day 1999). The ecological metaphor brings with it the notion of ecological failure due to environmental destruction. Nardi and O'Day believe that similarly, there is the possibility that unless we take control of our information ecologies and inject our own values and needs into them, we will be overwhelmed by some of our technological tools. They suggest that it is possible to gain beneficial and positive uses from technology if we do not simply allow it to 'wash over us'.

Clearly the vastness of the potential stakeholder population makes a nonsense of designing global systems with the participation of all citizens. Achieving citizen engagement/participation in the creation of desirable digital futures will depend on achieving the right scale for the process. Adopting an information ecologies perspective to the design of sociotechnical systems helps to identify the appropriate focus and scope of initiatives in which citizens will be able to participate effectively. Locality is a particularly important attribute in the concept of information ecologies. For positive outcomes to result, decisions about the design and application of technology need to be made in the context of settings in which the individual plays an active role and has an active say it what happens: *"our leverage point lies in acting within the spheres where we have knowledge and authority. (...) These sites of local participation offer both opportunities and responsibilities for shaping the way technology works in our lives.*" (Nardi and O'Day 1999).

7.2.4 A Participatory Approach to Design

Enid Mumford reminds us that "*the one thing that can be said with certainty about participation is that it is not a new concept, although it may sometimes have been given other names such as democracy, involvement, sharing, co-operation, etc. The Greeks used it to describe a certain kind of decision taking. For them a decision was participatively taken if the answer to the question 'who takes it?' was 'more or less everybody'. This kind of democratic decision taking contrasted with meritocratic forms in which decisions were taken by an elite, and with an autocratic form in which they were taken by one person*" (Mumford 1983).

In the specific context of design, Participatory Design (PD) has emerged as a recognized body of practice. The key objectives of participatory design are to ensure that those who will be impacted by a system are empowered to participate directly in decision-making about that system, not only in relation to computerized aspects but also in the design of work systems and policies. Muller (2002) characterizes the PD field as follows: "*researchers and practitioners are brought together – but not necessarily brought into unity – by a pervasive concern for the knowledge, voices and/or rights of end-users, often within the context of software design and development, or of other institutional settings (e.g. workers in companies, corporations, universities, hospitals, governments). Many researchers and practitioners in PD (but not all) are motivated in part by a belief in the value of democracy to civic, educational and commercial settings – a value that can be seen in the strengthening of disempowered groups (including workers), in the improvement of internal processes, and in the combination of diverse knowledge to make better services and products*" (Muller 2002).

The approach emerged in Scandinavia in the 1960s, initially in building design (Granath et al. 1996), but was then adopted by a series of projects undertaken by the Norwegian Computing Centre in the 1970s and 1980s (Keul 1983; Thoresen 1992; Clement and Van den Besselaar 1993). In these projects, researchers worked with trade unions to provide them with knowledge about how the use of new information technology could affect their working conditions. The aim was to encourage the unions to develop and implement their own technology control activities and policies. These projects, which included manufacturing, office work, public administration and health care, inspired similar projects in other Scandinavian countries and beyond.

A further defining feature of participatory design approaches is the use of methods and tools which promote communication between stakeholders. This enables joint exploration of design problems, and the generation and evaluation of solutions. This is important because the involvement of a wide range of stakeholders, with different knowledge bases and skills, requires mechanisms to facilitate the sharing of knowledge and understanding, and developing a consensus regarding design solutions. Thus, whilst historically, the concept of PD has been imbued with commitment to the ideal of democracy in work organizations, proponents now believe that it also offers a mechanism for drawing together the knowledge from different domains which is needed to solve complex, real world design problems. Muller for example cites Fowles, who writes about "*transforming the 'symmetry of ignorance' (mutual incomprehension between designers and users) into a complementary 'symmetry of knowledge', through symmetries of participation and symmetries of learning*" (Fowles 2000). Muller goes on to say that most of the theories and practices in PD "*require the combination of multiple perspectives – in part because complex human problems require the combination of multiple perspectives (e.g. software expertise and work-domain expertise) for good solutions (...) and in part because the workplace democracy tradition requires that all of the interested parties (or stakeholders) should have a voice in constructing solutions*" (Muller 2002). It is apparent then that a participative approach to design of desirable futures brings with it the benefits of promoting democracy, and of creating a shared knowledge pool from what have traditionally been quite separate domains.

An important advantage of the kind of engagement embodied in participatory design is that it achieves stakeholder 'buy-in' to the outcomes that are developed. This is clearly important for information systems success within organizations, but is perhaps even more necessary as computers are becoming an integral part of society. Systems such as e-government and e-commerce and the many other e-applications can only operate on the basis of citizen/consumer 'buy-in', acceptance and take up. Thus, powerful drivers now exist for active citizen engagement where there were few before.

7.2.5 Inclusive Design

So far, we have identified frameworks which place the focus of design on sociotechnical systems, located in their own information ecologies, and which promote a participatory process to both engage and empower key stakeholders. A further useful contribution comes from the inclusive design movement. This takes as its starting point the recognition of the diversity of the human population as users and consumers of products, systems and services. Inclusive design emphasises the need to identify and cater for this diversity. Not only is this with a view to creating designs which are well matched to the needs of their intended users, but also to ensure that designs do not exclude particular types of potential users, such as those with disabilities. An inclusive design approach enables the risk of exclusion to be minimized or eliminated by ensuring that unnecessary barriers to access are not built into technology and its provision at the design stage. Furthermore, designing for 'extra-ordinary users' may lead to positive enhancements to design by developing features which facilitate effective use for many, if not all, potential users.

As we note in Chapter 3, there are now significant legislative and business drivers for an inclusive design approach. As a result, considerable information, in the form of guidance, tools and techniques, has been generated to promote and to support inclusive design. These are intended to help designers to meet the diverse needs of citizens. The tools seek to provide information to designers about the physical parameters of specific groups within the population such as older people and disabled people ('extra-ordinary users' – Newell and Gregor 1999) who may have special needs compared to the 'ordinary' population. An inclusive design approach has been used effectively to identify the design constraints associated with specific types of user impairment (e.g. Eisma et al. 2003). However the design outcomes have generally been limited, e.g. to the design of products and aspects of ICT systems such as web pages.

There are mutual benefits to be gained by incorporating inclusive design principles and methods within a sociotechnical and participative approach. Inclusive design offers detailed practical methods and guidance to ensure that design solutions meet the needs of the broadest range of citizens. Equally, inclusive design is likely to have greater impact as a result of a shift in focus from detailed aspects of product design towards sociotechnical systems design.

7.3 Facilitating the Transition: A Change Management Approach

The many benefits of citizen engagement have been revealed in earlier chapters. What then is required to achieve a shift in the focus of ICT design practice such that citizen engagement becomes a normal, mainstream part of ICT design practice? Clearly this will not be easy to achieve – given the entrenched barriers identified in section 7.1 above. But the fact that achieving the shift will be difficult does not mean that it is impossible - nor that we should be daunted by the challenge. The high costs of maintaining the status quo and the promise of rich rewards made possible by the shift are very powerful reasons for embarking on an ambitious programme for change. Change management theory offers a sound basis for developing strategies to make the transition towards a new integrated approach to ICT design, incorporating the principles drawn from the multiple approaches to design described above. Successful change strategies will deliver the following outcomes: (i) create the right culture; (ii) promote widespread knowledge and understanding of the benefits of engaging citizen/users in design - amongst all stakeholders in the ICT design process; and (iii) develop the capacity and capability to undertake effective citizen engagement.

There is a vast literature on change management which includes well-documented best practice and guidance on implementing change strategies. One accessible example is offered by Gleicher (n.d.). Informed by the research into resistance to change and change management, Gleicher proposed a formula to reflect the way in which change often comes about and to suggest how the process can be facilitated by managing the following constituent components appropriately:

D = *Dissatisfaction* with the status quo (pain)
V = a shared *Vision* of the future
K = *Knowledge* about practical steps
C = the *Costs* (economic and psychological) of change

The formula indicates that change will occur when:

$$D \times V \times K > C$$

In other words, the formula suggests that in many situations change comes about when **dissatisfaction with the status quo**, combined with **a desirable vision** of the future and **knowledge of the steps** required to reach the goal, are greater than the perceived **costs** (financial and/or psychological) associated with the change and its implications.

In applying Gleicher's formula to achieve change in the ICT design process, a first step would be acknowledgement of the seriousness and scale of the problems and limitations of the existing ICT design practice. There is already ample evidence, as we have cited in Chapter 2 and elsewhere, that current approaches to ICT design and development lead often to sub-optimal solutions. Citizens and consumers have often 'voted with their feet' by refusing to use poor systems and products. Despite this prevalence of evidence of problems, senior people in positions of leadership and influence in government and in industry (with some notable exceptions), have not generally sought to publicise the difficulties and limitations of current ICT design practices until expensive problems or failures force their hand. An important objective of this book is therefore to help to promote awareness of the need for urgent change and to make the reasons and the benefits very clear. Chapter 10 will pick up this theme again. To illustrate application of the formula to devise a change strategy, the components of such a strategy are described below.

7.3.1 Dissatisfaction with the Status Quo

Change often tends to be stimulated by dissatisfaction on the part of key stakeholders with one or more aspects of the current state of affairs – or with anticipated and unwelcome proposed changes to the status quo. For example, in work organisations, many changes are triggered by management or shareholder dissatisfaction regarding the performance of particular individuals, departments, or with the organisation as a whole. In the community, the situation is somewhat different in that dissatisfaction that prompts action for change is most likely to relate to proposed changes in the locality (such as a new housing estate in a rural area) which are perceived as a threat to established lifestyles or quality of life.

Common to both situations, achieving a groundswell of support for change generally requires that a critical mass of individuals feel sufficiently well-informed and concerned about the problems (current or projected) to be motivated to act to individually or collectively. The first stage in achieving such support is to promote widespread understanding of the nature of problems experienced (or anticipated) with the status quo and their implications for different stakeholders.

In both contexts, sharing this awareness and understanding is necessary to create recognition within a wider constituency of the reasons why change is required. For example, employees may need an understanding of the real nature of the problems that their host organisation is facing, if they are to accept and contribute to changes necessary to addressing the problems. Similarly members of a community may need to be convinced that there is good reason for them to become involved in local action. It is often the case that one individual or small group of stakeholders becomes motivated to achieve change by their strength of feeling and concern about an issue. For instance, a key trigger for the K-Net project in 1993-94 was the lack of any telecommunications facilities in many of the villages in the region (see Chapter 4). Major change has been brought about by engaging citizens in the communities concerned in identifying their needs, articulating their requirements, gaining the necessary resources, and implementing changes.

This 'dissatisfaction with the status quo' component of Gleicher's formula, which we can describe as the '**know why**' step, is essential for mobilising people and gaining their 'buy-in' to the change. As is the case for every step in any successful change strategy, effective communication strategies and mechanisms are essential to articulate and share information and understanding among all stakeholders.

7.3.2 A Shared Vision

As suggested by Gleicher's (n.d.) formula, bringing about change requires more than sharing detailed analyses and understanding of the reasons for making changes. Equally important, if not more so, is to convey a powerful and compelling view of the advantages that will come about as a result of the proposed changes. For proposals for major change to gain support, those seeking to achieve change must create awareness, understanding and excitement regarding the potential benefits – promoting a real desire to experience them. This applies to those who can help to bring change about, as well as to those who will be impacted by it. In particular, achieving the buy-in of those in positions of influence (formal and informal) and in authority is very important for gaining legitimacy for the change, active support and necessary resources.

In the community context, awareness and real understanding of proposed developments and their implications are essential if consultations about planning are to be genuine democratic processes which enable citizens to influence decisions that impact upon their lives. This means that achieving commitment to change will depend on revealing issues and problems – as well as 'selling' the advantages of a new way of doing things.

Promoting a vision of the future which has perceived relevance, value and attraction for the individuals or communities involved is therefore essential. Clear articulation of achievable and tangible goals is particularly important if achievement of the proposed outcome is to be credible and perceived as worth the effort involved. This means that the outcomes illustrated should relate directly to the interests of as wide a cross-section of stakeholders as possible, indicating the advantages and benefits to different groups. Sharing the vision provides the '**know what**', i.e. the knowledge of what potential outcomes and impacts people can anticipate coming from the proposed changes. Envisioning a positive future and beneficial outcomes in a rich and compelling way is also important in achieving support for the change programme when problems (which will inevitably crop up during implementation) arise.

7.3.3 Knowledge about Practical Steps

To give credibility to the idea of attaining the envisioned future, the practical steps to be taken towards achieving this desirable vision will need to be made clear and tangible. A key part of a change management approach is to give confidence that the intended goal will reached. Such confidence is enhanced by a well-publicised, robust and practicable plan to achieve the goals. This component of the strategy can be described as the '**know how**' step.

Gaining the active involvement of key stakeholders who will be affected by the implementation of the proposed plan in its formulation will increase the chances of producing a robust and practicable action plan. Once the steps in the action plan have been determined, then a powerful communications strategy is necessary to share knowledge and understanding of the plan with all stakeholders.

7.3.4 Costs (Economic and Psychological)

Much of the psychological 'cost' of change stems from fears and apprehensions about change that is imposed upon us – and particularly about the loss of control this implies. Allaying fears about the consequences of the changes wherever possible is a key component of any successful change strategy. This is especially the case where profound impact on our personal lives, on our performance and on our ways of doing things is anticipated. These fears may not be justified and it is important to counter them where appropriate and provide reassurance that new prospects are at least as attractive as the familiar ones about to be lost. Positive actions, for example, the provision of learning opportunities and good support to individuals in making required changes, developing new skills and new ways of working can significantly reduce the 'pain of change' and encourage support for change.

7.4 Conclusions

We propose that an integrated approach to the design of digital systems, building on the successes and expertise in existing but, until now, separate domains, offers a route towards the creation of desirable digital futures. The different theoretical and conceptual frameworks described above enable the formulation of a multi-faceted strategic approach to ICT design which puts citizens/users at 'centre stage' – and engages them appropriately throughout the planning and development cycle. The robustness of the proposed strategy and framework and their potential power to achieve significant change stems not only from their foundation in influential and well-tested theories, but also from the fact that there are many established methods and techniques already developed and readily available to support implementation. Table 7.3 summarizes the key contributory principles that each approach has to offer.

Table 7.3. Key Contributory Principles of each Theoretical Approach

Theoretical Framework	Key Contributory Principles/Features
Sociotechnical theory	Social and technical systems are interdependent and need to be co-optimized
	Principle of minimum critical specification
	The design process should be compatible with design goals and outcomes
Information Ecologies	Specific focus on a particular environment/context
	Co-evolution
	Interdependency
Participatory Design	Involvement of stakeholders in decision making
	Combination of multiple perspectives
	Empowerment through use of envisioning/exploring techniques
Inclusive Design	Focus on identifying needs of widest range of users – emphasis on extra-ordinary users
	Provides methods to aid design
Change Management	Understanding the need for change
	Communicating vision
	Providing knowledge of practical steps
	Overcoming resistance
	Promoting ownership

The steps required to reach the goal of an integrated ICT design process enriched by the contributory components discussed above are shown in Fig. 7.2.

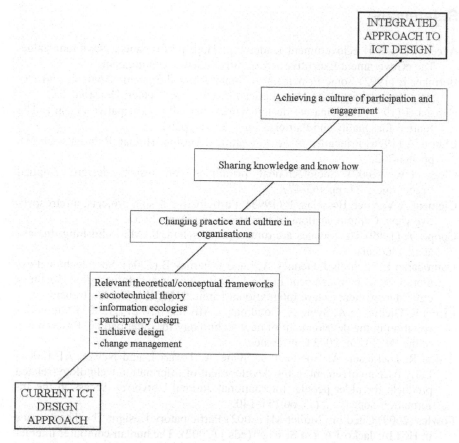

Fig. 7.2. Transforming the approach to ICT design.

As described in 7.3, change management theory indicates that awareness of the limitations of the existing approach, together with a clear vision
of the tangible rewards from a new approach (e.g. new markets, improvements in quality of life for many citizens), and knowledge of the practical
steps which must be taken for this to happen, will in combination provide a
compelling pull to transform the design process. The know-how exists to
achieve this transformation, as we explain in the following chapters. The
challenges are undoubtedly enormous and profound – but realizable if we
collectively have the courage and foresight to pursue the vision.

References

Accenture (2004) eGovernment leadership: High performance, maximum value. The eGovernment Executive series. http://www.accenture.com.

Berniker E (1992) Some Principles of Sociotechnical Systems Analysis and Design. Productivity Brief 25. American Productivity Center: Houston, TX.

Cabana S (1995) Participative design works, partially participative doesn't. The Journal for Quality and Participation, 18 (1), pp 2-11.

Cherns A (1976) Principles of Socio-technical Design. Human Relations, 29 (8), pp 783-792.

Clegg CW (2000) Sociotechnical principles for system design. Applied Ergonomics, 31, pp 463-477.

Clement A Van den Besselaar P (1993). Participative design projects, a retrospective view. Communications of the ACM, 36 (6), pp 29-37.

Cooper A (1999) The inmates are running the asylum. SAMS Publishing, Indianapolis, Indiana.

Damodaran L, Nicholls J, Henney A, Land F Farbey B (2004). Sociotechnical explorations of eGovernment in the UK. Behaviour and Information Technology, Management Centre International Limited (MCIL), Dublin, Ireland.

Eisma R, Dickinson A, Syme A, Goodman J, Mival O Tiwari L (2003) Mutual inspiration in the development of new technology for older people. Proceedings of the INCLUDE 2003 Conference.

Eisma R, Dickinson A, Goodman J, Syme A, Tiwari L and Newell AF (2004) Early user involvement in the development of information technology-related products for older people. International Journal Universal Access in the Information Society, 3 (2), pp 131-140.

Fowles (2000) Cited in: Muller MJ (2002) Participatory Design: The Third Space in HCI.In: Jacko J A and Sears A (eds.) (2002). The human-computer interaction handbook: fundamentals, evolving technologies and emerging applications 2002, pp 1051-1068.

Gleicher D (n.d.) Cited in: Buchanan D Huczynski A (1991) Organizational Behaviour: An Introductory Text. Prentice Hall Europe.

Granath JA, Lindahl GA Rehal S (1996) From Empowerment to Enablement. An evolution of new dimensions in participatory design. Logistik & Arbeit, 1996.

Gyi D, Cain R Campbell I (2005) Users, co-designers, stakeholders or partners? A case study in flexible packaging design http://www.hhrc.rca.ac.uk/ programmes/ include/2005/proceedings/pdf/ gyidiane.pdf.

K-Net (n.d.) Homepage. http://knet.ca/.

Keul V (1983) Trade union planning and control of new technology. In: Briefs U, Ciborra C. Schneider L., (eds). Systems Design for, with, and By the Users. Proceedings of the IFIP TC9/WG9.1 Conference (Riva del sole, Italy). North-Holland, Amsterdam, 1983.

Klein L (2005) Working Across the Gap : The Practice of Social Science in Organisations. H. Karnac, London.

Klein L Eason KD (1991) Putting social science to work. Cambridge University Press, Cambridge.

Mumford E (1983) Designing human systems. Manchester Business School Publications, Manchester.

Mumford E (1991) In: Shackel B Richardson S (1991) Human factors for informatics usability. Cambridge, Cambridge University Press.

Muller MJ (2002) Participatory design: The third space in HCI In: Jacko JA Sears A (eds.) (2002) The human-computer interaction handbook: fundamentals, evolving technologies and emerging applications 2002, pp 1051-1068.

Nardi B A O'Day V L (1999) Information ecologies: Using technology with heart. MIT Press, Massachusetts.

Newell AF Gregor P (1999) Extra-ordinary human-machine interaction - what can be learned from people with disabilities? Cognition Technology and Work, 1 (2), pp 78-85.

Norman DA (2000) The Design of everyday things. MIT Press, London/New York.

Office of the Deputy Prime Minister (ODPM) (2003) Local e-Government: process evaluation of the implementation of electronic local government in England. CURDS, Newcastle upon Tyne.

Seely Brown J Duguid P (2002) The social life of information. Harvard Business School Press, Harvard.

Sims R (2003) Design for all: Methods and data to support designers. PhD Dissertation, Loughborough University, 2003.

Thoresen K (1992). Principles in practice, two cases of situated participatory design. In: Schuler D Namioka A (eds.) (1993) Participatory design: principles and practices. Lawrence Erlbaum Associates.

Trist EL Bamforth KW (1951). Some social and psychological consequences of the longwall method of coal getting. Human Relations, 4, pp 3-38.

Von Bertalanffy L (1976) General system theory: Foundations, development, applications. Braziller (George) Inc, USA.

8 Strategies for Citizen Engagement: (i) Shifting the Focus of ICT Design Practice

For citizens to be actively engaged in shaping their digital futures requires that they have both the opportunity and the capacity to do so. This, in turn, means that governments, ICT system providers, manufacturers and other agencies need to recognize the sociotechnical implications of strategics and plans, and the need to engage with citizens in making decisions and shaping solutions. This requires a change in focus from the traditional view of either policy making or ICT design, which can only occur if it becomes part of the culture and routine practice of society and of organizations. A further requirement is to build the capability of citizens and other stakeholders, giving them the knowledge and skills to work in this new way.

Modern life places heavy demands on its citizens. Spending time and effort to engage in informing ICT design decisions is an additional demand which many may not welcome – however desirable the long-term benefits. Equally, those with job responsibilities for achieving the engagement of members of the public and relevant others in projects and exercises may find this an onerous task. The inherent difficulties are often exacerbated by the lack of guidance available on either the purpose of engagement/participation or on how to achieve it.

The aim of this chapter and Chapter 9 is to make accessible to those who need it, the available knowledge for embedding citizen engagement as a normal part of ICT development projects – i.e. institutionalizing it. The final chapter in this suite of three considers the challenging issue of bringing about culture change throughout society to alter thinking about the role of technology in society and the part citizens play in defining that role. Thus these last three chapters describe complementary strategies for achieving citizen engagement/participation.

8.1 Introducing the Strategies

The strategies discussed in these chapters are instantiations of the application of change management principles encapsulated in Gleicher's formula which is described in Chapter 7. Their function is to inform the definition, content and structure of change programmes necessary to bring about the required shift in ICT design practice. Although the strategies do, of course, offer guidance, they differ fundamentally from countless 'design guidelines' published over the past decades in their underlying assumptions. The distinction is important and warrants further explanation. Many guidelines, developed with the best of intentions to improve ICT design from a human-centred perspective, have failed to have significant impact. This is despite the fact that the advice is often sound and based upon valid research data. The lack of impact is because ICT designers generally find their customary ways of doing things satisfactory and comfortable from their perspective. Change theories tell us that human beings are unlikely and reluctant to change unless we see compelling reasons for doing so.

Guidelines by their nature are not appropriate or effective as persuasion techniques. The content of most design guidelines comprises details of steps to take – and sometimes on how to do this. The formulation of design guidelines is often driven by the conviction of their developers that they are needed to improve shortcomings in ICT design. This is not a perception generally shared by the intended users of the guidelines. Developers of guidelines see their purpose to be the provision of evidence-based instructions and have achieved this very successfully in many cases. Their guidelines have generally been offered up into a vacuum where there is no 'user pull' from the design community. This helps to explain the lack of impact.

In the terms of Gleicher's formula (see Chapter 7), there are three crucial components in achieving successful change: **dissatisfaction with the status quo, sharing the vision** and **knowledge of the practical steps** necessary to progress towards the vision. In the context of ICT design, guidelines are the knowledge component which indicate the practical steps necessary for the change. The two other components are generally missing from projects which generate design guidelines. Without awareness and understanding of the limiting effects and costs of current design methods, there is no reason for designers to be dissatisfied with how things are and no motivation for them to change their methods and approach. Equally, the vision of the attractive rewards and benefits which are likely to follow for them as a result of the shift towards engaging with stakeholders, especially with citizens, has not been effectively communicated to the ICT design community. The crucial message is that for guidance to be applied appropriately and to achieve the change intended, it has to be incorporated into a coherent change programme. The same principle applies to the strategies presented in this book: they can only succeed within the context of planned systemic change.

Following from the above, the assumption underlying the strategies formulated in these three chapters is that knowledge and understanding of the reasons and the need for change supersede and underpin everything else. Education and organisational support to develop human skills and institutional resources are seen as essential for achieving the envisioned scale of systemic change involved in achieving a shift in focus of ICT design methods and approaches. In other words, building capacity and developing organisational infrastructure must take priority.

To effectively 'embed' citizen engagement into ICT development projects it must become a mainstream, rather than a marginal or peripheral part of the development process. Transforming ways of doing things throughout an institution usually comes about through a gradual evolutionary process. Thus, strategies for building capacity and developing organisational infrastructure must also take account of the need to achieve longer-term cultural change.

The proposed strategies apply at three different levels: **the institution** (e.g. local council, government department, hospital, retail business etc), the **ICT project**, and **wider society** respectively. This chapter addresses the process of institutionalizing changes at the organizational level which are necessary to bring about a shift in focus of ICT design. Chapter 9, 'Tools and techniques' presents staff working at the project level with an awareness of the very many, highly varied and innovative resources available globally. These are valuable in developing their capacity to carry out job responsibilities relating to citizen engagement/participation.

The final chapter 'Achieving a culture of participation and engagement' considers strategic change of a quite different kind and of a far greater magnitude than is required at project and organisational levels. To fundamentally alter the way we all think about technological development and our role in the future shaping of our digital world is clearly extremely challenging. Change on such a scale cannot happen without the high level leadership and the support of very many stakeholders – both individuals and institutions. Only with the leadership and enthusiasm of influential bodies and individuals with the power and political will to transform established ways of doing things can ambitious institutionalized change occur on a societal scale. Some possibilities for embarking on this journey are discussed in Chapter 10.

8.2 Institutionalizing the Shift in Organisations

The content of this chapter applies primarily to institution-led citizen participation and engagement. This is because most large-scale ICT developments intended for the public take place in institutional settings (whether public sector or private sector organizations are involved). It is staff who work in these organizations who are likely to have responsibilities for gaining the participation and engagement of members of the public in different aspects of an ICT design and development project. There are, of course, generic aspects to the guidance. For example, the processes involved in communication and in envisioning alternative futures described in Chapter 9 are equally applicable in citizen-led activities. However, they are unlikely to be supported with the necessary resources more usually associated with institution-led initiatives.

Achieving a shift in ICT design away from its technical focus towards a sociotechnical focus (where citizen engagement is the norm) will draw heavily from good practice in civic planning and community development contexts. There are however some important differentiating characteristics of citizen engagement in ICT development contexts which we have taken into account in formulating the strategies presented here. Most ICT developments start with a concept (usually technological, usually developed by technologists). Then typically follow a logical sequence of steps in which the requirements are specified, the hardware and software are designed and the outcome is then implemented – again, usually by technologists. Where a user-centred approach is applied (which does not happen in all cases), then users may become involved in specifying their requirements at an early stage in the development cycle. Then, at a later stage, in testing a solution – possibly a prototype – defined and developed by ICT developers. By this second stage it is often considered too late to make more than minor modifications to the design. By contrast, when citizens are engaged successfully in public policy making and planning, following established good practice (e.g. National Forum on Health – Canada, Wyman et al. 1999) the objective is often to allow people to identify and explore alternative options at an early stage. This means that further development is focused upon preferred solutions – and avoids the wastefulness of developing 'solutions'. Which are seen as lacking in relevance or usefulness by those in whose interests they have been developed.

In an analogous way, an approach to ICT design which involves citizens and focuses on creating sociotechnical solutions could similarly involve people in identifying and exploring options in ICT provision, envisioning outcomes and achieving consensus on preferred solutions. The preferred solutions could then be developed and tested with greater confidence that they will successfully meet the needs of the people for whom they are intended. Engaging in technology shaping is not something with which people are generally familiar. This means they need concepts, knowledge, language and tools to be able to do this. Some of the many possibilities for enhancing understanding, envisioning, communicating and sharing ideas and so on are identified in the next chapter.

There are a great many actions required to begin the shift towards making stakeholder participation/engagement a mainstream activity in ICT projects. This includes taking a number of steps at the earliest possible stage – desirably before most decisions have been made. Examples of preparatory steps which are often relevant are the following:

- recruit a leader/champion for the engagement process;
- communicate to create awareness of the need for a new, integrated approach to ICT design (aims, approach, expected benefits etc.);
- provide education and learning opportunities;
- secure resources;
- implement a sound organisational infrastructure to support the project or initiative;
- build confidence (both of staff in the institution and of citizens in the community);
- encourage a strong 'user pull' for making citizen participation mainstream and for sharing knowledge and expertise relating to civic participation in ICT development;
- encourage greater application of an integrated design approach to enhance significantly the quality and relevance of ICT provision for citizens.

8.2.1 Action Plan for Institutionalizing Citizen Participation/ Engagement

The action plan presented in this section draws on many years of our experiences working with client organisations in both the private and public sectors. To present a rather mechanistic-looking plan may appear to contradict our earlier assertion that guidance developed out of context is unlikely to be accepted or to be relevant. However, we are frequently asked to provide planning aids which indicate the steps to take and therefore offer this as a starting point for developing a context-specific action plan, tailored to the specific circumstances of use. A four stage, twelve point Action Plan for institutionalizing the proposed shift in focus of ICT design is therefore described in subsequent sections.

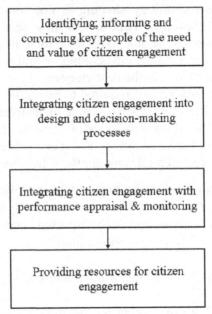

Fig. 8.1. Action plan for shifting the focus of ICT design.

8.2.2 Identifying, Informing and Convincing Key People

This stage is crucial as it seeks to achieve 'buy-in' of people in key roles to the concepts and values underpinning the engagement of citizens in ICT design and development. Powerful communication and knowledge sharing methods will be essential.

To ensure that citizen contributions inform the activities and decision-making associated with ICT developments, widespread awareness of the value and importance of citizen engagement is needed. This is especially the case among the membership of relevant steering committees, project groups, etc. where many key role holders/stakeholders have responsibility, authority or influence over decisions. People with expertise in public participation processes could be invited to promote such awareness and understanding.

To achieve such changes in mind set may need to be reinforced through formal education and training. Understanding the need for a new approach to design will be strengthened by an awareness of the theories and concepts of the social sciences, from which the principles underpinning the

integrated design approach are drawn. Opportunities for learning basic social science concepts and participatory principles do not generally form
part of the curriculum for computer scientists and engineers. Yet the applications which they design have significant human and social implications.
Excellent multi-media tools are now available which could support education and training in concepts and approaches relevant to citizen engagement. Designers, developers and providers would all benefit from learning
these. Experiential and immersive techniques (see Chapter 9 for examples)
offer powerful means of promoting rapid learning regarding perspectives
of people in different roles and circumstances.

Action Points: Steps 1-4

1. Mobilize for change: identify 'change champions' who recognise the need for change in the design approach in the organisation - appoint one as a leader for the change process.

2. Identify relevant key people and consult to make changes to
   job descriptions/terms of reference to include citizen engagement activities and responsibilities.

3. Develop and deliver learning opportunities (desirably using
   experiential learning techniques) for senior people.

4. Develop and deliver awareness and education programmes
   (e.g. in social science concepts) and, where appropriate, opportunity for skills acquisition in citizen engagement (e.g.
   facilitation) for middle management and staff members including ICT design/development staff.

8.2.3 Integrating Citizen Engagement with ICT Design Methods

Participation/engagement of citizens in ICT design needs to occur throughout the development cycle. Citizens should be involved early in decisions,
when ideas are still at the vision stage, "*before political interests and professional input dominate debate*" (Demos 2004). It therefore needs to be
planned carefully in relation to the design methods currently in use in the
organisation concerned. It may well be the case that those undertaking an
ICT development project are following one of the many available methodologies, some of which are mentioned in Chapter 2. In some cases (such as
in the UK public sector) there is often a formal requirement to follow a
particular methodology. This may specify citizen/user involvement activities

and the stage at which they take place. The adequacy and appropriateness of this needs to be reviewed. It is also important that other experts, particularly external consultants, recognise the need for these in the activities they have been contracted to carry out. It is especially important in the award of major contracts for ICT development projects that the tender evaluation criteria include preparedness and capability to ensure genuine and active participation and engagement of users/citizens in the project.

In traditional approaches to ICT design, user input is often not sought until there is a technological concept which is to be developed. In this engineering model the purpose of the involvement is to define user requirements for the technology to be developed – leaving potential users with no 'say' in whether or not the proposed technology is appropriate or desirable. In the examples of best practice in public policy making and planning context however, citizens are likely to be consulted and engaged in agenda setting. This gives them the opportunity to define their priorities and to influence the scope, rather than the detail, of policies and plans. In ICT development projects, citizens need to be engaged at the equivalent of this agenda setting stage, i.e. earlier than is normally the case.

In the later stages of the lifecycle, there is recognition, in both the systems development context and in the public policy making and planning context, of the benefits of testing possible solutions with users/citizens through pilot projects. However, in technology development projects, the focus of testing is usually on the performance of the technology, rather than on the wider implications of the technology for its intended users. Opportunities, and support for, exploration of these human and organisational implications – in terms of project resources, skills and job design of participants – need to be built into the design process.

Action Points: Steps 5-7

5. Review membership of key decision-making bodies to ensure citizens are fully represented and engaged.

6. Incorporate citizen engagement processes and values into ICT design methods.

7. Review contractual terms/procurement criteria for employing external ICT consultants. Revise as necessary to ensure that citizen engagement processes are included as part of the terms of reference and contractual conditions.

8.2.4 Integrating Citizen Engagement with Performance Appraisal and Monitoring

The ability to engage effectively with citizens in the course of normal working must be recognised in any processes for assessing and appraising the performance of those responsible for developing ICT for the public. Only by emphasising a positive approach to the process will 'in-house' expertise and acceptance of citizen contributions develop. Additionally, the design outputs (including proposals) from every stage should be reviewed to check that they have been informed appropriately by citizens.

Evaluating the impact of ICT on people requires monitoring to ensure positive effects and to see how well the citizen engagement strategies and mechanisms are working. Audits can be undertaken to provide information to the providers, designers, developers and manufacturers on the success of the ICT delivered.

Action Points: Steps 8-10

8. Through consultation and negotiation, include citizen engagement criteria in annual assessment/performance appraisals.

9. Include citizen engagement criteria in quality assurance protocols and procedures.

10. Conduct long-term auditing of the effectiveness of citizen engagement to assess the impact of ICT and its acceptability.

8.2.5 Providing Resources for Citizen Engagement

It should be recognised that resources will be required to support the transition to the new ways of working implied by the change in focus of ICT design. Key requirements are for education, skills and a budget to support participation/engagement processes.

- *skill support.* To support citizen engagement projects in the short term, whilst expertise develops within the host organisation, experts in public participation may be required. These specialists could be external or part of an in-house group;

- *budget planning.* For a citizen engagement strategy to become a reality, adequate resources of skills, time and facilities are required. These need to be costed and given appropriate budget allocations.

In organisations where citizen participation/engagement needs to be conducted frequently, it may be worthwhile to set up a group which specialises in these processes. There are precedents for this, such as the Participation Services Unit of the Scottish Parliament (2004).

Action Points: Steps 11-12

> 11. Consider establishing an in-house unit of citizen engagement specialists, especially facilitators if this appears appropriate; decide location (dispersed or localized), staffing, equipment, etc.
>
> 12. Review relevant budgets and schedules to see that citizen engagement activities are included.

Table 8.1. Summary of 12 point Action Plan for Setting up Citizen Engagement

1	Mobilise for change: identify 'change champions' who recognise the need for change in the design approach in the organisation – appoint one as a leader for the change process.
2	Identify relevant key people and consult to make changes to job description/terms of reference to include citizen engagement activities and responsibilities.
3	Develop and deliver learning opportunities (desirably using experiential learning techniques) for senior people.
4	Develop and deliver awareness and education programmes (e.g. in social science concepts) and, where appropriate, opportunity for skills acquisition in citizen engagement (e.g. facilitation) for middle management and staff members including ICT design/development staff.
5	Review membership of key decision-making bodies to ensure citizens are fully represented and engaged.
6	Incorporate citizen engagement processes and values into ICT design methods.
7	Review contractual terms/procurement criteria for employing external ICT consultants. Revise as necessary to ensure that citizen engagement processes are included as part of the terms of reference and contractual conditions.
8	Through consultation and negotiation, include citizen engagement criteria in annual assessment/performance appraisals.
9	Include citizen engagement criteria in quality assurance protocols and procedures.

10   Conduct long-term auditing of the effectiveness of citizen engagement to as-
      sess the impact of ICT and its acceptability.
11   Consider establishing an in-house unit of citizen engagement specialists, es-
      pecially facilitators if this appears appropriate; decide location (dispersed or
      localised), staffing, equipment, etc.
12   Review relevant budgets and schedules to see that citizen engagement activi-
      ties are included.

8.3 Capacity Building

Successes in civic participation – whether in impoverished communities in
the developing world or in leading, developed nations – are characterized
by the development of skills and capabilities of the participants. Successful
participation projects report the growth in confidence of participants in
articulating and sharing their views and experiences, their increased
knowledge and understanding of issues under consideration and ability to
contribute to debate and decision-making. This contrasts with the frequently voiced expressions of concern in the media about voter apathy and
cynicism of the public, especially of the young. In fact, there is considerable evidence to show that, in the right conditions, there is positive enthusiasm, commitment and a surprising willingness to spend time preparing
for consultative exercises on issues of significance and relevance to participants (The National Forum on Health – Canada, Wyman et al. 1999).
Capacity building is defined in different ways, depending on the context.
One common element is the change and development which takes place as
individuals learn new skills and gain in confidence.

In the context of involving citizens in shaping the digital technologies
that underpin the information society, some important objectives of capacity building among the individuals responsible for achieving and managing
engagement include the following:

- promote widespread understanding of the need for change;
- promulgate awareness of the wide-ranging benefits of participa-
  tion/engagement for individuals and their communities;
- provide realistic and flexible guidance on how to achieve such understanding;
- promote the development of skills and knowledge necessary for citizens
  and other stakeholders to make a meaningful contribution to ICT design –
  tailored to the needs and context;
- enable citizens and relevant others to arrive at consensus on design decisions;

- promote understanding of sociotechnical concepts, i.e. the relationship between different elements of the system such that policy can influence technology and vice versa;
- give confidence in asking 'know why' questions before jumping to the 'know how'.

Preparing staff to carry out their responsibilities for involving members of the community in an ICT development project will be helped by an imaginative awareness and education programme. This should be defined and designed wherever possible in consultation with the people for whom it is intended. Those responsible for leading and managing the change need leadership and facilitation skills.

Equally, preparing citizens is an essential part of capacity building in society. The quality of their contributions to design outcomes is of course determined by the capacity of participants to engage in the various stages of a typical design life-cycle. Developing this capacity begins with giving confidence to members of the public that they have a significant part to play. Through understanding that they really can participate usefully in areas where they probably feel they have little to contribute – and would probably not be heard anyway – is a critical step in eliciting willingness of citizens to engage with an ICT project. It is therefore important to show that citizens can and have played a constructive part in project processes such as the following:

- activities which shape the social context in which ICTs are used;
- the evaluation of technological solutions at the conceptual stage – evaluating the potential implications not just in terms of functionality or ease of use, but for quality of life, sustainability, ethical issues etc.;
- identification and specification of their requirements (as input to the detailed shaping of socio-technical systems);
- evaluation of detailed sociotechnical design options against their requirements;
- developing 'ownership' of the sociotechnical solutions which are implemented;
- monitoring progress and contributing towards further evolution where appropriate.

Clearly the language used above would need to be 'translated' into meaningful colloquial language used by the intended participants. Appropriate real-life examples of actual contributions made by other citizens with whom they can identify, are particularly motivating and reassuring. Seeing the outcomes and impacts that are possible are powerful ways of changing perceptions and expectations.

It is important to make clear to potential participants the difference between those activities which will benefit from the knowledge, skills and capabilities that most people already have – such as those listed below and those where some preparation and opportunities for learning are required e.g. in areas associated with technical aspects of ICT developments. Regarding the skills which citizens have in abundance, it will be important to emphasise that it is capacities such as those listed below – and not their knowledge of ICT – that are most relevant and important in shaping ICT developments.

To inform ICT design decisions citizens/users can do the following:

- use their imagination and creativity as well as their knowledge of their context and experience to envision the possibilities;
- consider the implications and the potential of emerging technologies for their lives;
- be demanding, informed and willing to 'co-create' the systems, products and services best suited to their lives;
- exert their power and influence to significant effect by asking critical questions;
- engage in considered reflection to pre-empt or reduce the negative unintended effects of new technologies;
- provide inputs to the design decision-making process that reflect the diversity and richness of their own experience.

In addition to the above capabilities, there are some specific skills which are frequently of value and relevance in design exercises of many kinds. These include envisioning, knowledge sharing, requirements shaping, consensus building and conflict resolution. It is has already been indicated that an active educational process and appropriate learning opportunities, supported by tools and techniques described in Chapter 9, may be required to promote development of these skills.

As indicated above, an appropriate organisational infrastructure will be essential to launch a viable citizen engagement strategy and to support engagement processes. Setting up organizational infrastructure to facilitate and enable citizen engagement processes in the context of on-going ICT projects is best done in advance of launching engagement processes. More typically, this happens as an ad hoc response to developments. For example, pressures from national government to implement local e-government in the UK has required local councils to find their own ways of developing structures and procedures to support the implementation. The trial and error involved has been an expensive process and slowed up the delivery of e-services. For example, people who are in job roles that require them to interact with citizens – gathering opinions, eliciting information needs, or seeking participation of the hard-to-hear, have in many cases, lacked the necessary guidance and training. (This issue of improved sharing knowledge and experience will be addressed in more detail in subsequent sections).

8.4 Changing Organizational Culture

Shifting the focus of ICT development projects from the technical to the sociotechnical represents a significant change in culture for many IT departments and organizations engaged in developing systems and services for the public. For citizen engagement to become a routine and, more importantly, a valued part of ICT developments, the organisational context must be one that promotes, supports and rewards citizen engagement activities.

A first step is to create readiness for change and for this to happen requires that there is understanding of the need to change. Achieving the shift in ICT design focus, like any other major change, will be facilitated by using an established change management approach. This involves the three steps (see Gleicher's formula – Chapter 7) to be addressed at the project level, within the organizations where ICT developments take place, and in wider society. Essentially, everyone involved in making the shift towards citizen participation/engagement in ICT development needs to have the opportunity to develop the following:

- understanding of the need for change – the 'Know Why' of Citizen Engagement in ICT design;
- knowledge of what needs to be done to achieve the vision – the 'Know What' of Citizen Engagement in ICT design;
- knowledge and skills to carry out the necessary steps – the 'Know How' of Citizen Engagement in ICT design.

As already described in 8.2.2, an important precursor to achieving the engagement of citizens/users as a routine matter in ICT development projects is achieving a shift in the design focus of key stakeholders (e.g. senior managers, project managers, IT development staff, practitioners) from a technical to a sociotechnical one. This requires changing attitudes and perceptions. With the objective of persuading these role holders to take account of human, social and organisational concerns as a normal part of the project agenda throughout the development cycle. Educational processes such as those outlined in the Action Plan are likely to be essential to succeed in meeting this objective.

To prepare people, such as staff in local councils, to engage with citizens in the context of ICT projects there is an abundance of educational and experiential learning material which is described in Chapter 9. Following good practice in change management it may be helpful to begin the educational process by communicating some key learning points such as those presented below. It is important to stress that these are for illustrative purposes only – and not to be regarded as a prescribed or standard approach to apply in all situations. For new information and concepts to be heard and taken on board, material has to be tailored to context and to the people it is intended to inform. In all cases presentations should be used only as an introduction and as a catalyst for discussion to help people to think through and explore the ideas and their implications and to articulate their ideas. They can helpfully set the scene for further learning opportunities but are far from adequate without a supporting programme for building capacity.

8.4.1 Key Learning Points: The 'Know Why', 'Know What' and 'Know How' of Citizen Engagement

Understanding the need for change – the 'Know Why'

Why the need for a shift to involve citizens?

- high cost of disappointing delivery of ICT

- poor match with needs of citizens

- dissatisfaction of citizens/users

- low level of take-up of electronic services

Limitations of current ICT design approach

- focus is on the delivery of a technical solution

- traditional design roles (software designer, programmer etc) predominate

- limited and low level of citizen/user influence or shaping of ICT design decisions

- lack of awareness and skills of participatory methods for involving citizens/users

---

- perceived high costs and risk of delays associated with involving users are deterrents of a change in focus

The benefits / outcomes of involving citizens – some examples

- better understanding of citizen's needs and priorities

- design outcomes meet the needs of citizens better

- greater satisfaction with ICT-enabled services

- improved take-up of services

- greater confidence and empowerment of citizens

- enhanced democracy

Sharing the Vision of what needs to be done – the 'Know What'

What needs to be done?

- gain the 'buy-in' of key role holders (CEO, IT managers, etc) to achieve the shift

- gain support and resources to: build the capacity, i.e. develop knowledge, understanding and skills of all stakeholders (e.g. citizens, ICT project staff, customer liaison personnel etc.), and create the infrastructure to support the participation/engagement of people in ICT developments

What all key stakeholders need to know

- the costs/consequences of the current approach (the need for change)

- the advantages of doing things differently (the benefits of involving citizens)

- different ways of doing things successfully (good practice exists)

- how to do things differently (tools and techniques)

- opportunities and support to learn new ways of doing things will be available (training and coaching etc.)

- success will be recognised (performance appraisal will include citizen participation/engagement activities)

Providing knowledge and skills to carry out the necessary steps – the 'Know How'

How to create the infrastructure for citizen engagement?

- define roles required – recruit and train people to fill them

- define and develop relevant learning opportunities for citizens and other stakeholders

- select appropriate tools and techniques to support the participation/engagement of citizens and other stakeholders

How to build capacity – essential skills include:

- leadership

- facilitation

- envisioning

- knowledge sharing

- requirements shaping

- consensus building

- conflict resolution

8.5 Sharing the Knowledge

There is now extensive knowledge available about effective citizen engagement. Promulgating the learning is most pressing in order to make more visible and tangible the limitless potential of the vast pool of human knowledge and diverse capabilities of people everywhere. This rich resource residing in citizens is available to inform and enhance the design of digital futures but is largely unappreciated and untapped. An effective citizen engagement strategy will need to include a wide variety of multimedia education and communication material tailored to convey and share the knowledge and learning of the processes involved. It is often the case that the most effective way of persuading individuals to do things differently is to show them a different approach in action. This may involve demonstrating the methods used, the processes involved, the issues arising including problems encountered, and how these were tackled and the outcomes and impacts. Showcasing best practice can be particularly powerful and effective. As an example of this, Chapter 4 reports on a major undertaking in Canada (K-Net) (see Beaton (2004) which was selected for government funding as an exemplary 'Smart Community' project and which has been extensively documented and reported.

8.6 Conclusions

The strategies presented in this chapter will establish processes for engaging citizens and delivering more effective systems and services for the public. An impressive array of techniques and tools are available to support the strategies and these are examined in the next chapter. The know-how presented has been distilled from examining examples of citizen participation and engagement worldwide and from developing the integrated theoretical framework described in Chapter 7. It is likely to have resonance and relevance to many people in the public sector, in e-business and in a variety of other contexts who are actively engaged with design and delivery of ICT-based developments for use by the general public.

Some of the individuals involved are already acutely aware of the limitations of current approaches and open to the idea of doing things differently. In such cases, individuals need support and guidance, tools and techniques, and new approaches to find and adopt appropriate new ways of working which embrace the principle of citizen engagement. Others may not yet be persuaded of the need for change. For example, the Demos Project, co-funded by the European Commission, had the primary aim of increasing and enhancing citizen participation in local government. The project linked eight city councils in seven countries with research organisations across Europe. One of the findings of the research was that "*the attitude of government officers loath to share control with citizens*" was a barrier to citizen engagement (Demos 2004). These findings are not consistent with the authors' experiences of working with local councils on e-government implementations in the UK. We found local government staff working at grass-roots in the community are committed to consulting and engaging with citizens – especially the 'hard to hear' groups – but expressing uncertainty about how to go about this and apprehensive about the adequacy of their skills for this process.

Beyond this, for digital technologies to begin to transform lives in significant ways on a societal scale, involves both major institutional change and behavioural change of people. It is often the case that such changes come about reactively as institutions and individuals strive to exploit and accommodate new technologies in their lives. Now, in the early 21st century a far more pro-active approach is within our grasp. The convergence of telecommunications and information technologies alongside the burgeoning knowledge and interest in promoting participation of citizens in civic society means that it is timely to find new answers to old problems. A great diversity of wired and wireless technologies to enable fundamentally new ways of working, learning, communicating and influencing are coming on stream with great rapidity. Harnessing these to create desirable digital futures requires a major shift in culture surrounding the developments of ICT systems, services and projects. What is needed now for this to happen is leadership in society and the political will to take action to achieve this change. How to achieve this is discussed in the final chapter.

References

Beaton B (2004) The K-Net Story: Community ICT Development Work. The Journal of Community Informatics. 1 (1), pp 5-6.

The Demos Project (2004). Homepage. http://www.demosproject.org/.

Gleicher D (n.d.) In: Huczynski A and Buchanan D (2001). Organisational Behaviour: An introductory text. Prentice Hall. Harlow, pp 589-621.

Scottish Parliament (2004) The Participation Handbook. <http://www.scottish.parliament.uk/vli/participationHandbook/index.htm>.

Wyman M, Shulman D, Ham L (1999) Learning to Engage: Experiences with Civic Engagement in Canada, Canadian Policy Research Networks http://www.cprn.com/en/doc.cfm?doc=87.

9 Strategies for Citizen Engagement (ii) – Tools and Techniques

In Chapter 6 we have described how the creativity, know-how, interests and values of citizens have been harnessed to generate a range of desirable outcomes – thus shaping aspects of their digital futures. For this to happen routinely, as we have already indicated in Chapters 7 and 8, requires a shift in focus of the ICT design process. Such a shift is essential not only for making citizen participation/engagement in ICT projects the norm, but also to empower citizens to contribute to decision making about meeting their information and communication needs. This paves the way for debate and selection of appropriate social and technical solutions suited to a particular context. Having set out in Chapter 8 the actions to achieve such a shift in focus within individual organisations, this chapter considers the practical issues associated with engaging citizens in the context of specific projects and initiatives. Emphasis is placed on building the capacity of all stakeholders to contribute effectively.

9.1 Methodologies or Toolkits?

There is in fact a myriad of tools and techniques available to support both citizen engagement and user-centred ICT design. It is tempting to try to pull these together into a methodology, which spells out step by step the way to go about citizen engagement in the context of ICT design. However we have resisted this temptation because the research evidence, and our own experience, makes clear that such methodologies usually do not work. By this we mean that few of the many 'new' design methodologies which have been developed, often from the best of intentions and on the soundest of theoretical foundations, have been widely adopted by the ICT design community. The lack of 'user pull' from the design community has already been cited as one of the reasons for the low uptake of such guidance. Another reason is the sheer diversity of ICT design projects. Projects will vary by purpose, budget, timescale, scope, skills, feasibility, working styles and preferences of the designers to name but a few factors; creating a methodology which can be sensitive, responsive, relevant and appropriate to all these variable factors has been shown to be an almost insuperable challenge.

Nor is it possible to specify a 'right' or 'best' way to 'do' citizen engagement. The numbers and types of citizens who should be involved in a project will depend on the aims and scope of the project. Sometimes it may be necessary to make particular efforts to engage with specific groups, such as the 'hard to hear'. It is also the case that citizens' skills and knowledge bases will be very diverse, depending on the context and communities in which they live. This means that the techniques needed to recruit, inform and empower them to contribute effectively to an initiative will be very different.

With regard to methods used to recruit participants, contrast, for example, the German Bundestag website project, (which sought to consult a sample of German citizens about ideas for the design of the Parliament website), with the UK Womenspeak project, (which sought input to policy from those who had personal experience of domestic violence). Appropriate ways of seeking out relevant participants will need to be selected on a case by case basis, bearing in mind the characteristics of the people involved and the purpose of the intended participation/engagement.

Informing and empowering different groups of citizens will also take may different forms. Clearly the pictorial methods used for people without literacy skills in villagers in Africa and India, for example, in the *Reflect* ICTs project, are very different from the nature of the briefings and documentation used in preparing citizens to participate in such initiatives as the Canadian National Forum on Health. For the Womenspeak project, the only knowledge which participants needed to make an effective contribution was that of their own experiences. Their learning need would be to develop the confidence and trust necessary to convey real understanding of their situation and needs. Learning opportunities and materials will only succeed in building the capacity of people to participate effectively to the extent that they take into account the different levels of skills, knowledge and experience of the individuals concerned. Equally, the purpose of the engagement and the characteristics of the participants (both citizens and ICT designers or policy makers) will have implications for the kinds of tools that will be helpful in equipping people to engage effectively. For instance, to contribute constructively to the Bundestag website design project, citizens needed some prior knowledge and understanding of the nature of the Bundestag in order to identify the kind of information that they would wish to receive on the website. They may also have needed some understanding of the generic nature of websites so that they could contribute practicable ideas for content which could feasibly be included.

For the *Reflect* ICTs project, villagers needed ways of communicating their own needs and values to the facilitators drawn from the local community who were working with them to develop solutions to local problems. Indeed, perhaps the only universal imperative to follow in seeking citizen engagement is to begin at the point where potential participants are (Klein 1976).

It seems therefore that a 'toolkit' approach, which identifies candidate tools for particular tasks and objectives, is one which can offer the kind of flexibility which is needed to support engagement with diverse citizens in diverse contexts. The aim of this chapter is not to provide an exhaustive list of the tools which might be included in a toolkit – because there are dozens, if not hundreds available – but to identify some of the criteria for selecting them. The key functions to support citizen engagement in ICT design will be outlined and the way in which some of the many available tools and techniques might meet these requirements will be highlighted.

9.2 Resources to Support Citizen Engagement

There are numerous, easily available resources – many published on the Internet – which provide compilations of relevant tools and techniques for citizen engagement. The majority of these have been produced by public sector organizations or NGOs for those working in these domains. Some examples of these include the Handbook of Information, Consultation and Public Participation in Policy Making (2001) published by the OECD, the Participation Handbook, produced by the Scottish Parliament (2004), the Citizen Science Toolbox produced by the Australian Coastal CRC (2004), and the Guide to Effective Participation produced by David Wilcox. Table 9.1 lists the 63 tools and techniques included in the Australian Coastal CRC toolbox. Most of the resources provide instructions for how to apply the tools and techniques which they describe. Others provide an evaluation of different tools in relation to their ease of use and impact for citizen engagement, and several also provide case studies of their use in practice. In addition to compilations such as these, there are numerous texts which describe relevant tools and techniques in detail. For example, Merrelyn Emery and Ronald Purser have written several books about the Search Conference method that they have developed (e.g. Emery & Purser 1996), providing extensive practical detail about one of the techniques which is included in many toolkits.

The tools and toolkits mentioned above are not directed specifically at the design and development of digital products or systems, although some of them have been appropriated for such purposes to good effect.

For example, focus groups, which began as a tool for market research, are now regularly used by some designers as both a way of eliciting requirements and as a way for designers to gain additional insight into the needs and aspirations of users. One example is the UTOPIA project (UTOPIA 2004) described in Chapter 5 (See also Bruseberg and McDonagh Philp 2001).

Table 9.1. 63 Tools for engaging, interacting, lobbying and creating dialogue with stakeholders (Citizen Science Toolbox, from the Australian Coastal CRC)

Backcasting	Information hotline	Public meetings
Brainstorming	Information repository	Questionnaires / responses
Briefings	Interactive TV	Role plays
Citizen committees	Interactive display kiosks	Samoan circles
Citizen juries	Key stakeholder interviews	Scenario testing
Civic journalism	Kitchen table discussion	Search conference
Community fairs	Media release	Shopfront
Community indicator	Meditation and negotiation	Simulation (electronic)
Conference	Multi-objective DSS	Sketch interviews
Consensus conference	Newspaper inserts	Snowball sampling
Deliberative opinion polls	Nominal group	Speakouts
Delphi study	Open house / open days	Stakeholder analysis
Design charrettes	Open space technology	Study circles
Displays and exhibits	Participant observation	Submissions
Electronic democracy	Photovoice	Surveys
Expert panel	Planning for real	Technical assistance
Field trips	Poster competitions	Technical reports
Fishbowl	Printed information	Telephone trees
Focus groups	Prioritization matrix	Visioning
Future search conference	Public conversation	Websites
Information contacts	Public volunteers	Workshops

There are also numerous other tools and toolkits which have been developed specifically for the purposes of developing user-centred, inclusive ICT products and services (see, for example, the I~Design toolkit for inclusive design – available at: http://www.inclusivedesign.org.uk, or the RESPECT Handbook of User-Centred Design Methods produced by Maguire et al. 1998).

It is not the aim of this chapter to reproduce the material which these resources already provide. What is intended here, is to show how different tools and techniques can support the transformation of citizen inputs into an array of positive outputs and outcomes (as shown in figure 6.1, in Chapter 6), in the particular context of the creation of digital futures.

9.3 Preparing the Ground

An important precursor to effective citizen engagement is to recruit citizens to participate in a specific initiative or project. As we have already indicated above, the selection will depend on features of the project itself (e.g. scale, scope and the likely impact that it will have on citizens). However the approach to selecting and recruiting citizens to participate will also need to take into account factors such as their diversity, motivation and readiness to engage.

9.3.1 Identifying Stakeholders: Who Needs to be Engaged?

In order to engage the relevant and appropriate stakeholders for a particular design or development project, the first step clearly is to discover who they are and to begin to understand something about the nature of their stake in a project or initiative. Stakeholder identification can simply take the form of a list of all the possible people or organisations that might be affected in some way by a particular product, system or service. However this simplistic approach may fail to identify significant and critical categories of stakeholders. To reduce this danger there are other ways of identifying stakeholders. For example, in a participative 'cascade' approach, an initial group of stakeholders (perhaps representing the most 'obvious' ones) then identifies and defines other groups of stakeholders. These additional people can then be approached and their participation invited. Talking with members of a target stakeholder group can additionally provide useful information about that community.

There is a need for both quantitative information e.g. how many stakeholders in a given category, and for qualitative information, e.g. what are the important distinguishing features of any given stakeholder group. Building up a stakeholder 'map' or profile of stakeholders for a target project is an important research exercise. It involves a review of a range of data sources to build a picture e.g. of the demographic or geographic makeup of a particular community. This could include for example, population trends, business and employment patterns and available infrastructure.

Other methods for gaining useful information about the issues which are important to a particular group of stakeholders include scanning stored print and electronic media articles. This may help to identify key spokespersons, and indicate community attitudes and values (Queensland Government: Department of Communities 2004). Such research can be done in the traditional way, or it can now be done electronically. For instance, some organisations offer a stakeholder mapping service based on data collected by a computer program. It searches the Internet and then creates an actual 'map' or visual representation of the different stakeholders who may be interested in a particular concept and their relationship to each other.

The identification of stakeholders, their diversity and their different requirements is important in defining issues of relevance for them. It also gives a starting point for collaboratively identifying appropriate citizen engagement activities. Clearly, stakeholder analysis needs to be thorough. It should be undertaken as early as possible at the very start of the design process so that stakeholders can be recruited to participate from the outset. This enables them to inform decisions from the conceptual stage of design onwards. Engaging with stakeholders after decisions have been taken can run into problems since the early decisions may constrain or limit what will eventually be possible. These limitations and constraints may subsequently be challenged by the stakeholders. There is also the danger that stakeholders may be misled (consciously or otherwise) about the amount of influence that they will be able to exert over the design process. The sense that 'there is no point' can become a serious disincentive for citizens to participate.

9.3.2 Revealing Stakeholder Diversity

User-centred approaches to ICT design tend to assume that it is easy to identify the potential user population for a product or service, and then to engage with a sample of those potential users to define their requirements or evaluate potential options. The reality is not so straightforward. The pervasive and ubiquitous nature of technology means that everyone in the population is a potential user of, for example, e-government services. As members of the population differ vastly on a range of characteristics, which ones will be significant for the design of effective, accessible and popular e-services? Those involved in marketing, policy making and planning recognize the diversity in the population. In these domains, increasingly sophisticated and detailed understanding of different categories of citizens and stakeholders has been built up, and ways of recruiting, communicating and engaging with them devised accordingly. Comparable in-depth understanding of the diverse characteristics of stakeholders is needed to inform ICT design decisions and solutions. Such knowledge and information is necessary to ensure that design outcomes are desirable, easy to use and accessible to the widest possible constituency. It is also necessary to identify and develop an appropriate approach to participation/

engagement and to the selection of a representative sample of participants from relevant diverse sectors of society.

Stakeholders can be categorized or segmented in many different ways for different purposes. For example, market and social research organisations have developed classifications by profession and income level. For ICT developments, distinctions are typically drawn between primary stakeholders (e.g. those who might be 'users' of a product, system or service) and secondary stakeholders (those who may not use it directly but have some other relationship e.g. customers, agents, maintainers, etc.). Because each group is likely to have different kinds of requirements. Characteristics of stakeholders that may be relevant to design decisions include:

- age and gender;
- education and levels of literacy (including ICT literacy);
- socio-economic profiles (income, employment, housing etc.);
- language;
- ethnic groups, faith and cultural differences.

Chapter 5 has already highlighted the value and benefits of engaging with 'hard to hear' stakeholders. Often such stakeholder groups have specific needs and requirements which are not likely to be identified and met if they are not explicitly sought. Special efforts should therefore be made to identify and engage with such categories of citizens e.g. young people, ethnic minority groups, people with disabilities and the elderly (Demos 2004).

In the case of design for people with 'extraordinary' characteristics there are many tools available which can be used to identify some of their distinguishing characteristics and limitations which can influence their requirements for design – e.g. Older Adultdata (Smith et al. 2000) There are also analytical techniques that can be applied to design concepts to identify those whose physical and/or cognitive characteristics would put them at risk of exclusion by a particular design feature (e.g. Structured Assessment, see Keates et al. 2000).

9.3.3 Stakeholder Readiness to Engage

The readiness of citizens and of other stakeholders to engage in planning or design will be influenced by a raft of factors including their experience, attitudes and skills in relation to engagement. Positive experiences of engagement will reward and encourage citizens to continue to participate and to seek opportunities for further engagement (e.g. *Reflect* ICTs project).

Lack of experience or negative experiences will discourage engagement. Some of the most relevant factors to consider are:

- starting from the point where people are (Klein 1976). The capacity to listen and to develop understanding of the world that participants occupy is crucial;
- capacity for engagement – do stakeholders have the *knowledge* needed to participate (e.g. to critique planning models), the *resources* needed to participate (e.g. time, internet access), and the *skills* needed to participate (e.g. public speaking)?;
- access to necessary *infrastructure* necessary to support participation (e.g. child care networks, transport and disability access)?;
- preferences for engagement – have community members expressed particular preferences regarding engagement (e.g. to be involved in information sharing, consultation or active participation)?;
- previous experience(s) with engagement – has any previous engagement been particularly positive or negative?;
- are there factors that could prevent trust and connectedness being achieved between stakeholders and designers?;
- what motivation and incentives are there for engagement?

9.3.4 Motivation for Citizens to Engage

With regard to the issue of motivation, one of the paradoxes of new technology is that it *"connects the connected more than the peripheral"* (Norris 2001). In the same way, and for some of the same reasons, efforts to involve and engage citizens face the danger of including those who are already willing and able to engage rather than those who are uncertain and lack experience of engagement. This can mean that those with a vested interest will be motivated to engage – potentially driving the agenda and exerting undue influence.

There are some important lessons to learn regarding motivation to engage from cases where unprompted or spontaneous engagement of citizens has arisen. This generally occurs in response to a particular issue they regard as significant in their lives or that of their community. The drivers for this can usually be readily identified. Typically the motivation to take action will be prompted either by a high level of dissatisfaction with the status quo (e.g. poor housing conditions, the high cost of fuel for transport, a failing local school, crime or anti-social behaviour in the neighbourhood) or by fear of a proposed change and perceptions of likely negative impact (e.g. erection of a telephone mast, creation of a holding centre for asylum seekers, a new housing or commercial development). In other words, where there is a strongly felt personal reason for the citizen to become engaged, people are motivated to become actively involved to address the issues. It is often very difficult to generate interest and involvement in projects which are perceived to have little immediate relevance.

Extrapolating from the phenomenon of citizen-initiated action, Coombs (2003) suggested that in the quest to gain citizen engagement in changes it is proposing, government should *"tap into their passions at a personal level"*. This suggestion is supported by Randell (2003) whose first rule of engagement is to enable citizens to *"define their own decision making process."* Both identified the need to go to the citizen at a local level and not expect the citizen to move to the 'authorities/experts'. A fundamental element underlying both these points is the importance of building the relationship/communication with the citizen. Such processes require time and resources both from the stakeholders and the participants (Coombs 2003). Special skills in facilitation may also be essential. Randell (2003) reports that involvement at a local level broadens through time to extend to wider public issues in society. She suggests that people need to be given time to participate and to experience the rewards and satisfaction associated with working together. Findings from projects engaging citizens clearly identify the need of the citizen to know they have actually been listened to and that their participation has influenced the process and outcome. The Demos project (2004) makes the further point that citizens need feedback about their contributions in order to sustain motivation to participate, i.e. to be able to see the effects of their inputs.

Building the confidence of citizens to engage effectively in a change process or design activity happens in stages. Confidence comes from individuals having the insight to see that they possess unique knowledge and insights that others cannot contribute – because they have not 'travelled the same path' and therefore have not gained the same knowledge and experience. The point is made powerfully by Nardi and O'Day (1999), who regard as most important the idea that strategic questions demand local knowledge both to formulate the right questions and to develop answers to them. Further they stress that local knowledge is distributed throughout an information ecology with the consequence that *"no single person can know enough to ask all the right questions. A diverse set of perspectives is needed to develop a healthy information ecology. This means that everyone should be encouraged to ask questions, not just those with highly visible technical knowledge or management responsibility"* (Nardi and O'Day 1999). An excellent example of the benefits of such an approach being applied to deep-rooted social problems associated with poverty is reported by Lister who describes the major and highly positive impact of engaging people living in poverty to contribute to the formulation of policy intended to reduce poverty (Lister 2004).

9.4 Supporting Citizen Engagement in Sociotechnical Decision Making

To enable citizens to contribute effectively to the decision making stages involved in the creation of sociotechnical systems, the primary requirement is for them to be able to fully understand the context. That is, the problem or situation which gives rise to the need for decision making, and to be able to freely explore the possibilities for, and implications of, different decisions. The key processes which will support them in these activities will include:

- communicating and knowledge sharing;
- envisioning;
- consensus building;
- creativity and problem solving;
- requirements surfacing.

These processes will be involved at different stages of the decision making/development lifecycle, as shown in figure 9.1.

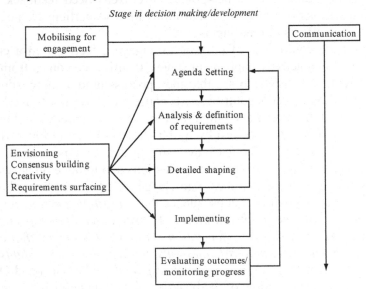

Stage in decision making/development

Fig. 9.1. Key processes to support effective citizen engagement in sociotechnical systems development.

As we have already indicated, there is a variety of tools and techniques available to support and facilitate these processes. Some examples of these will be discussed in sections 9.5-9.10 below, where we shall identify the contributions which each can makes to an effective citizen engagement process.

9.5 Communication and Knowledge Sharing

Good communication is of course essential throughout any successful project which involves different individuals working together, whatever its purpose and whatever their roles. It is especially important to engage citizens and to empower them in the context of a technology development project.

To enable citizens to participate effectively in a dialogue, they need firstly to have confidence that if they express their views these will be listened to and valued, and secondly to understand and be understood by other stakeholders. The concept of engagement implies that there is a two-way process where an understanding of the individuals that are being engaged is essential (Hashagan 2002). Good communication and knowledge sharing also reduce the risk of misunderstanding and lack of trust which mitigate against successful and effective engagement of citizens (Public Agenda 2003).

Knowledge sharing becomes critical where stakeholders come together from diverse perspectives and experiences. In ICT projects adopting an integrated approach to design, there will be people with technical skills and expertise in different aspects of the development of ICT-based systems and services. There will be others with responsibility for implementing and delivering policies and services (e.g. within local communities, local authorities or even central government), project managers, facilitators and possibly other domain experts too. Each type of participant will have their own frames of reference, jargon, and norms of communication. Add a wide range of citizens to this gathering and it will be evident that the potential for poor mutual comprehension and for misunderstanding between participants is significant.

Communication mechanisms are therefore needed that enable knowledge to be shared easily between the different participants in the process, and which do not depend on understanding particular jargon or technical concepts. Mechanisms must also allow both for one-way transmission of information between participants, but crucially also for two-way dialogue, so that clarification can be easily sought and given, or opinions expressed and discussed. To achieve such open communication, a mixture of different communication channels and mechanisms are likely to be needed.

9.5.1 Communication Techniques and Channels

A wide range of appropriate techniques are available. Examples from the Australian Coastal CRC Citizen Science toolbox shown in Table 9.1 include:

One-way (information passing)	Two-way (enabling dialogue/interaction)
Briefings	Conferences
Information hotline	Focus groups
Media releases	Kitchen table discussions
Printed information	Public conversation
Submissions	Study circles
Surveys	Websites (interactive)
Websites	Workshops

A communication strategy can be developed which will deliver information tailored to the audience and provide a range of opportunities for dialogue before and after key decisions are reached. Effective public consultation and engagement will exploit communication channels and media which are familiar and appropriate to their target audience, building for example on:

- networks, committees, structures which could support engagement within a particular community;
- newsletters, radio stations, websites etc. that the community already use.

A study by Myhill et al. (2003) examined how police authorities in the UK engaged with the public in dialogue and identified the benefits to the police service. It also aimed to identify how best to direct improvements to this area of activity. The report describes various communication methods which were used by the police authorities to consult with the public. The traditional public meeting was still the main form of consultation for many authorities, but other methods had increasingly been adopted. Surveys were also used by the majority of authorities and over half had used focus groups. Other techniques included market research and electronic methods. Analysis of the effectiveness of the different mechanisms led to the conclusions that:

- methods must be tailored to suit the audience;
- community factors and personal contacts played the largest role in stimulating participation;

- utilisation of more than one method was important to achieving consultation and engagement aims;
- the public is more engaged when engagement is done on their terms.

The Myhill study also outlined measures which were used to encourage engagement. These included the use of mobile units (advertised on press and radio) which would be driven to publicly accessible areas where engagement could easily take place, including areas where there were likely to be groups of people such as barber shops and hair salons. Efforts were made to target shows or special events in the community by setting up stalls with promotional materials at these events.

Of the different methods tried, surveys were found to be useful in targeting citizens, using online or conventional methods as appropriate. Although surveys can be expensive, the responses are generally helpful in giving an overall assessment of a situation. Citizen panels on the other hand were found to be less effective as they failed to reach important segments of society such as 'hard to reach' groups.

On this point, a study done by Communication Canada (2002) helps to identify strategies for effectively reaching out to young people. The study suggests that factors which enabled successful communication with young Canadians included the following:

- communicate about what matters to them;
- break through the advertising clutter and grab their attention;
- use spokespeople young adults admire;
- tell real stories from people their age;
- project an image of the Government that is consistent and sustained;
- use a variety of media, with an emphasis on the Internet.

9.5.2 Knowledge Sharing

One of the barriers to effective participation described in Chapter 7 is that participants lack appropriate knowledge or believe that they do not have appropriate knowledge to contribute. Designers and system developers will have technical expertise and knowledge which citizens most likely do not. Conversely, citizens' needs and requirements will be rooted deeply in their own personal experiences, and it may be difficult to express and communicate these in a form with which designers can understand and empathise.

We have already mentioned the growing use of the focus group. This is one example of a communication medium in which groups of citizens can meet with designers, policy makers etc. or their representatives, to discuss and comment on topics, design ideas etc. The group setting can give participants confidence to contribute views and opinions which they may be reluctant to do as lone individuals.

The use of pictorial techniques, such as mind mapping (Buzan & Buzan 1995), or 'rich pictures' (as in Checkland's Soft Systems methodology 1981) can be particularly useful in helping stakeholders to map, explore and understand a complex 'problem space'. The K-Net project adopted the 'rich pictures' approach in workshops to explore problems that could be resolved through the application of new technologies in their local communities. They describe rich pictures as simple pictorial diagrams, "*using as many drawings and icons as possible to convey information. Each line drawn should include details on what the linkage is about, what is exchange, what communication tool is used, etc. The names of people and organizations that should be involved in further planning also begin to appear. The rich picture is the transition from the brainstorming to the next step where specific activities are worked on.*" Furthermore, it is a tool that is "*fun to use*" (K-Net 1999). Similarly, the *Reflect* ICTs projects used a range of pictorial techniques to help the teams explore aspects of their community.

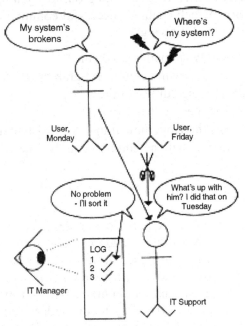

Fig. 9.2. Example of a simple 'rich picture' (http://www.ideagenerationmethods. com/images/rich-picture.gif).

Stakeholders also need to be able to understand possibly unfamiliar, even complex, concepts in order to make informed evaluations, for example of different technical options or plans and policies. Citizens must believe that there is a 'level playing field' if they are to contribute fully to the development process, and this includes being able to have a dialogue with designers. Techniques are therefore particularly needed which bridge the gap between designers' knowledge and citizens' knowledge, breaking away for example from technical jargon and the complex text-based descriptions which characterize many if not most large scale ICT development projects.

9.6 Envisioning

As a precursor to contributing to design decisions, citizens have to develop an awareness of the potential of technological capabilities available. Then, crucially to perceive that the emerging capabilities have relevance to their lives, are suited to their needs and capacities, and are affordable and accessible. The requirement here is for techniques which not only allow stakeholders to visualize the form of design solutions, but which provide sufficient detail for them to be able to assess the 'impact' of the design at different levels – at the individual level, for ease of use, joy of use, etc. and at the collective level for organizational and/or social impact.

9.6.1 Visual Representations

Sketches, prototypes and mock-ups have long been a part of the designer's repertoire of tools. Each of these forms of representation offers stakeholders the opportunity to explore and evaluate aspects of design. Lower-fidelity representations such as sketches or diagrams may be better for testing out concepts because they are seen as more 'disposable' and less costly. However, they are only capable of conveying superficial or limited aspects of a design, and may be capable of being interpreted in widely different ways by different stakeholders. Scenarios and use-cases have become popular in the requirements engineering community as a way of exploring and defining requirements, but these too can lead to different interpretations and resulting requirements.

Such techniques have often been used in an evaluation context, i.e. to present the potential user with a representation of a future situation on which they can comment. Prototypes and simulations can be a good way of finding out from users whether the features of a design meet their needs, and the more realistic the representation, the easier it is to evaluate. But research also shows that as design representations become more 'concrete', evaluations become more focused, i.e. the scope for imagination of alternatives becomes much more limited. Through successive iterations of prototyping and evaluation it may be possible to ensure that qualities and features that the evaluators do not like are designed out. However, it is harder to ensure that qualities and features that they may have liked are 'designed in'.

An example of a technique which enables citizen engagement in envisioning is Planning4real. This technique uses simple physical models as a focus for people to put forward and prioritise ideas on how their area can be improved. It is a highly visible, hands-on community development and empowerment tool. It has been used in a wide range of settings and it appears to be easy and enjoyable to use by people of all abilities and backgrounds. The method uses three-dimensional materials or models for people to see potential changes in their community. Comments and opinions are then written on cards or post-its and added to the model. Other comments then build on these. This method is particularly appropriate for stakeholders who are less comfortable with written material. Often the model is set up in a community venue and worked on over a number of days (Scottish Parliament 2004).

9.6.2 Experiential Approaches

Experiential approaches enable the participant to envision a particular situation more fully than simply looking at a visual representation of it. Examples would include role playing, theatre, and high-fidelity simulations such as can be provided with virtual reality. Virtual Reality (VR) technology is increasingly being used as a tool for this purpose. Davies (1999) for example describes the 'Envisionment Foundry' – a virtual reality tool which has been developed to support the participative design of work environments. Several organisations have developed simulated environments in which new products can be evaluated in 'realistic' settings (e.g. the ID Studiolab at Delft University of Technology). Simulation environments such as this may be relatively costly to set up initially, but the representations they enable have the twin benefits of being highly realistic and yet relatively easy and cheap to change.

There are other approaches which give the participants the direct opportunity to experience different ways of 'being and doing'. One example of such an approach is the Third Age Suit (Hitchcock et al. 2001), a design aid which aims to provide designers with some insight into a range of functional limitations associated with ageing. The suit was developed after a thorough review of the physiological effects of the ageing process and its consequences for older drivers, such as reduced mobility of joints and impaired vision. The aim was to enable engineers in the vehicle design industry to immerse themselves in 'being a third ager', wearing the suit to climb in and out of vehicles and to drive them. The impact of the Third Age Suit on design practice has yet to be systematically assessed, but anecdotal evidence suggests that wearing the suit sensitizes designers to the reality of having special needs, and the importance therefore of designing to accommodate 'extraordinary' users.

9.7 Consensus Building

The myriad of different perspectives that the different stakeholders bring with them to a design project means that there is potential for conflicting views about their needs and priorities, or what constitutes the 'best' or right solution in any given situation. Tools and techniques which help to expose these differences and enable participants to discuss them and build consensus will be important at different stages in the decision making process. As Chapter 4 has shown, there are many examples of good practice in engaging citizens in shaping aspects of their own future. A first step in creating technologies that positively contribute to a desirable future is to enable participants not only to imagine and envision what a desirable future might be for themselves, but to discuss, negotiate and arrive at a consensus with other stakeholders about what it should be. Subsequently stakeholders will need to achieve consensus about the way forward. While positive endorsement of all aspects of a plan by stakeholders may not be feasible, the process will expose disagreement or dissent which can then be discussed and used to inform plans further.

9.7.1 The Search Conference

An effective participatory technique for this process is the Search Conference (Emery and Purser 1996) – sometimes called a Future Search Conference. This approach was used in the Macatawa Area Coordinating Council case. A Search Conference is a participatory event that enables a group to create and implement a plan. Based on the view that people have a desire to make decisions about their own lives and futures, a Search Conference brings together between twenty and thirty-five people who work together as a group to develop strategic plans for a system they share. (This system can be a corporation, a geographic region, an organisation or association of any kind). Those selected to participate are chosen because of their knowledge of the system, their potential for taking responsibility for implementation, and to reflect a wide range of viewpoints. The Search Conference usually consists of a two or three day event, which is facilitated by a specially trained facilitator. Search conferencing results in action-based strategies. This is because participation in the decision-making process creates a sense of ownership which in turn motivates participants to implement plans emerging from the process. The plans and strategies in a Search Conference reflect the unique character of each organisation or community, thereby increasing the probability that effective implementation will follow.

Search conferencing has been successful in a number of areas. Emery and Purser (1996) report that: *"organizations have found that it is an effective method for fast-paced, participative strategic planning in today's turbulent environment. Communities have used it for bringing diverse groups together to work on issues and areas of common concern. It is an excellent means of planning large-scale systems change in real time, and it generates excitement, energy, and purposeful behaviour."* Emery and Purser (1996) report a number of examples of successful search conferences including: mergers of hospitals and companies, community-based planning and development, establishing new policies for governing institutions, and development of system-wide plans for reinventing government (e.g. Macatawa Region Project).

Although primarily used for community and organisational planning situations, the search conference approach has the potential to be extended so that participants consider the types of technologies that could be created to help make the vision of a desirable digital future a reality. However, one of the difficulties which consistently arises when people are asked for their requirements for new technologies is that they feel hampered by not knowing what is technologically feasible. At the same time, considering the current limits of technological feasibility can create constraints and limitations on imagination. Therefore use of envisioning techniques could supplement this process.

9.7.2 Citizens' Juries

While techniques such as the Search Conference seek to achieve a shared vision of the 'right way forward', there are often competing and conflicting views amongst stakeholders about desirable futures. Techniques such as the Citizens' Jury can be helpful in achieving conflict resolution, or to develop a transparent and non-aligned viewpoint. *"Citizen jurors bring with them an intrinsic worth in the good sense and wisdom born of their own knowledge and personal experience. The Citizens' Jury provides the opportunity to add to that knowledge and to exchange ideas with their fellow citizens. The result is a collective one, in which each juror has a valuable contribution to make"* (Jefferson Center 2002).

In a Citizens' Jury, participants are a representative sample of citizens. The participants are briefed in detail on the background and current thinking relating to a particular issue, and asked to discuss possible approaches, usually in a public forum (occasionally even televised). Jurors are required to make their judgement in the form of a report, as they would in legal juries.

9.8 Creativity and Problem Solving

For citizens to become actively engaged in shaping their futures, techniques are needed which help participants to explore problems and develop ideas for solutions. Rather than presenting them with 'ready made' solutions or options developed by 'experts' for them to comment upon and evaluate.

9.8.1 Brainstorming

Brainstorming (e.g. Bolton 1979) is a technique which has been used in a wide variety of different circumstances to generate new ideas and solve problems. Brainstorming is a group activity in which participants are encouraged to come up with as many ideas as they can, including 'wild' ideas. The 'rules' of brainstorming are that participants must not evaluate ideas as they are generated, nor should they seek clarification. Further, while all ideas are recorded, names are not attached to them. Participants are encouraged to build and expand on ideas generated by others.

9.8.2 Workshops and Games

An innovative approach to participation has been developed by Mackie and Wilcox (2003), in the form of a workshop-based game (Making the Net Work), which can be used to plan the development of technology systems, online communities and learning materials. Workshops and games provide informal settings, which promote and facilitate exploration in a "*safe*" environment. The co-design workshop is an approach which has been successfully used in a product design environment (e.g. Gyi et al. 2005) and again has potential to be used for aspects of ICT design. Such events allow the opportunity for citizens to give in-depth feedback on products and to share, communicate and discuss ideas through 'designing and making'.

9.9 Requirements Surfacing

As we note in Chapter 2, the most difficult challenge for those designing ICT systems is to properly and fully elicit the requirements of potential users. Conventional approaches to systems design have tended to be aimed at eliciting, and satisfying, functional (task related requirements) and have ignored other kinds of user requirement. However, as we also argue in Chapter 2, the non-functional requirements which users have – such as for security procedures which are robust but which at the same time do not place high loads on our memory or capability to enter accurate strings of numbers on keypads – can actually be equally or even more important for the effectiveness as well as the desirability of the system.

Robertson (2001) proposes that requirements can fall into three categories: conscious requirements, unconscious requirements, and undreamed of requirements. Conscious requirements are those that stakeholders are particularly aware of, and which are therefore relatively easy to elicit. Unconscious requirements are those that stakeholders do not realise that they have. Reasons for having unconscious requirements might be that stakeholders are so used to having a requirement fulfilled that it does not occur to them to express it. These are harder to elicit because they relate to what may be deeply ingrained beliefs about what technology 'can do' or 'should do'. Undreamed-of requirements are those, which do not occur to stakeholders because they cannot imagine what it might be like to have access to a new kind of technology or product. One of the major problems with requirements such as these is that they are hard to elicit. In many cases they cannot be directly observed or easily articulated. They may for example relate to our wishes and aspirations for quality of life – issues which we are not necessarily used to discussing with others, and which may appear to have no relevance to the design of technology. In other cases, requirements arise as a result of seeing and exploring possibilities: new technologies for example can offer new ways of doing things.

Unless these requirements can be elicited or brought to the surface during the design process, there is no prospect of designing products and systems, which deliberately aim to meet them. Designers therefore need tools which help people to imagine or 'surface' their requirements. The techniques described above under 'Envisioning' e.g. prototypes and simulations, can be used not only to give participants a vision of a different way of being or doing, but also to help elicit aspirations, wishes and requirements.

9.9.1 Challenging Stereotypes

One way of bringing unconscious requirements to the surface is to challenge them – i.e. to create prototypes or simulations of technologies or products which are very different from the norm, and encourage stakeholders to express their views and opinions about them (see section 9.6). Conversely, as we have already noted in section 9.6.1, presenting stakeholders with options which are very similar to previous technologies will not challenge underlying assumptions and therefore may not bring these to the surface to be tested and, if appropriate, changed. The most important features of successful techniques for supporting imagination and surfacing requirements is that they should enable people (not just stakeholders, but also designers) to break away from the constraints which tend to arise from the existing situation or current ways of doing things ('out of the box thinking'). Brainstorming is another possible technique (see section 9.7.1).

9.9.2 Surfacing Assumptions and Attitudes

Techniques which can help to reveal our unconscious assumptions and attitudes that may give rise to requirements can be drawn from diverse fields. For example techniques that help to expose the thinking which might underlie a particular expression or thought could be drawn from family therapy approaches (e.g. Satir et al. 1991), or neuro-linguistic programming (e.g. O'Connor & Seymour 2003). Other approaches include theatre, dramatization and storytelling.

9.10 Developing Outputs to Inform Design

The outputs of these multi-faceted analyses generate invaluable data to inform the requirements specifications for the proposed systems. To ensure that the citizen engagement process feeds into the shaping of digital technologies, it will be important to capture the outputs of different activities and present these in a way that designers of ICT systems can use. This can be problematic. For example, some designers have used approaches drawn from ethnography to get a deep understanding of their users in order to derive design requirements. However, it is recognized that this approach is time-consuming and needs trained researchers to analyse and interpret the data which is obtained, particularly to derive design requirements from it (e.g. Lebbon et al. 2003 in Clarkson et al. 2003). Transforming this kind of rich data into outputs that can be used by designers is not straightforward and has often proved elusive to achieve. Examples of outputs which can be informed by rich qualitative data include:

- a stakeholder 'map' of all stakeholders (including those at risk of exclusion);
- a description of citizens' priorities and goals;
- a skill profile of citizens in terms of ICT preparedness;
- a profile of local context;
- ICT options and alternatives;
- identification of interdependencies.

The products such as those listed above will complement and enrich those carried out in conventional system analysis. These information-rich outputs greatly enhance the validity of specifications of citizens' requirements and are therefore likely to significantly improve specific design attributes such as the relevance, ease-of use and utility of the products of ICT development. (For further examples of the outputs and outcomes see Chapter 6).

9.11 Conclusions

We have considered here the processes which are necessary to support effective citizen engagement/participation in ICT design such that socio-technical systems evolve into desirable digital futures. But bringing about a significant change in the way in which ICT design is approached needs more than just tools. The final chapter discusses the changes required for this process to become institutionalised in all development processes which involve the public.

References

Australian Coastal CRC (2004) Citizen Science Toolbox. http://www.coastal. crc.org.au/ toolbox/index.asp.

Beardon H (2005) ICT for development: Empowerment or exploitation. Learning from the Reflect ICTs project. ActionAid, London.

Bolton R (1979) People Skills. How to assert yourself, listen to others and resolve conflicts. Simon & Schuster, UK.

Bruseberg A, McDonagh-Philp D (2002) New product development by eliciting users' experience and aspirations. International Journal of Human-Computer Studies, 55 (4), pp 435-453.

Buzan T, Buzan B (1995) The mind map book. BBC Books, London.

Clarkson PJ, Coleman R, Keates S, Lebbon C (2003) Inclusive design: Design for the whole population. Springer-Verlag, London.

Checkland P (1981) Systems Thinking, Systems Practice. Wiley, Chichester.

Checkland P, Scholes J (1990) Soft Systems methodology in action. John Wiley & Sons, London.

Communication Canada (2002) Canadian Government Department of Public Works & Government Services, Communications Survey. Fall 2002. http://www. communications.gc.ca/survey_sondage

Coombs A (2003) Re-engaging with citizens: Taking an issue to the people on the street. Online Opinion, 4 August 2003. http://www.onlineopinion.com.au/ view.asp?article=591

Davies RC (1999) The Envisionment foundry – a virtual reality tool for the participatory design of work environments. Workshop on User Centred Design and Implementation of Virtual Environments. King's Manor, University of York. pp 23-43.

The Demos Project (2004) Homepage http://www.demosproject.org

Emery M, Purser RE (1996) The Search Conference: A Powerful Method for Planning Organizational Change and Community Action. Jossey-Bass, San Francisco.

Gyi D, Cain RB, Campbell I (2005) Users, co-designers, stakeholders or partners? A case study in flexible packaging design http://www.hhrc.rca.ac.uk/ programmes/include/2005/proceedings/pdf/gyidiae.pdf

Hashagan S (2002) Models of community engagement. www.scdc.org.uk/ resources_reports/models%20of%20engagement%20web%20version.doc

Hitchcock DR, Lockyer S, Cook S, Quigley C (2001) Third Age usability and safety - an ergonomics contribution to design. International Journal of Human-Computer Studies, 55(4) 635-643.

Hoffman L (1981) Foundations of Family Therapy. New York: Basic Books.

i~design toolkit (n.d.) Homepage http://www.inclusivedesign.org.uk/

ID Studiolab, Delft University of Technology. http://studiolab.io.tudelft.nl

Jefferson Center (2002) The Citizen Jury Process. Jefferson Center for New Democratic Processes, Minneapolis, MN. USA. http://www.jefferson-center.org/citizens_jury.htm

K-Net (1999) Step 4 Creating Rich Pictures. http://smart.knet.ca/archive/fsworkshop/step4.html

Keates S, Clarkson J, Harrison LA, Robinson P (2000) Towards a practical inclusive design approach. ACM Press, New York.

Klein L (1976) A social Scientist in Industry. Gower, Epping.

Lebbon C, Rouncefield M et al. (2003) Observation for Innovation in Clarkson PJ, Coleman R, Keates S, Lebbon C (2003) Inclusive design: design for the whole population. Springer-Verlag, London.

Lister R (2004) Poverty. Polity Press, Cambridge.

Mackie D, Wilcox D (2003) Workshop games: Making the Net work. http://www.makingthenetwork.org/pgame/whygames.pdf

Maguire M et al. (1998) RESPECT User-Centred Requirements Handbook, EC Telematics Applications Programme, Project TE 2010 RESPECT, Deliverable D5.3, HUSAT Research Institute, July, 1998. http://www.ucc.ie/hfrg/projects/respect/urmethods/index.html

Myhill A, Yarrow S, Dalgleish D, Docking M (2003) The role of police authorities in public engagement – Home Office Online report 37/03. http://www.homeoffice.gov.uk/rds/onlinepubs1.html

Nardi BA, O'Day VL (1999) Information Ecologies: Using Technology with Heart, Massachusetts: MIT Press.

Norris P (2001) Digital Divide: Civic engagement, information poverty and the Internet. Cambridge: Cambridge University Press.

O'Connor J, Seymour J (2003) Introducing Neuro-Linguistic Programming. London, Thorsons.

OECD (2001) Handbook of Information, Consultation and Public Participation in Policy Making.

Public Agenda (2003) http://www.publicagenda.org/pubengage/ pubengage_questions.cfm

Queensland Government: Department of Communities (2004) Engaging Queenslanders: a guide to community engagement methods and techniques. Queensland: Australia.

Randell M (2003) How to engage citizens? Well a good start is to treat them like people! Online Opinion, 4 August 2003. http://www.onlineopinion.com.au

Robertson S (2001) Requirements Trawling: Techniques for discovering Requirements. International Journal of Human-Computer Studies, 55(4) pp 405-422.

Satir V, Banmen J, Gerber J, Gomori M (1991). The Satir Model – Family Therapy and Beyond. Palo Alto, CA. Scence and Behaviour Books.

Smith S, Peebles L, Norris B (2000) Older Adultdata: The Handbook of Measurements and Capabilities of the Older Adult: data for designing safety. Department of Trade and Industry, UK.

Scottish Parliament (2004) The Participation Handbook. http://www.scottish.parliament.uk/vli/participationHandbook/index.htm

UTOPIA (Usable Technology for Older People: Inclusive and Appropriate) (2004). Publications page last updated 6th April. http://wwww. computing. dundee.ac.uk/projects/UTOPIA/Publications.asp
Wilcox D (n.d.) Guide to Effective Participation. http://www.partnerships.org.uk

10 Achieving a Culture of Participation and Engagement

The central theme of this book is that ICT design and development practices informed by citizens and enriched by principles drawn from several design approaches – especially a sociotechnical one – promise wide-ranging and rich rewards for 21st century society. Yet we reported earlier that we could find few cases of citizen participation/engagement in ICT development and delivery, beyond website design projects. This was surprising given that early participatory design initiatives were very promising in organisational contexts. It seems that the custom and practice of participation has not spread to influence the design of large scale ICT systems used by the public. This is disappointing and suggests we have a long way to go to embed participation and engagement in integrated ICT design approaches. Substantial funding of effort in countless projects to generate design guidelines over more than three decades has failed to achieve significant change in ICT design practice. The time to take a new approach is long overdue. In the *zeitgeist* of the early 21st century a major shift seems timely and eminently possible as several disparate strands are coming together: sound research and good practice (the necessary 'know-how') in projects and initiatives around the world; important drivers for change in society (the momentum); and, perhaps most significantly, enthusiasm for change within the IT profession offer unprecedented opportunities.

Some of the barriers to participation/engagement in the ICT context have been described in Chapter 6. In addition to these, another stumbling block which the authors have encountered but for which we have no documented research is the sheer tedium associated with 'user issues' in the minds of some managers and IT professionals. The problems of poor usability, lack of relevance for users, especially members of the public, negative user responses and limited uptake are so familiar and have been around for so long that they have become a tedious backcloth to the use of ICT. The rhetoric of user participation as a solution has become boring and it seems that for many ICT designers, engrossed in demanding, technically complex software design, it is unwelcome and unrewarding. While this is entirely understandable, it is a position that denies designers the advantages of citizen/user participation and the rewards associated with delivering what people want. The challenge therefore is to find innovative and compelling ways to radically change mindsets and working arrangements so that ICT design can benefit from contributions of citizens/users. Breathing excitement and interest into new ways of doing things which enable businesses, governments and citizens alike to reap the rich rewards offered by successful ICT developments must surely be worthwhile. This is the challenge that this chapter addresses in the following sections:

- drivers for action;
- the rewards for changing the focus of ICT design;
- leading the way;
- enabling the transition;
- roles of key stakeholders;
- scaling the process;
- conclusions.

10.1 Drivers for Action

The drivers for citizen engagement have been considered at length in Chapter 3 so will not be repeated here. Clearly a number of them are also drivers for a shift in design approach. One particularly powerful catalyst for change is the financial incentive to increase significantly the return on investment in public sector ICT developments. A current example of the problem is provided by the limited success so far with implementing local e-government in the UK. The evidence suggests that the public is not buying in to this on the scale required to make the efficiency savings anticipated. Nor are citizens gaining the projected benefits of the enhanced services developed for them.

We know that this pattern of high investment and disappointing return is nothing new. We have noted earlier that over several decades such outcomes have been attributed in part to inadequate user involvement and consequent poor user requirements specification (Kearney 1984). The authors suggest that the costs of allowing this pattern to continue are becoming prohibitive both in economic and in social terms. Investment in achieving new ways of designing ICT products, systems and services can reasonably be expected to pay for itself over the medium to long-term. This would come about as a result of delivering ICT design outcomes which successfully meet the needs of the public and fulfil the objectives of other stakeholders. Some savings are also likely from increased knowledge sharing. This should reduce some of the duplication of effort currently in evidence. For example, the move towards local e-government in the UK means that every local council is having to discover for itself how to encourage citizens to use e-services, and especially how to reach the 'hard to hear'. This is wasteful and unproductive as there is considerable well-established practice and knowledge available; Lisl Klein captures the essence of the issue: *"the challenge is to produce forms of institution-alization that provide appropriate opportunities for development and guard against inflexible and inappropriate application, but do not require everybody to rediscover the wheel"* (Klein 1976). Sharing available knowledge as described in section 10.2.1 could cut down some of the unnecessary effort and reduce costs.

10.2 The Rewards for Changing the Focus of ICT Design

Achieving the shift in ICT design to embrace wider design principles and citizen contributions will bring important and valuable rewards. In Chapter 3, we describe the high level functions and drivers for citizen engagement. Some of these, e.g. narrowing the digital divide, increasing social inclusion and enhancing democracy and citizenship, are benefits for society as a whole. Others however bring rewards directly to those involved in ICT design and implementation, and indirectly to everyone else. These include:

1. an enriched knowledge base and pool of resources;
2. improved systems and services (i.e. better matched to citizen/user needs);
3. faster adoption and more widespread use;
4. reduction in the risk of error or failure.

10.2.1 Enriched Knowledge Base

A significant benefit of the proposed shift in ICT design is the expanded knowledge base that will become available to inform the entire design and decision process. This will come in part from the integration of knowledge from two particular domains. Earlier chapters have referred to two parallel universes of discourse and activity, namely the ICT design domain on the one hand and the public participation domain on the other. Both domains are characterized by significant human endeavour, which has led in each case to a considerable literature of published knowledge and information. Both domains consume significant amounts of public funds through government departments, agencies and research funding bodies. Yet the output of these two rather diffuse communities generally takes little or no account of the other. Their separateness may help to explain why we seem to be such a very a long way from reaching the vision of human-computer symbiosis anticipated by Sackman in the mid 1960s (Sackman 1967). Bringing the knowledge base from the public participation domain together with ICT design expertise will greatly enrich the resource pool available to designers. Adding contributions from citizens to this expertise will further enhance the resource pool accessible to the ICT design process.

10.2.2 Improved Systems and Services

The expanded and enriched knowledge base will greatly increase the likelihood of achieving a good match between the design outcome and citizens/users' needs. Better informed design is likely to produce better systems and services from the perspective of the citizen/user as they will be closely matched to their needs and requirements as depicted in Fig. 10.1.

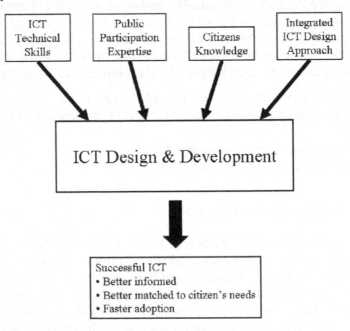

Fig. 10.1. Enriching the Knowledge base for ICT Design.

10.2.3 Faster Adoption and More Widespread Use

Successful systems, services and products attract users and promote continued use. In Chapter 3 we discussed the success criteria for gaining customer loyalty. It is worth repeating that meeting these criteria (for relevance, accessibility, value for money etc.) demands good knowledge of the needs of prospective users in society. This is where the citizen contributions are of particular value to the developer. Direct engagement with potential users is the most effective way of gaining insights into what matters to them and their priorities regarding electronic services. The point is worth reiterating here that the economic benefits of 'getting the design right first time' can make the difference between a business prospering or failing. When services are well-matched to the real needs of their intended customers, take-up will reflect this. Valued systems tend to be well-used systems. Comparisons of government website usage make this very clear. A recent report in the Guardian (Guardian 2005), revealed that many government websites are failing to attract readers despite extensive spending. Figures show that many of the UK government's internet operations are under-performing despite vast funding and investment. One website, UK World Heritage Sites, for example, received only 77 visitors in the previous year. By contrast, some other government websites have been overwhelmed by demand e.g. the website for the 1901 census. These extremes suggest a lack of prior research to discover citizens' interests and user needs, and therefore to predict likely demand, before investing in website developments.

10.3 Leading the Way

10.3.1 Role of Influential Leaders

Those best placed to initiate change are the most powerful stakeholders involved in determining our futures, that is, governments, shakers and movers of the telecommunications sector, and especially the ICT professionals and the bodies that represent them. Setting major change in motion requires an appropriately high profile initiative with influential leaders and key stakeholders in society. Putting in place a process to institutionalize a new approach to ICT design is clearly a very major undertaking. Success will require strong political will, commitment and understanding of three key facts:

- ICT applications for use by the public will inevitably and unavoidably have technical, human and social components and should therefore be designed as sociotechnical systems;
- citizen engagement in defining and developing these is crucial to their success;
- the rewards (outlined 10.2 above) are very significant and attractive – in both social and in economic terms.

10.3.2 Publicising the Value of Citizen Participation/ Engagement

At least one precedent has already been set for a senior government minister to recognize and acknowledge publicly the benefits of citizen engagement in decision-making. This occurred in the context of local health provision. Regarding the role seen for citizen juries in the UK, in a speech on the 23rd June 2005, Patricia Hewitt (Secretary of State for Health) highlighted the benefits of 'Citizen Juries' in Leicester, UK. She recalls: *"the health authority was grappling with the problem of how to recognize services across three acute hospitals. Their proposals were leaked – and the public were confronted with a plan to close a highly successful and much-loved hospital and replace it with what looked like a glorified old people's home. Within a few weeks, 120,000 people had signed a petition to save the hospital. I persuaded the health authority to establish a citizens jury and, for a week, in the full view of the local paper, a panel of local residents interrogated the experts on their plans. The results were extraordinary. The part of the plan that had attracted most opposition – the 'care and rehabilitation centre' – was welcomed with open arms by the people's panel. But they were equally firm that they were putting it in the wrong place. The authority, sensibly, accepted the people's verdict and amended their plans"* (Hewitt 2005). It will of course be some years before the impact of this particular citizen jury can be assessed. The fact that it took place at all suggests the stirrings of a change in culture towards acknowledging the value of citizens' knowledge and experience and accepting these as significant contributions to decision-making processes. What needs to happen now is the extension of this growing awareness of the benefits of citizen engagement into the domain of ICT development. We have described some of the instances where this is already happening. Often however, as we have noted, the engagement relates to a very specific aspect of technology such as creating and designing a website (e.g. Germany's Bundestag website project). Often too the intention has been specifically to engage with hard-to-reach groups (for example, the Surrey

Over 50's website developed as one part of the UK's local e-Government pilot projects) rather than with citizens more generally. There is a need to build on this good practice, publicising both the benefits and the processes used, to encourage adoption of the approach more widely.

10.3.3 Role of the IT Profession

Public acknowledgement of the benefits of citizen engagement by influential leaders in society is of course only one of several thrusts required for transformational change to follow. Equally important is that the leadership in the IT profession and in the telecommunications sector consider the case for ICT developments to be conceived and planned as integrated socio-technical systems right from their inception. The foundations for such developments appear to be present already in professional bodies such as the United Kingdom Academy for Information Systems (UKAIS), the Worshipful Company of Information Technologists, (WCIT) and the British Computer Society (BCS). For example, in the case of WCIT, the 100th livery company of the City of London, it has through its charitable activities brought to bear the experience of senior IT professionals in several programmes involving citizen participation and engagement – notably the Lifelites scheme which is currently installing specially designed computer networks in every children's hospice across the country, enabling children with serious illnesses to continue their education, keep in touch with family and friends and access the Internet (The Worshipful Company of Information Technologists 2006). It also supports the *"Carers on Line"* project offering advice, information and support to carers across the country (Milner 2005). In addition, WCIT has played a key role in the development and launch of IT4Communities, a national initiative to promote volunteering by IT professionals, using their skills for the benefit of local communities. WCIT is an example of a voluntary professional organization which can bring IT skills to the aid of the disadvantaged in the community.

Part of the remit of the BCS also reflects a wide societal perspective. In its terms of reference the BCS states that *"The Society also acts to generate public awareness and appreciation of the associated social and economic benefits in IT"* (British Computer Society n.d.a). Further, part of its stated mission is that *"The BCS will lead the change in the standing of the IT profession by creating an understanding of what is required to implement successful IT projects and programmes, and to advise, inform and persuade industry and government on what is required to produce successful IT enabled projects"* (British Computer Society n.d.b). Allied to this is an explicit objective *"to provide leadership in industry, government and trade and regulatory associations"* (British Computer Society n.d.b). It therefore appears that there is a readiness on the part of the BCS to engage with the kind of change which would result in more successful ICT developments. Its objective to 'Encourage creativity' also has important relevance for a change process where new ideas and new ways of doing things will be key to success. One more piece of evidence of the preparedness of the IT professionals represented by the BCS to fully engage in achieving the proposed shift is the existence of the BCS Sociotechnical Specialist Group. This group is concerned with human and organizational issues that arise in developing, implementing, using and evaluating information systems and in the wider use of ICTs. The aims of the group are to integrate the social and technical aspects of ICTs, and of systems more generally, and to promote sociotechnical principles, methods and ways of thinking. The BCS Sociotechnical Group promotes the view that in developing, using and studying ICT systems, it is essential to give due weight to both social and technical factors.

Since IT professionals are such key stakeholders in ICT developments they are of course well positioned to support and encourage the engagement of citizens at all stages of design decision making. Many will be well placed to be influential role models by engaging with citizens/users themselves and following good practice to achieve a good experience of participation and worthwhile outcomes.

10.3.4 Starting the Dialogue

Identification of some of the key players to engage in debating the issues and possibilities associated with the major change proposed is a first step towards planning action. The next consideration is how to begin a dialogue on the merits of the case for achieving a shift in the focus of ICT design. The initial task here is to persuade a number of influential individuals that there is a worthwhile issue to consider in some depth and in an informed consultation. To this end, we hope we have developed through the course of this book a sufficiently convincing case for a sociotechnical focus of ICT design and associated participation/engagement of citizens/users. In particular we hope we have convinced our readers that there is real value and benefit to derive from enabling citizens to inform ICT design decisions that profoundly affect their lives.

Assuming there is a nucleus of interested relevant parties, the next step is to decide how to host and conduct such a consultation. There are excellent precedents for creating the 'spark' which ignites a process of systemic change in society. For example, St. George's House at Windsor in the UK has an honourable history of hosting inspirational and productive events to address complex issues in society. Since 1966 the members of St George's House have invited people of influence (for example, national leaders, senior members of governments, of the armed forces, of emergency services, leading figures in the voluntary sector, management and technical experts, to name a few of the types of participants at past consultations), from all parts of society to attend consultations on the challenges faced by today's world. One example of a consultation convened in January 2004 sought discussion on the 'Introduction of a Single Three-Digit Non-Emergency Number for Accessing Local Services'. The consultation was chaired by the Chairman of Motorola, with distinguished participants drawn from local Councils, UK Youth, the Independent Police Complaints Commission, Help the Aged, academia, Government Departments (E-envoy, DTI, Home Office and Crime Reduction), the National Farmers Union, the Neighbourhood Watch Association, schools, the Jersey Ambulance Service, the Strathclyde Fire Brigade, NATO Consultation, Command and Control Agency, West Midlands Police, and the Diocese of Oxford. This particular event resulted in a report which informed the deliberations of the Home Office and the drafting of a consultative document published in 2005 (Office of Communications 2005).

Another UK institution which affords opportunities for debate and exploration of societal issues is Goodenough College, London (see: http://www. goodenough.ac.uk/). As part of its mission as a college, it offers through the medium of a conference series *"to debate issues of concern to the leadership of the contemporary world"*. These allow complex real-world issues and problems to be examined and appropriate actions and methods of approaching them to be considered and reported to inform planning and policy-making.

Although both of these examples are based in the UK, there are no doubt equivalent institutions in other countries which host exploratory consultative events which can lead to important initiatives being launched in society. It is also the case that both St. George's House consultations and Goodenough College's conferences and debates enjoy contributions of participants from the wider international community.

Such consultations allow participants to discuss freely, in a congenial environment away from day-to-day demands, major issues of social concern. The generic objective of hosting such events is to contribute to the betterment of a rapidly changing world through the publication of influential reports and briefings for key people in positions of power. The participation of key people who are in positions of authority where they can support and facilitate the progress of initiatives agreed upon in consultations clearly adds impetus for effective implementation of changes proposed.

Taking such opportunities for high level strategic consultations would seem to offer a powerful way of exploring the issues and proposals raised in this book. In particular such consultations would test the level of interest, and, potentially, achieve the buy-in and positive backing of many relevant stakeholders. These would be essential prerequisites for beginning a movement of sufficient standing and influence to begin to shift the focus of ICT design. Participants in any such event would need to include thought leaders from many domains. Examples of relevant domains include government, government agencies such as the Audit Commission in the UK (e.g. authors of the Comprehensive Performance Assessment guidance for government), industry – especially the telecoms industry, professional bodies such as the British Computer Society, other institutions representing designers, academia, the voluntary sector and other groups representing members of the public. It would be for the participants to debate the issues to decide whether action should follow and what form any action might take.

10.4 Enabling the Transition

Assuming there is sufficient support to take up the challenge to shift the focus of ICT design to incorporate citizen engagement, then utilising numerous channels and mechanisms for promoting and facilitating change becomes possible and necessary.

Enabling the transition will require change at several levels. For institutions there are many changes to achieve in the culture of IT departments, mindsets of software developers, education and training of IT professionals, accreditation and so on. With regard to citizens, participation and engagement are not familiar activities for many. Building capacity to equip citizens to contribute effectively will be an important function which Government will need to fund. This will be considered briefly in section 10.5 where the role of government in this venture is outlined.

10.4.1 Institutionalizing the Changes

'Know-how' is readily available to achieve the changes that are urgently needed. A great deal of good practice in participation strategies and the management of change has been documented in Chapters 8 and 9. Utilising the ideas and research findings presented in this book implies vision, understanding, infrastructure and institutions. We have attempted to lay out our stall regarding each of these in the course of this book.

For citizen engagement and participation to become the accepted norm in shaping our digital futures requires that these processes are also institutionalized in society. Lisl Klein provides an excellent example of institutionalization in describing a familiar everyday context: *"society has made a policy decision, crystallised in law, to restrict driving to one side of the road. This apparently simple decision is supported by a surprising number and range of institutions: the assumption that it must happen is built into the design of vehicles. It is built into the training of drivers, as well as into their legitimation (licensing). It is built into the formulation of codes and standards (the Highway Code, standards about the width and layout of roads, and so on). Then there is the continual reinforcement of seeing that others do it, and, finally, sanctions (punishment) if it does not happen. These institutions, in turn, are supported by funds, training establishments, staffing, and monitoring (traffic police). Together, these institutions are very powerful, and they have been in force for a long time. In addition, a breach of the policy is generally clearly visible and unambiguous. As a result of all that, the policy is mostly carried out: drivers are not in the position of having continually to decide on which side to drive"* (Klein 2005).

As already discussed, to put in place a comparable set of mechanisms to institutionalize citizen engagement and embrace a range of new design approaches requires a groundswell of support and action at many levels and in many sectors. The pervasiveness of the problems and issues associated with large scale ICT systems means that there are many in society who would like to see significant change. This means that there are likely to be influential thought leaders willing to make the case for citizen engagement and the allied need to change the focus of ICT design. Through sharing their vision and understanding with many others in central and local government, in telecommunications, manufacturing and retailing sectors, in academia and in the design community, preparedness and enthusiasm for change can be expected to grow.

10.4.2 Giving Citizens a Voice

Another separate, but closely related, aspect to explore is how citizens at large can begin to become involved in influencing decisions to shape our digital futures. The World Wide Web is an awesome symbol of human creativity and people power. It is the world's largest ICT system, continuing to grow on a scale so vast that it is hard to conceive its true proportions, and it is arguably making the greatest contribution yet to human development. However the Web as it now exists was not 'designed' – the original concept devised by visionary technologists and scientists has simply been appropriated by the rest of the world. It is a unique example of participative development undertaken by countless individuals. The freely accessible and open nature of the Web has empowered citizens and engendered extensive engagement, with highly visible and influential outcomes. This power and influence is at odds with the limited power and influence citizens typically have in the design and shaping of many of the other ICTs they use in their daily lives. Although citizens are major stakeholders in systems for public use, their high importance to the success of such systems is not matched by their opportunity to influence critical variables – e.g. access, ease of use, usefulness, entertainment value or desirability – all of which will promote adoption.

Members of the public, along with many relevant professionals in a wide variety of roles, have significant and often unique contributions to make in shaping digital futures. To achieve their participation in the design of ICT systems, services and products will require not only a shift in the focus of the design process, but also special capacity-building initiatives. A groundswell of support and understanding of the issues is essential in gaining a critical mass for major change to begin to come about. It is not possible or appropriate to attempt to offer an exhaustive list of relevant participants who have significant contributions to make to bring about change. Some examples of professionals to include are social scientists, psychologists, software developers, HCI designers, change management specialists, experts in participation strategies, along with government agencies, voluntary agencies representing the interests of many 'extraordinary users' among the population, and, above all, citizens themselves as crucial stakeholders in society.

10.4.3 Enabling Role of Technology

There will of course be a role for technology-enabled debate to cascade discussion of the issues and involve citizens in examining ways in which they wish to engage with the design of our digital futures, what they see as the benefits and the pitfalls, their priorities, and the preparation they need. Some new mechanisms might well emerge to support this process. For example, a 'civic commons' conceived of as a trusted public space where dispersed discourse can be concentrated to allow government to inform itself regarding concerns and views of its citizens would offer one context for debate for people who are comfortable conversing on the Internet. For others, there are tried and tested hybrid environments such as those offered by 'America Speaks' which combine traditional 'town hall' meetings with the use of ICTs to allow votes to be counted and reports of deliberations to be compiled in real time.

10.4.4 Investing in the Transition

Achieving the proposed shift in focus of ICT design and development will require commitment of substantial resources to implement governmental strategies at both national and local levels. There is often reluctance to invest in the citizen participation/engagement aspect because of the high perceived cost (see Chapter 7). In contrast it seems that we simply accept the escalating costs of large scale ICT systems and the huge investment in the technological aspects of ICT development projects – despite their unsatisfactory record of delivery. There is now a need for comparable commitment of resources to the social, human and organisational aspects if the reluctance to engage with citizens is to be overcome. The risks and costs of failure to do this successfully are proving just as significant. All the key stakeholders will have a part to play in resourcing the transition.

The reality is that investment in the human aspects or 'soft issues' has for decades persistently remained at very low levels compared with the vast investment in information and communications technologies. The investment in the technology escalates for each successive public sector ICT development, (£6 billion for the latest NHS system in the UK, which is intended to make patients records more accessible, to enable GP's to book hospital appointments, and to develop a system to store and send prescriptions and x-rays electronically). Thus it is to be hoped that in such a crucial area as health provision, that good practice will be the norm and set a precedent in participation and engagement to ensure an excellent match between ICT provision and user requirements. This will reverse the pattern of inadequate involvement of stakeholders, including citizens as patients, documented in the failures of ICT systems cited earlier in the book (National Audit Office 1999; Bourn 2000).

10.5 Roles of Stakeholders

Although this book is focussed upon the importance of the role of citizens in shaping technologies and determining their application, there are many other stakeholders with a part to play in debating and planning a shift in focus of ICT design. Successful institutionalization of sociotechnical thinking and associated citizen/user engagement within ICT design will require the active participation of very many role holders, especially from the ICT design community, the technology providers, ICT manufacturers and retailers. Government will also have a significant role as a major initiator of large scale ICT developments, a major customer of ICT systems, services and products and as guardian of democracy. The roles of these key stakeholders in achieving the shift in focus of ICT design is considered next.

10.5.1 ICT Designers

One of the themes of this book has been the importance of having ICT systems, services and products that are well matched to the characteristics of citizens. We have suggested that this will be achieved successfully by integrating into ICT design principles from the five complementary approaches of sociotechnical theory, participatory design, information ecologies, inclusive design and change management. New challenges along with new rewards are likely to characterize this new way of working. Giving designers the confidence and enthusiasm to work within an integrated design approach will be a key part of the institutionalization process.

An important consideration in the preparedness of designers to adopt the suggested approach is their skill and knowledge. There are important ways in which the skills of ICT designers need to be extended and complemented by those of other professionals to meet the needs of 21st century society. University degree courses for software designers and for product designers have for many years included teaching in human-computer interaction (HCI). This has helped to improve interface design considerably from the users' perspective. Teaching of inclusive design principles is still far from standard practice. This is despite moves in the European Union several years ago. In February 2001 the Council of Europe Committee of Ministers passed a resolution that introduces the principles of 'Universal Design' into the curricula of all relevant occupations in member countries. (Council of Europe 2001). While such principles are already part of the teaching in centres of excellence in design and education in the UK and in other countries, the principle of inclusive design is still something of a novel concept elsewhere.

Concepts which relate to social psychology and human interactions with other people and with technical systems – in other words, sociotechnical thinking – are even less likely to be part of the curriculum of courses for designers. Yet knowledge about citizen's concerns, attitudes, and needs regarding many aspects of their lives would seem highly relevant to design decisions about digital products, systems or services. Knowledge which provides an holistic view into citizens' lives – and not simply an analysis of the tasks people carry out, will have generic relevance in designing for whole communities. In our experience, the values and cultural attributes inherent in the design process of systems, services and products for the citizen, are a dominant influence in determining whether or not citizens embrace the resultant digital technologies with some degree of preparedness and acceptance.

Designing to meet the needs of diverse populations requires designers to have education and training in the concepts and theories of all five components of the integrated approach to design proposed in Chapter 7. The principles need to be taught, in order that the concepts and approach can be institutionalized. Product managers, service developers, design engineers, marketing professionals and others involved in any of the stages of the ICT design and development cycle need an understanding of the basic concepts. Having an understanding of the principles underpinning a sociotechnical approach to design will help designers and others to see the central part that participation and engagement of citizens/users play in an integrated approach to ICT design.

The future holds countless opportunities for designers to use their skills in innovative ways. Their design ingenuity has perhaps never been as important in terms of its influence over the quality of life of citizens of the world. Enlightened managers can provide a supportive environment in which the designers' skills and creativity have full reign in the rich design context envisioned here. Designers will of course have their own perspective on the proposed changes and ideas for making the change work for them. They will have a crucial role in planning the transition.

10.5.2 ICT Manufacturers

The importance of allowing market forces to prevail is frequently voiced. The essential premise in this model of a market-driven economy is that well designed products that meet consumers' needs will sell successfully and those that do not will fail. In reality, life is not so simple. There are many circumstances when consumers/citizens do not have the freedom of choice or sufficient influence or knowledge to guarantee that this will happen. Advertising can motivate consumers to buy new products and services. Sales are achieved but, once purchased, goods or services are often under-used and sometimes even abandoned. Shifting the focus of ICT design towards a sociotechnical systems perspective requires a different model of how the market operates. In the case of manufacturers, they will need to recognise that adoption and successful usage of products depends not only on the quality of their design, but also on consumers' awareness, attitudes and understanding of their products. Wider potential roles for the manufacturer are suggested below.

Part of the role of manufacturers is to see the commercial advantages of designing to meet the needs of our highly diverse populations. Engaging directly with citizens and hearing expression of their very different needs and wants is a far more powerful way of becoming aware and responsive than simply reading consumer survey data. Manufacturers have much to gain in learning from those with experience in public participation exercises about how to elicit ideas, hopes and aspirations of citizens. As understanding develops of the powerful business case for designing for diversity (e.g. Keates et al. 2000) together with realization of the bigger markets to be created globally, responsiveness of manufacturers is also likely to grow.

To ignore significant sectors of the population is to restrict market opportunities as well as to increase the risk of exclusion. Ensuring that ICT systems/services/products become accessible and desirable for a wide range of the population, immediately broadens the market to which they can be sold. It also increases the likelihood of their take-up in European and worldwide markets. Using just one segment of the population and one ubiquitous product to illustrate the point: imagine if a company were to invest in designing and manufacturing a TV remote control to operate digital television which was truly easy to use – both cognitively and physically, by most older people. It would have a huge potential market. The design challenge is to recreate the simplicity and ease of use of the first handsets introduced for analogue televisions.

To be responsive requires the identification of market segments and of the gaps in existing research into attitudes and needs. Filling the gaps in research is likely to reveal potential new markets and opportunities for innovation. This knowledge enables new business opportunities to be identified – including the potential to use the internet and local intranets as a means of reaching new markets (e.g. isolated older people), and opening new routes to market. Greater responsiveness to needs of consumers may be reflected in a growth in development of inclusive systems, services and products. Developing successful products that are inclusive will be facilitated by collaborative arrangements with designers, special interest groups, media companies, retailers and citizens themselves. Sharing and using knowledge and understanding of citizens and how to engage them in design and testing of systems/services/products will therefore have mutual benefit for all the stakeholders. In addition, the need for acquisition of social science skills mentioned above in relation to ICT designers, applies equally to the engineers and product developers in the manufacturing sector.

With regard to consumers/citizens, many lack confidence in their skills in using ICTs, and their ability to operate new technology. Manufacturers have a role to play not only by ensuring that their products and services are designed to be easy, reliable and safe to use, but also in providing accessible help, support and even learning or training packages for their products. For example, advertising material could include information on newly-designed helpful features of new products/services, on how to use them, and the fact that these were designed with the participation of people from appropriate user groups. Such measures will serve not just to inform consumer/citizens – but also to promote business success.

10.5.3 Government

Crucially, the role of national government will be to create an environment in which technology 'push' and user 'pull' strategies are encouraged. For example, government is well placed to promote and reward appropriate activities in society both in terms of technology design and civic participation. The allocation of realistic resources explicitly for the process of stakeholder participation and engagement – including the crucial opportunities for education and learning – is clearly critical. Further, some of the principles and values of public service, reflected in a commitment to consultation and public participation, offer a substantial and valuable legacy of expertise in the processes involved.

A highly influential role for government will be to encourage the institutionalization of relevant criteria in the commissioning process for all ICT systems for the public. Government is a very large customer for countless products, systems and services. To the consultants commissioned to develop ICT systems, government is the customer, not the citizen. Government however is a complex and multi-faceted customer; project specifications result from a sequential process, overseen throughout by Treasury. This process starts with a political act, which is then converted into a legislative or regulatory scheme, which then requires an administrative process and organization to be defined. This is then translated by an ICT Department into a user requirement, which in turn results in the selection of an industry vendor, which then proceeds to design and implementation. After delivery, staff in government departments and agencies have to actually use the system. At the end of the process the real customer – the citizen – has to bear the consequences, intended or otherwise. Only rarely are those who have to use the system, or who are likely to be affected by the system, involved in the process of specification and design. This means that acceptability to the citizen stakeholder and usability by the departmental staff are only really put to the test at the conclusion of the project after implementation when, all too often errors, inconsistencies and unintended consequences emerge. Part of government's responsibility is to close this gap by ensuring (e.g. through their procurement practices) that external ICT developers have explicit responsibility to apply best practice in achieving successful engagement of users and citizens throughout the ICT development cycle – especially in eliciting needs and in evaluating design solutions. Such a shift in the focus of design would identify and obviate errors, increase relevance, test acceptability and usability.

So the extent to which government requires ICT manufacturers and suppliers to adhere to relevant design principles and policies can have great influence in regard to promoting good design practice. Requiring suppliers to comply with standards for usability for example would be a major incentive for companies to meet them and provide a new and level field to stimulate competition which can drive prices down. Government is not generally providing this pull perhaps because of pressures to accept lowest price tender bids in any current spending round. A broader assessment of the real medium and long term costs arising from products/ systems and services that do not meet usability and other human-centred criteria would reveal this stance to be counterproductive and short-sighted.

Governments across Europe have a real opportunity to push for national adoption of the EU resolution for the implementation of inclusive/ universal design/'Design for All' in all design curricula. This would serve to institutionalize some important design principles throughout the European Union. The enhanced design outcomes are likely to offer powerful competitive advantage to the European economy.

10.5.4 Creating Capacity for Engagement/Participation

It should give pause for thought that few of us as citizens in technologically advanced nations appear to have any part to play in the technology shaping process. As the opportunity to influence design decisions opens up to citizens it will be important for people to develop the skills and capabilities. Creating capacity to participate and engage in technology shaping and design will need to be actively developed. Indeed this is an explicit objective in exciting and innovative community development projects in the developing world, e.g. the ActionAid *Reflect* ICTs Project (Beardon 2005). In these projects, there are facilitated opportunities for citizen learning through discussing and analysing local issues. The possibilities for economic and social change are opened up by learning of the rich possibilities and alternative ways of harnessing ICT capabilities in the community.

Crossing boundaries of knowledge domains relating to such areas as culture, perspective, context (e.g. home, educational setting, place of employment), location, (e.g. private space or community–based) will demand new ways of communicating to achieve real sharing of knowledge and perspectives. This is likely to be a necessary precursor to development of mutual understanding and respect amongst participants.

Achieving all this is far from easy and will often require facilitation skills and learning on the part of many of the participants. There are many techniques for these processes, ranging from those used in conflict resolution processes (see Chapter 9) to techniques such as knowledge cafés, which place emphasis on the active listening of the receiver to extract meaningful knowledge from the source, rather on the more usual delivery of information in a format planned by giver of information. These skills need to be embedded in education and training at all levels in schools and colleges, e.g. in the citizenship classes introduced in the UK. The importance of training in relevant skills for all professionals involved in ICT development projects has already been emphasised. Creating awareness and confidence of citizens in participation and engagement is a determining factor in the shaping of technology to achieve desirable digital futures. This is therefore an essential challenge to meet!

10.6 Scaling the Process

As 'e-everything' prevails in the information society, everyone 'is a stakeholder in our digital world. However, because of the scale of the potential stakeholder population, the idea of designing whole global systems with the participation of all citizens in one great collaborative endeavour would be nonsensical. Achieving widespread participation will depend on, among several other things, achieving the right scale for the process.

While the message is to involve and include citizens in ICT design and development and appropriately use their unique contributions, there is no single 'right way' to do this. Tailoring the approach to the context is essential for success. Applying the concept of information ecologies (Nardi and O'Day 1999), described in Chapter 7 establishes the contexts in which issues of real concern in communities throughout the world can be addressed effectively and enabled by technology where appropriate.

Citizens can become involved in design and development activities at a local level, and on a small scale, making it initially more manageable and allowing citizens a voice. Some successful examples were reported earlier (see Chapter 4) and demonstrate that citizens can contribute to novel solutions and assist in innovation. Successes with starting small means that such participation can evolve into something bigger. In the Jhai Foundation project described in Chapter 4, the importance of a gradual process is emphasized: *"Jhai helps create change that is sustainable, because it is locally conceived and implemented to be that way, with minimal interference and direction from outsiders. And we always try to start slow, making sure everyone is on board, building momentum as we go"* (Jhai Foundation n.d.).

10.7 Conclusions

Shifting the focus of ICT development processes to incorporate a variety of design approaches and especially to engage citizens in these processes will have a transforming effect. It is an immense undertaking with many ramifications and it is worth reminding ourselves of the challenge of major change, described vividly in 1505 in the words of Niccolò Machiavelli (1469-1527), Italian historian, statesman, and political philosopher: *"there is nothing more difficult to arrange, more doubtful of success, and more dangerous to carry through than initiating changes...the innovator makes enemies of all those who prospered under the old order, and only lukewarm support is forthcoming from those who would prosper under the new. Their support is lukewarm partly from fear of their adversaries, who have the existing laws on their side, and partly because men are generally incredulous, never really trusting new things unless they have tested them by experience. In consequence, whenever those who oppose changes can do so, they attack vigorously, and the defence made by the others is only lukewarm so both the innovator and his friends are endangered together"* (Machiavelli, originally published c.1515).

This quotation sums up eloquently some of the likely obstacles that are likely to crop up. In this chapter we have considered some of the ways to begin the shift. We are fully cognisant of the complexity, the scale and effort involved in making the changes we suggest. We are equally cognisant of the unsatisfactory nature of current design practice. Working – sometimes as researchers and sometimes as consultants – with ICT project managers, designers and developers and users in many different contexts over many years has given us first hand experience of the realities. We have seen the enormous effort and technical skill committed to improving the user experience and ability to carry out work tasks. Too often we have witnessed the distress caused to the designer when users criticise and complain about design features which have taken countless hours of pains-taking writing of code to create.

Another obstacle is the sheer enormity of the undertaking. Recognising the sense of futility that many of us experience in contemplating attempts to change huge, impersonal systems, Nardi and O'Day encourage and inspire us: *"While a local information ecology might seem too small a leverage point, consider these words of Margaret Mead: 'Never doubt that a small group of thoughtful, committed citizens can change the world; indeed, it's the only thing that ever has.'...As we confront the rhetoric of inevitability and the steamroller of technological change, it is good to remember Mead's optimism and her own unique, committed contributions"* (Nardi and O'Day 1999).

Evidence of the potential for significant change stemming from similar modest beginnings is beginning to appear in the context of ICT develop-ments as local councils in the UK strive to implement e-government. The technology has tended to dominate the national strategy for local e-govern-ment. Despite this, change has already started at grass roots with local coun-cils making significant efforts to achieve a shift of focus towards the needs of users. In defining and developing e-services, they have been consulting with citizens in the community regarding their needs of the council.

We anticipate with enthusiasm and optimism the growing focus on the needs of people and on their unique and diverse qualities and contribu-tions. Our vision is that such a focus will be nurtured in an integrated de-sign approach which draws from the different approaches according to the needs of a particular design context and to the design challenges encoun-tered.

The harmonising impact of a holistic, integrative approach was antici-pated by Margaret Mead. In 'The Future as the basis for Establishing a Shared Culture' (cited in Bennis, Benne and Chin 1969 p. 532) she notes *"the agglomeration of partly dissociated, historically divergent and con-ceptually incongruent patterns of culture and sub culture which now block men and women in their search for a better future for mankind"*. Miss Mead envisioned a future united society founded upon the collective ef-forts of young and old, men and women, people of various nationalities and religions, scholarly and non-scholarly. She envisaged individuals and communities transcending the existing cultural divisions to create a shared culture. She emphasised the value of inclusion and sharing knowledge. Her interest was much less in predicting changes in society in the future but to focus upon the potential for invoking and shaping the future *"The fu-ture, unlike the past is always newborn. To involve all living persons in constructing the future is to release and facilitate growth and change all round."*

In conclusion, citizen engagement strategies offer a potent way forward for the Information Society of the 21st century to inform desirable digital futures. These are likely to be most fruitful within a design framework that integrates a number of approaches including a sociotechnical perspective.

The challenges in achieving such a shift in focus of design are enormous and profound but realizable if we collectively have the courage and foresight to pursue the vision. The tantalising potential rewards for vast numbers of the world's citizens, for governments, for societies and for economies make the striving towards the vision worthwhile. We shall leave the last word with other authors:

"*...the worst thing we can do is to ask too little of the future – and ask too little of ourselves in determining the future...*" (Nardi and O'Day 1999).

References

America Speaks (n.d) Homepage http://www.americaspeaks.org/

Bearden H (2005) ICT for development: Empowerment or exploitation? ActionAid, http://www.reflect-action.org/

Bennis WG, Benne KD & Chin R (1969) The Planning of Change. Holt Rinehart & Winston Inc., USA.

Bourn J (2000) NAO Report - (HC 25-III 2000-01): Report of the Comptroller and Auditor General on Driver and Vehicle Licensing Agency (DVLA) Appropriation Accounts 1999-2000.

British Computer Society (n.d)a. BCS and society. http://www.bcs.org/server.php?show=conWebDoc.2417

British Computer Society (n.d)b. BCS mission and values. http://www.bcs.org/server.php?show=conWebDoc.1586

Council of Europe (2001) Resolution RESAP (2001) On the introduction of the principles of universal design into the curricula of all occupations working on the built environment. http://wcd.coe.int/viewdoc.jsp?id=186495&BackColorInternet=9999cc&BackColorIntranet=FFBB55&BackColorLogged=FFAC75

Guardian Unlimited (2005) Government websites attract few visitors Bobbie Johnson and Michael Cross. http://politics.guardian.co.uk/egovernment/story/0,12767,1661852,00.html

Hewitt P (2005). Speech by Rt Hon Patricia Hewitt MP, Secretary of State for Health 23 June 2005; Britain Speaks. http://www.dh.gov.uk/NewsHome/Speeches/SpeechesList/SpeechesArticle/fs/en?CONTENT_ID=4114050&chk=%2Bsw3kj

Jhai Foundation (n.d.) Homepage http://www.jhai.org/commitment.htm.

Kearney AT (1984) The Barriers to Information Technology. Institute of Administrative Management, Orpington.

Keates et al. (2000) Towards a practical inclusive design approach. ACM Press, New York.

Klein L (1976) A Social Scientist in Industry. Gower, Epping.

Klein L (2005) Working Across the Gap: The Practice of social Science in Organizations. London: Karnac.

Machiavelli N (2003) The Prince. Penguin Books Limited, London.

Mead M (1969) The Future as the Basis for Establishing a Shared Culture. Science and Culture. 94 (1).

Milner J (2005). The Community Panel – Panel of the Month. Monitor: The newsletter of the Worshipful Company of Information Technologists, 38, p 7. www.wcit.org.uk/Publications/ main_content/MonitorJuly2005-1.pdf

Nardi BS, O'Day VL (1999) Information ecologies: Using technology with heart. MIT Press, Cambridge, Mass.

National Audit Office (1999) The passport delays of Summer 1999: Report by the Comptroller and Auditor General. HC 812.

Office of Communications (2005) National Single Non-Emergency Number Proposals for Number and Tariff. http://www.ofcom.org/consult/condocs/snen/snen.pdf

Sackman H (1967) Computers, System Science and Evolving Society. New York, Wiley.

The Worshipful Company of Information Technologists (2006) Charitable Projects. http://www.wcit.org.uk/whatwedo/charitableprojects

Index